The "Sunny" Side of Cancer

A rare form of incurable cancer cannot destroy
a wife and mother's desire to live her life with happiness

by Sunny Jennings Carney

SUNNY CARNEY CARCINOID CANCER FUND
VERONA, PA 15147

All Rights Reserved
Copyright © 2011 by Sunny Carney

No part of this book may be reproduced or transmitted, downloaded, distributed, reverse engineered, or stored in or introduced into any information storage and retrieval system, in any form or by any means, including photocopying and recording, whether electronic or mechanical, now known or hereinafter invented without permission in writing from the author.

Sunny Carney Carcinoid Cancer Fund
sunnycarneycarcinoidcancerfund.blogspot.com/

ISBN: 978-0-9848139-0-2

Life is not measured by the then number of breaths you take,
But by the moments that take your breath away.

~unknown~

To my husband Mark
and the joys of my life, Austen, Logan and Nolan,
for all the moments you take my breath away!

Introduction

Sunny's husband Mark tells their story…
May 2008
A mother of three boys, a daughter, the baby sister to a large family, an aunt, a godmother to several, a trusted friend to more then I can count, an outreach volunteer, a business owner and my wife. Sunny Carney lives up to her name every time someone speaks to her; she is beautiful both in and out. She has been my biggest motivator, my rock and my inspiration in tough times, my biggest fan in good times, and most importantly my best friend. Told 14 years ago that having children may not be part of our future because of ovarian tumors, she kept the faith, and is a wonderful mother to our three sons, Austen, Logan, and Nolan. She is always ensuring that they know the Lord, love of life, kindness to others, hard work, and occasionally when to "shape up."

Her boundless energy, healthy lifestyle and positive attitude are infectious. When she walks into a crowd everyone that does not know her wants to because those she is with seem so happy. She has served as president of our children's PTA, organized committees that benefit those who are less fortunate in the community, chaired several non-profit events to help so many people in need and led fundraising drives for those who have been caught up in unfortunate situations. She has done so much for others, usually without letting anyone ever know, I could not begin to list them. Her strong faith in God and modest upbringing has given her a sense of giving that only she can explain. When she successfully started her own photography business, she also started a non-profit division photographing family portraits for area families fighting cancer. Her friends say she is amazing and she simply shakes her head and wonders what all of the fuss is about.

Her mother, sisters, brothers and large extended family will tell you she is the one you can count on to lend an ear when needed and never judge. Just when you think you know what she is going to think or feel she seems to surprise you with her words. She was raised by her loving mother and her father who was the warden of the Allegheny County Jail and actually spent most of her childhood in the residence connected to the jail. At a young age she witnessed more of life's tragedies and obstacles through her neighbors, the prisoners, than most of us can imagine. I have heard stories over and over again about Sunny befriending prisoners and never judging them. As a little girl she would give prisons handfuls of candy when her father would walked her through the cells with him. Her brother once told me she would beg her father to be taken in to the prison so she could jump from cell to cell saying hello to all those incardinated in her carefree cheering voice because she felt bad that many did not get visitors. Even today when we talk about her experience growing up in a prison system she never disrespects the prisoners rather believes they where in unfortunate situations.

Although all of the aforementioned is remarkable it is not what makes her truly special. Sunny is a two-time cancer survivor and is currently fighting for a third time. After beating ovarian carcinoid cancer (at least that is what we think it was…doctors cannot agree if it was the start of carcinoid cancer or not) and undergoing serious surgery for carcinoid tumors in her right lung just three years ago, the carcinoid tumors returned in her lymph nodes, liver and bones. The size and proliferation throughout the liver of these tumors mandates immediate chemotherapy in four treatments over the next few months as well as monthly octreotide treatments. These painful treatments will hopefully stop the growth, but are not a cure. There are numerous tumors in her spine, her skull, her hip, her leg, and her shoulder…all in the bones and she will wait on potential radiation to fight those.

What my wife has is Carcinoid Cancer Syndrome, an endocrine disease that is rare and spreads from organ to organ. As of right now the only known treatment for remission is administered by renowned clinics in Europe. Our doctors have encouraged us to start raising money and preparing for the several trips to Europe. Her lead oncologist strongly believes that Sunny would be a prime candidate to be a voice to get the message out regarding carcinoid cancer syndrome, bring this treatment to the United States and encourage approval from the FDA. Without this treatment, the tumors most likely will continue to metastasize in other organs and her fight will be ongoing. She believes that once she beats this cancer she can make a difference to others also suffering from Carcinoid Cancer. As if she has not already made a difference in so many lives.

Mark A. Carney

Prologue

Most of us know that there are thousands of books on the subject of cancer. Some talk about kinds of cancer, how to live with cancer, cookbooks for cancer patients, life after cancer, fighting cancer with faith, curing cancer without doctors, how not to get cancer (missed that one), and the list goes on. I have probably read or at least skimmed through 80% of them. Some were helpful, some were rife with medical jargon that I could not even begin to understand, some were nonsense, many were written by those who never had cancer, and more then I want to remember some were just plain depressing. The above-mentioned reasons however are not why I decided to put my personal journals and blog into a book. I decided to publish my blog and journals because I want people to see that everyone has their own cancers that they are trying to battle and you are not alone in your difficult times. I hope that this book inspires everyone to live life joyfully no matter what obstacle or problem you are fighting. I never had any intention on publishing anything I have written nor do I claim to be a professional author. I am just a terminal cancer patient that has found a way to live an amazingly happy life despite my obstacles and difficulties.

After months of journaling and blogging I have had several people ask me to write a book. Out of nowhere I would receive letters and emails asking me to continue to blog because it changed their outlook on life. I started my blog a few months after I was diagnosed with an advanced rare form of neuron-endocrine cancer called Carcinoid Cancer. This was mainly to keep my family and friends updated. My loved ones wanted to keep up with my diagnosis and my day-to-day situation as I lived with this cancer. Coming from a large family and having several different groups of friends that wanted to stay in touch with my doctors' appointments and treatments, a blog was the easy way to keep them informed. Surprisingly enough, my blog also took some of the pressure off my husband and kids when they were asked, "How's she doing?" I also needed a way to let people know how much I loved and appreciated their support. So a friend and colleague, Susan Jordan, helped me design and start up my blog.

After a few weeks of writing updates, I started realizing that writing posts about my treatments, scan results and doctors appointments was not only beneficial in getting the word out about Carcinoid Cancer, but was extremely therapeutic. As I continued to write, not always publishing, it began to become a way of emotional therapy for me. Each post got deeper and deeper. I learned to use my computer keyboard as a way to sort out all my anxieties and feelings. At the time, I was completely unaware that people were moved by my blog.

Then I started getting some wonderful feedback with emails and letters. Hundreds of people, not just cancer sufferers but for others who were facing adversity, were writing to tell me my blog has gotten them through days they thought would be impossible to overcome. Realizing this little blog turned into something much bigger than my need to feel, I began to feel obligated to keep posting. At least that is what I kept telling myself. But writing was truly a release of my reality. Once I jotted down all my thoughts and feelings I was then able to go back and live a life where cancer was not in control. I would write a post, many times not even publishing it, and it was like leaving the cancer on that computer. Cancer comes and destroys more than just your body, it takes over every aspect of your life. So as the other problems would appear—like strain on my marriage, financial disaster, or my children's fears—I would blog. Writing these problems on a computer screen allowed me to sort out solutions and get on with my life beyond my terminal disease. I was then able to return to my life like cancer had never been a part it. Several times when I was going through some tougher than normal periods I would post three to four times a day. Sometimes I would never hit the publish button, yet feel so refreshed when I was done.

I am told that my blog posts inspired those going through difficulties. I did not set out to be an inspiration. It is just something that happened because of the way I choose to fight this incurable disease. At times I pinch myself to make sure I am still living the life that I was told would be a nightmare. I cannot believe what my struggles and efforts to stay alive so that I can be a positive influence to my boys have done for others. Sometimes, I have trouble understanding how I have gotten this far by doing what I have always done—giving my all and believing in the impossible. I would have never guessed that I would have articles written about me, partake in interviews by both radio and news shows, work with Senators to speak in Congress, have a blog that is read by thousands across the world or even be asked to write a book. I am no more special than anyone holding this book. Instead, I am going to live my life with a "Sunny" attitude despite my challenges of life expectancy. I choose to believe that *I* control my happiness, not the cancer that I am plagued with. I've been told that my blog and postings have inspired others to change their lives in order to see the good in all difficult situations. If my outlook can inspire just one person to never doubt the power they have over their life and to know that God is always with them, then writing this book will be worthwhile.

As I continued to write my blog, I was encouraged by several to publish it in a book. Then Tracy Reedy, a local friend, asked if she could be a part of a project to get the message of my blog to more readers. She encouraged me to reach out to other carcinoid cancer patients through my blog. As a book designer she knew that if she helped me to communicate my passion to help others with this unknown cancer, a book collecting my blog could have a strong impact on people. I was finally convinced that this book needed to be written when she said, "even if you don't sell one book, there are at least three copies that will be treasured forever… The three you will give to your sons."

So you see, this book is not meant to be preachy or a lecture about how positive thinking will bring good things your way. Nor is it an unrealistic story of a cancer patient fighting a losing battle with a remarkable attitude and because of that is she is now cancer free. It is not a bunch of theories about sending good vibes and your cancer will miraculously disappear. It's about living a wonderful life even when you know it will be over soon. It is about a mother, wife, daughter, friend, sister, aunt, neighbor, business owner and more, dealing with her destiny the best she can. It's about me and how extremely blessed I am despite the cards I have been dealt. It's about how I try to find the good in my death sentence.

This book is not just for those who are going through the CANCER journey. This book is for everyone who is going through LIFE and the difficult journey it is.

Chapter 1: Reality

Reality leaves a lot to the imagination. ~John Lennon

May 14, 2008
Telling My Sons
It's hard to believe that it's only been a few days since the cancer card was dealt to us once again. I am not sure how I am supposed to feel…other than sick. I am not sure what I am supposed to say when people ask how I am feeling…or when people want to tell me how sorry they are…or when they want to know if there is anything that they can do. I am not sure how to say thank you for the cards and meals that keep coming. I am not sure how to wipe away my loved ones tears, when I cannot wipe away my own. I know that it takes a ton of courage for my friends and family to approach me and try hard to find something to make me feel better. It's awkward, like when you wish someone best wishes and prayers at the funeral of their loved one and the next morning comes and your life is back to normal and the other person's hell is only beginning. When they want to know what they can do, I just want to explode sometimes and tell them "yea you can take this disease away from me." But that's not who I am. That's not going to get me through this…get US through this.

It's strange how life can turn seemingly upside down in an instant. When I went through this the last time it was over. It physically and emotionally beat me up and it almost destroyed our family. It tore us in all different directions and my marriage was hanging on by a thin string. This destruction that cancer did to our family…my marriage…my children…is far worse then anything I could ever imagine. Three years and we are just starting to build it back up. The surgery was successful, the year long recovery was over, and I was convinced that my "cancer" chapter was closed in my little book of life. So after my too long recovery and finally fixing myself, I started to focus on fixing Mark and the boys again. I put the cancer behind me and threw myself into rebuilding a family that had crumbled to pieces. I was and still am determined to fight with all my heart to get this family back to the perfect life we once had—the life that I worked so hard to have and my children deserve.

I had back pain. How the hell does back pain…a pulled muscle…become a life threatening stage 4 incurable cancer? My head still spins when I think about the past few months of quiet torture. I kept treating my pain with heating pads, meds, physical therapy and visits to my chiropractor. There were times when I could not even walk, yet I trucked my butt through Disney World on our family vacation just to bring back some of the happiness that was lost by the last bout of this monster. How could I have not seen it? Mark tells me not to beat myself up but I wonder if deep down he is thinking the same thing. I know he is thinking, "I am not sure I can do this with her again. But, I'm not sure I can stand to lose her either." I went to the doctor several times in the past six months but she just kept saying it was a pulled muscle because the x-ray showed nothing (carcinoid cancer does not always show on x-rays). Why did I not push her for more tests? Would catching it earlier have made it stage 1 or 2? Maybe, deep down, I did not want to know. I will live with this guilt forever…however that may be.

Breaking the news to my three boys was the most difficult thing I have ever had to do. Giving birth to them was painful, but there was a joy to the end of that pain. Holding each of them for the first time made all that pain disappear. I remember those three "birth" days so vividly with such indulgence. Unfortunately, I will also remember this day so vividly with such pain. There are no guarantees that I can give them. Just like the doctor yesterday could not give me any guarantees. There is nothing fair in this for them. Mark and I both knew that we had to address this immediately. Family, neighbors and friends were stopping by with food, flowers, gifts and offers for help were pouring in. We could not hide this from them, nor should we. Hearing the severity of this from someone else would just crush them. The last time they were younger, we were cancer "newbies'" and thought it was better, for their sake, not tell them everything. In fact, I think we kept the seriousness of the cancer from many of our loved ones. Not by Mark's choice, but by mine. However, when their teachers started calling at home and emailing about the meltdowns they were having and the nightmares were a nightly event, we both realized, too late, that it probably was not the right way to handle it. So this time we decided to handle with complete honesty and let them in on every detail.

Experts on child development, or whatever a person needs to be an expert in to deal with children who have a parent with cancer, may disagree with how we are going to handle it this time but it is what we feel is best. Mark and I agreed that we should be open with them, to the extent we know what's going on, and to let them know it's okay to cry and be scared. We also made sure that they knew we had beat this once before and we would do whatever it takes to do it again. We told them over and over again that this is not just happening to Mommy but to all of us and we are all in this together.

We called them into the family room and all of us sat together on the couch. This is something we don't do often so they knew that it was something serious. Logan, my middle son, automatically said, "It wasn't me. I swear." If only it was a punishment conversation. Mark did some of the initial talking. He had scripted it out in his head, rehearsed it with me, and yet I could tell even as his lips were moving he was actually as numb as I was. He tried to be strong and positive but I could see the fear on his face. I have seen this look many times before. As he talked, the fear went from his face to their beautiful, innocent, freckled faces. My eyes filled with tears that I struggled to hold back. They immediately remembered the lung cancer, the surgery and everything that came with it…the dinners…the family sleeping over and getting them off to school…not seeing me for weeks when I was in the hospital…and then when they did it was with tubes and IV's…and I was not able to function properly, let alone be the mom they expected me to be. I can't even begin to fathom what was circling through their little heads as we explained as straightforward and dry-eyed as we could.

They say your true personality comes through in times of crises and I saw that clearly in each of my three angel's reactions. Austen, the oldest at age 11, was on the couch between Mark and I and he started to feel faint and anxious…he kept saying over and over again, "why twice mom, it's someone else's turn. Not you again mom." I was thankful he was sitting because he is known to pass out under stress. My heart ached as I rubbed his head and he bravely tried to say "it's okay mom." He actually slid down partially off the couch as Mark and I jerked him back up. As I tried to help him up I looked into his eyes and I wondered what freckles and cancer should ever have in common. Those sky blue eyes that had so many thoughts behind them should never have to feel this pain.

Logan actually had the most questions. He has always been the thinker of the three. They were serious…he was serious. He put his game face on, as much a 10-year-old could do. My heart broke for him because as intense and passionate as he is about the simple things and as anxious he is about adjusting to new jeans and shoes or just change in general, this was going to throw him to the edge. He is one who will withdraw into his own little world at times to escape stress (or from his teasing brothers) and it seems like we had just seen him come out of his shell. He was finally showing the independence and calmness that I prayed for him. After he fired off his questions, he started to head up to his room. I stopped him and gave him a hug. I noticed he pulled back a little for fear of hurting me, much like he does when he hugs his great grandma who is very fragile. As a baby he had the biggest puppy dog eyes and those eyes where now filled with tears. I held him so tight even though the pain intensifies when I am hugged, tears running out of the corners of my eyes. All I could do was wish we could go back to simpler times…back to our small house in Greenfield (where the boys were originally born). I wish we could go back to when the biggest problem we had was potty training three boys with one bathroom. God only gives you what you can handle, but apparently he doesn't wait for you to raise your arm and say "Okay, I am ready, give me some more."

Nolan is the family clown. He takes after Mark in that aspect. He, like his father, prefers to treat things with humor and just like his dad, can sometimes pick the wrong time or the wrong joke. He sat on the arm of the couch next to me and once again I can't even pretend to know what was going through his nine-year-old head. True to form he made a stab at humor, something about at least you can be blond now mom with a wig (we told them about the chemo and hair loss). My heart cried for him as Mark and I tried to fake a laugh, and as his brothers told him to "shut up." He had tears in his eyes…the "crying comic." As a mother, it ripped me apart to not be able to grab his little arms, kiss him, look him in the eyes, and tell him that there was nothing to worry about…mommy was going to be fine. But I wasn't going to lie or try to oversimplify things this time. He sat there…actually silent…knowing that being funny wasn't the right thing to do and not knowing what the right thing to say or do was. He is nine. At this point, I was really trying not to lose it because there is no way my kids deserve this. Does God know when he "gives us what we can handle" that other people may have a hold on the same handle. What else can they go through?

The doctors are trying to give me answers to this rare and difficult neuroendocrine cancer but I don't think they know where to turn. Mark and I are both on the internet getting re-acclimated with Carcinoid. There is a plan for treatment set up, but deep down I am feeling like the doctors know this is a death sentence. I think they are just humoring me. All I can think of right now is how is my marriage going to last through this again? How are my kids going to make it through this again? How strong am I? And how am I going to control this like I do everything else? God don't leave me now.

I am closing this with the realization that life is precious, and when I beat this, my priorities will be refocused. My energies re-employed. Not sure to what—other than my kids and family—but I have to do something if I beat this. I have to stop others from going through this torture of "Life With Cancer."

May 17, 2008
I Lay Down To Sleep

Reality has finally hit me. I HAVE CANCER, AGAIN!!! For the past few days I have been in a fog. I know this is my world but I seem to be looking in at it from the outside. Numbness is all I can feel. Last night while I lay in bed, I finally took the time to comprehend everything that has gone on in the last few days. I reviewed my treatment plan over and over again in my head. I thought about how sick I will be from the poison they will be giving me to kill the enemy. I formulated ways to handle those side effects the doctors are promising me I will have soon…meditation, herbal substitutes, vitamins, relaxation, pain pills, but mostly prayer. Yeah, that is what I will do, PRAY. I ran through a game plan to fight this attacker, again. Then I comprised a plan B if that game plan did not work. Then a plan C in case B and A don't work.

All those plans put prayer on the top of the list and never quit on the bottom but surrender was never written or spoken.

    I tried to figure out how to help my children while they watch me fight this. I thought about my life and how much time I have wasted because I expected a tomorrow to come. I imagined this beautiful home with out me. What would happen to it? Who would keep in up? Will Mark follow the plans we had to remodel it into our dream home? Who will buy new towels when the old ones wear out? Who will change the sheets every week? Who will make the "honey do list" for a Saturday when there was nothing to do? Who will be there to make sure the "honey do list" gets done with no excuses?

    My boys' lives then ran through my head. I could not help but think what would happen to their future if I am not in it? Who will tuck them in at night and wake them up in the morning? Who would know which way each one of them liked their morning toast…one well done with just peanut butter, one medium brown with little butter and cinnamon sugar, and one very light with peanut butter and jelly? Will they remember to comb their hair and brush their teeth if I am not standing by the bathroom door reminding them several times? What happens if they forget their lunch or homework on the table…will someone from home bring it to them at school? Will they ever learn to match their shirts with their pants and know that when it's less than fifty degrees they need a jacket? Who will teach those table manners, kindness, respect for others, and how to give all you have to help someone else? Who will they share secrets or problems with? The kind of secrets or problems only a mother can accept and understand. Will they trust Mark like they trust me? Who will be there to hug them when they have their first heart break? Will they have someone to replace me to cheer them on at their sporting events… like only I can do? Can Mark motivate them to give everything they do their best or will he tell them average is okay? Will they learn to never give up on their dreams and remember that quitting is not an option? Will they keep their faith in the Almighty God and believe that anything is possible through Him…even after they see their mom die of a horrible disease? I have this urgent need to teach them everything before this cancer takes over my life. This urgent need to teach everyone who will be in their lives when I am gone. I have so much to teach Mark before I lose this battle. How will he raise them without me?

I closed my eyes to try to catch at least an hour or two of sleep before the alarm wakes me up again to be part of the nightmare I am living or dying in. I tried to go to my happy place which I found the last time I fought this enemy, but the comments from my original oncologist kept running through my head, "get your affairs in order. The degree of tumors in the liver is extensive. This is serious…this will progress quickly in the next six months. I am afraid there is nothing more I can do." He was once my hero, when he removed my lung three years ago to save my life. I now hate him with a passion. I know it's not his fault, but I hate that he lost faith in me. He pretended back then to know me and know my ability to fight with all I had. He would tell me I have what it takes to beat this disease. But now he just gave up on me.

Mark was lying next to me and I knew he could not sleep either, but I did not want to acknowledge it. So we both laid there with our backs facing each other afraid to break the silence. Breaking that silence would mean bringing all our fears to the surface. I am not sure we can take on each other's anxieties right now. We both know what this demon has done to our relationship and speaking about it would just make it worse. I am sure his mind was wondering like mine. He asking himself the same question I am, only in his voice. He is wondering where our future is going. *Or is he?* I thought.

At that moment I had an amazing feeling of power come upon me. A power that I have felt before when defeat was coming my way. An energy that has gotten me through so many competitions or struggles in my life. This power, sensation or awareness was so much more intense then any other time I have felt it. Maybe because this battle is so much more intense. However, at that moment I decided I can do this and do it with a positive attitude. I accepted my challenge that I was called out on and will look my antagonist, named cancer, in the eyes and fight with all I got. I am in control of this, not the enemy. I will not let cancer take my troops away from me. I will not let anyone I love…Mark, my boys, my family, the doctors, the cancer or the pessimist…go to the dark side. I will force them all to be on my team and not against me. I will be a winner even if I lose to death one day. It may take my life at one point but not without me winning all the battles to make a difference. This is what I need to do to fight this horrible invader of my life. I need to know that I am not just doing it for me but that I am doing it for everyone. I need to fight cancer with a "Sunny Side."

May 24, 2008
Change
Today was a day of change.

I made an appointment to get my hair cut by my friend Dawn at her shop. Dr. Friedland suggested that I get it cut short so that when it starts to fall out from the chemo it won't be such a shock to me, but mostly the kids. I was also told by other cancer patients that it becomes a huge mess when it starts coming out if your hair is long. Today this was difficult for me because my long thick auburn hair has always been my "trademark" so to speak. Mark told me that my hair was the first thing he noticed about me when we met. He would joke that he thought I was way too skinny and of course from the wrong side of the tracks. Just not his type he would say. Listen, I saw his type and his comment did not bother me a bit. But he could not resist me when I would wear my hair long without any fuss to it and no makeup…just natural. The boys, even at the age they are now, love to twirl it around their fingers. When they were little they use to laugh endless, the kind of laugh that you can only get from a toddler, when I would flip my head forward, bring my hair all over my face and pretend I was Cousin It from the 70's show "Adam's Family." As babies when I would rock them they would softly tug on my hair until they fell asleep. I guessed it soothed them. The three of them use to each grab a few strands when they all would be held at one time. I have not had a short hair cut since the 1970's when my mom decided to give my sister and I, a pathetic attempt to make it easier on her, the "Dorothy Hammil" cut. I think I was traumatized and decided never to look like a boy again. So I've had long hair ever since.

On my way to Dawn's shop I felt a tear roll down my face. I got so angry at myself for being so vain. This is hair and I am fighting for my life. Suck it up and get it done. When I got there I was greeted by the usual Dawn Lewis warm smile and I knew that there was no better person to share this moment with. At the same time my friend Angela was their just getting finished with her new high fashion cut and she stayed with me while Dawn did the deed. She put the hair in a pony to save it for Austen because he wanted it for some reason, and in one big hack off it went. I looked over at Ang, and tears filled her eyes. I knew what she was thinking and my heart ached for her. This is an example that cancer is so much harder on the ones watching the fight then the ones actually in the fight. I smiled at her with such conviction, and decided to show her I was okay with this. And it was not an act, I was okay. Dawn did her magic and I felt great, knowing that within a week it would all be gone.

We then looked through some wig magazines, yes a hair salon has wig magazines ironic, and we pick one. I almost fell to the floor when she told me the price. Mark and I have been down this road before and knew that financially this takes a toll on any family. I could not spend our mortgage payment on a wig for myself, so I asked her for a bargain wig book. She smiled at me and told me not to look at the price because group of my woman friends have already paid for whatever I wanted. I felt embarrassed and humbled at the same time. The same group of women that I spent so much of my time to look good in front of are now paying for my vanity. I knew that this was the beginning of my Sunny Cancer support group doing what they want to do. So with much hesitation, I accepted. For me, the hardest thing when fighting this cancer will be accepting help.

On the way home with my new young and hip reverse bob I called Mark at the office. He picked up in one ring so I knew he was sitting with his hand on the phone waiting for me to call. "I did it" I told him. I heard him let out a huge breath. He was probably holding it all day. "I am now official a cancer patient prepared to lose my hair." With his amazing positive voice he shouted out to his bull pin of sales men, "my wife is my hero and hot, too." He always seems to know strange things to say at awkward times. That was exactly what I needed to hear.

When I got home to the quiet house I stared in the mirror for almost an hour holding my pony tail of hair that Austen wanted to me to save. Not one tear fell, just pride that I am prepared to fight this disease. I sat on my steps waiting for the boys to jump off the school bus and react to my hair. The bus pulled up and they were the last three to get off the bus. I stood there with my legs shaking and my neighbors all staring my way. The boys ran off, dropped their backpacks at my feet and passed right by me to catch up with the other neighbor kids while yelling, "Love you mom, going to play." I got not one comment…not one look. I was just given the prize of carrying three backpacks into the house. All this fear I built up inside of me was for nothing. They did not even notice.

From outside the of the house I could hear the phone ring so I dropped the backpacks and ran as fast as a woman can with cancer in her bones, so I guess I hobbled, to answer it. I had been waiting all day for the doctor's office to call to tell me what time my treatments are starting tomorrow. I look down at the caller ID first before saying hello and saw UPMC Medical Center. As expected it was Dr. Frieland, not his nurse but him. After the "hellos" and "how are you" thing, conversation started in with we have a change of plans. I started shaking…they are giving up on me. After Dr. Friedland spoke with Dr. Gamblin, my liver oncologist, they decided standard chemotherapy will not work on me. So he cancelled my therapy for tomorrow. Before he could say another word I jumped in with a campaign not to give up on me. This had been my nightmare. All the research I read in the past few days said that there was no chemo that would kill carcinoid. I just thought that the docs new more. My voice started shaking in fear and tears were rolling done my face. I got louder and louder begging him to please let me try. I'll do whatever I need to do to make it work. The boys came in the house and saw me dropped to my knees the same spot that I answered the phone. Austen put his arms around his brothers and took them to the game room to play this week's new video game. He turned the volume up so loud that to drown out my crying and begging that the sound shook the floor but I don't think I even noticed it.

After about 2 minutes of listening to me ramble Dr. Friedland finally interrupted me by saying, "I will not give up on you, but we need to change the plans." I could not hear anything he said about the new game plan. To me he sounded like Charlie Brown's teacher in the Holiday specials. He realized that I did not comprehend what he was telling me so he asked if he could call Mark and go over things. I okayed it and click went the phone. The time it took Mark to call me back seemed like days but in reality it was only five minutes. His voice was calming as he told me the whole change of plan. There is a somewhat new treatment called Chemo-embolization of the liver. They go into a vein in your leg and they inject chemotherapy directly into the liver tumors. I felt that Mark was moving to the doctor's side and buying into the new give up plan. "Standard chemo does not work on carcinoid patients, Sun, even you," he rationalized with me. As he was talking to me he actually walked in the door holding his phone to his ear. He came home from work early, he knew I needed him. He fell to the floor next to me and wrapped his arms around my shaking body. He then whispered, "You are not a quitter and nobody will quit on you." Then he reached for my hair and realized it was gone. I felt overwhelmed with his worry. The worry he was hiding to comfort me. The worry that our lives are changing again…quickly…without our control. That is when it hit me to stop going to the dark side and stand up and fight. I will change my thoughts and that will change my situation.

May 29
Here I Go

Tomorrow I go for my first chemo-embolization. I will be admitted in the hospital for one to two days. I'm so anxious to get started with the battle. I want this disease out of me. Chemo-embolization is a targeted treatment to the liver. It combats the cancer in two ways. First, it injects a high amount of chemotherapy directly into the cancerous tumor. Then eventually it will kill of the blood flow to the tumor which will stop it from growing and in best scenario shrink it. Dr. Gamblin told me it's a simple procedure and I should be home having fun in a few days. "Just a walk in the park" he said in his golly gee manner. I am ready. Hit me with your best shot cancer.

My brother Happy's wife the grand Aunt Sue has decided to leave her family of three teenagers behind in Ohio to come and stay with me at the hospital and to help Mark out with the boys. She is planning on staying a few weeks until her son Jimmy comes home for summer break from college. Jimmy will then move in with us to help out with the boys until the fall semester starts. I had no chance to even ask for help. My family just stepped in and took over just when I need them to. I was having trouble just planning for tomorrow let alone the whole summer. They seem to know just what I need. I am so amazingly blessed.

June 3, 2008
Who Said A Walk in the Park?

Let me tell you that I am not walking in a park. I have given birth naturally three times, had 8 different surgeries, and had a lung removed and have never felt pain like this. I can actually feel the battle going on inside my liver. I feel like my liver is going to explode and all come pouring out. My 115 lbs. body is now about 130 lbs. because of the amount of chemo that was injected into me. I am not able to keep any food down so I am sure I will lose that chemo weight soon. Just what I need to worry about, I am dying from terminal cancer and I think I am fat.

I am unable to lie down, stand, sit or just walk. I cannot believe that something that is supposed to be saving my life is such hell. As I comb my hair chunks just keep coming out. Mark told me to just shave it and it will much easier to handle. I just cannot do that yet. I need it as long as I can have it. It's the only thing I have left of my old life…my BC life (before cancer).

I could not have done this battle without Sue. She stayed right by my side night after night in the hospital as I screamed in pain. A hospital stay of one night turned into three torturous nights of no sleep for either of us. Once again I am so blessed.

June 7, 2008
Chemo Embolization

I realized that I never really explained what chemo embolization is and why my doctors feel it's the best option for me. First, I am sedated, but not put completely out. I know what is going on, but it is almost as if I am there watching it happen to someone else. The doctor then takes a scalpel and makes an incision in the artery in my right groin. Then each tumor in the liver is located and the catheter was inserted into the tumor through the blood vessel that feeds the tumor. Chemo is shot into the tumor along with tiny beads that are used to block the blood flow. It is basically soaking the liver in chemo and trying to clog the blood flow so eventually the tumor will die. The side effects are about the same as traditional chemo because, over time, the chemo get's into the blood stream. However, the chemo works for a month instead of immediately so the side effects come slower. The pain that I have been feeling is from the enlarge liver. My abdomen looks like I am about six months pregnant. The advantage is about 200 times the usual amount of chemo can be shot into these tumors causing them to necropsy and die.

I am sure any doctor who reads this post will have a more technical way of explaining this procedure. But I am trying to reach others like myself, so I put it in normal human terms. Not to mention Medicalesse is not my lingo.

July 1, 2008
With Faith All Things are Possible

The last few weeks have been torture, but I kept the faith and got through it. I cannot imagine not having a relationship with God and going through this battle. This summer is one like no other. I have my 19-year-old nephew taking care of the boys because I am too weak and sick to do so. He will be leaving the first week of August to go back to college for football camp. I will truly miss him and the boys will miss him even more. He has been an outstanding help to me. He does all the dirty work with the boys while I spend the time I am feeling well just being with them. He is an amazing role model for them. His hard work ethic and kindness to me has taught my boys more then any nagging mom could teach them. I just love him so much.

I lie in my bed and wonder why I am so blessed. Why has God chosen me to have so many kind and giving people in my life? I can hear the laughter of happiness going on below me in my family room when their mom is upstairs fighting for her life. The doorbell rings everyday at 4:00 with a friend holding a gourmet dinner she had slaved over all day for my family. I have endless family members doing whatever they could to bring normalcy to my boys and husband. To make things even better my hair stopped falling out…completely stopped. I have a few bald spots but they are covered by the enormous amounts of hair God has blessed me with.

Cancer has taught me that life can never be that bad. Life is what you want it to be if you keep the faith.

July 4, 2008
Independence Day

Fireworks are so much brighter and amazing when you look at them with cancer glasses. It's like seeing them for the first time. However, the only Independence I want today is to be free from the monster that is taking over my body…taking over my life.

August 1, 2008
Escape to the Lake

Mark and I woke up this morning with a strange sense of anxiety. I could feel us both turning to the dark side. Medical bills are piling high in the bill basket, the horrible phone calls are starting, Mark's business is slowing down, reports on the news that we are in a recession, Jimmy will be leaving soon so we will be on our own, and the pain and sickness is getting worse. We need a day without cancer. We need to run away.

Our favorite escape for years has been a very simple beach called Morraine State Park on Lake Arthur. So we decided to pack a cooler with lunch, a hat and comfortable chair for me and off we will hide. Hide from this cancer world we have been living the past few months. It was in the 90s today in Pittsburgh so I prayed the whole one hour ride to the lake that I will make it through the day without incident. I wanted the kids to see me normal today.

Later in the Day:
Watching my boys play on the beach was what I needed to continue on this journey. Seeing them stick by each other and lean on each other even if it is only to build a city out of sand. I sat back and realized they

will be there for each when that day comes. They have each other to lean on. They need no one else but each other.

※※

August 21 2008
Tomorrow the Hell Starts All Over Again

There's been an awkward silence here at the Carney house. Mark and the boys are aware of what's to come in the next few weeks so I think they are preparing. The mom that they know will soon turn into a screaming pain maniac that will live in the room down the hall.

To lighten the solemn mood around the home the boys and I decided to write a little ditty about it:

The Night Before Chemo-embolization

It's the night before Chemo and all through the house
not a creature is stirring not even Oscar the dog who we call the louse.
The clothes for the kids are hung ironed with care
In hopes that Daddy will not have to check what we wear.
Daddy is nestled all snug in his bed
While visions of dropped off dinners dance in his head
With Aunt Sue, The General, ready for the fight
We are hoping we all sleep through the night.
Mom will be gone when we wake up for our day
"not ever given up," is what she would say.
She is doing this to save her life
Because nothing will stop her not even this strife.

I know this is very corny but it sure did break the tension we are all feeling. Keep me in your prayers.

※※

September 18, 2008
The Word's Getting Out

I cannot believe how this cancer journey has changed my life and what is important to me. Last week I was interviewed by both of our Pittsburgh local papers, the *Pittsburgh Post-Gazette* and *Tribune Review* because of my plight to find a treatment for this cancer. To my surprise, both papers published their articles today.

I have always wanted to make a difference in this world but never did I imagine trying to save my life would help other people. Strange is the only way I can describe the feelings I am having. As I read both articles, it amazes me how two reports can interview me and my family, yet twist the story so differently. I agreed to do these interviews to raise awareness of Carcinoid Cancer. I want to help others be aware of the cancer and teach others everything I have struggled to learn about this misdiagnosed cancer. I want others to know the symptoms of this disease so that they can direct their doctor to the correct test and scans. I feel the need to reach out to the public about the costs of medical treatments and about proven treatments in Europe. I expressed to both reports that I don't want this to be an article about a poor mother who is dying from an incurable cancer. Nor do I want them to talk about my children's pain watching their mother battle this disease. I stressed to the reporters that I want them to make the article positive, educational, and inspiring.

The *Pittsburgh Post-Gazette*, Kate Luce Angell, wrote an amazing article. Her facts were right on; she was informative and expressed my concerns about our nation's health care issues. She interviewed several of my friends and showed that you can live a full life even though you are terminally ill. She did research about the cancer and gave a ton of background information on the symptoms. She articulated my need for health care reform and help for those who have an overwhelming amount of medical bills…like me. She also communicated the need to be your own advocate and not to think the possible is impossible. The article accomplished everything I wanted to accomplish for the carcinoid community.

The other article however pulled at people's heartstrings. Even the photograph looked pathetic. Pity and shame is all I can feel when I read about this woman Sunny Carney dying from a hopeless disease. Wait, that woman is me. I felt like I was having an outer body experience. I looked at the photo and read the name in the article but it was not me. I am not helpless or desperate. I have not given up on my fight. Mostly, I sure don't want anyone to feel sorry for me. The article did however; raise awareness of Carcinoid Cancer and the lack of understanding of this incurable cancer. If that means I need to be humbled a bit then I will take that risk to help others.

Please take the time to read both articles, "Treatments For A Rare Cancer Could Banish Clouds for Sunny" and "Wiffleball Tourney to Help Plum Cancer Victim Pay for Special Treatments." I imagine by reading the titles you can guess which one is which. Educate yourself about this cancer, the symptoms, the cost of treatment and the hopes that our available. Send the articles to your family, friends and your doctors. If you have the symptoms ask your doctors for the necessary test to rule carcinoid syndrome out. Mainly, be inspired to never give up hope and faith.

※※

September 20
Today I was contacted by Senator Arlen Spector's office. Apparently, the articles that where published on September 18th, did what I intended them to do…reach out to those who can help me make a difference for Carcinoid Cancer. We will be meeting next month to discuss the European treatment, the FDA, and medical costs that are not covered my health care insurance. I am in awe at how God is working through me to help make needed changes.

Chapter 2:
Passion for Giving

"Act as if what you do makes a difference. It does." --William James

October 1, 2008
Thank you for the Wiffleball Tournament
It's amazing how family, friends, and two communities come together to support a family dealing with cancer and the financial burdens that come along with the journey. I would like to thank everyone who helped to make the "Take A Swing Against Cancer" Wiffleball Tournament fundraiser an amazing success. Watching all the planning going on in the past four weeks from Mark and his troops, I had difficulty comprehending how they were going to pull this whole event off. Then the day came and I must say it was more then I could have possibly imagined. The rain fell in the morning and cleared up before the games and festivities got started. People from all aspects of my life came rolling in. However, my truly unbelievable moment was when I walked on the field by myself with no one watching me and I took in all the sights. To the right of me were 63 teams of five players each laughing and smiling while they swung the yellow plastic bat to get a strike or collided with each other as they reached for the pop up that fell right next to them. To the left the grills were smoking and families where picnicking together with pure joy on their faces. Then in front of me was a group

of children with their faces painted and colored hairspray in their hair comparing notes on who looks the funniest. I then realized that cancer brought this whole event together. Cancer, the monster that I despise, has brought so much happiness to so many people in one field. Today, because of cancer, I feel so loved.

I believe we also succeeded in bringing awareness to this life threatening disease and the fact that the remission cure is not presently given in the United States. The day wouldn't have been possible if it weren't for the efforts of my family and friends and for generosity as a whole. Looking around that field on Sunday as the music played, the grill smoked, and laughter filled my ears, I felt overwhelmed by all of the love and goodwill. My family has been touched every time someone has sent best wishes and prayers. At the risk of leaving anyone out I want to thank my dear husband, my amazing family and great friends who helped to plan and organize this "Little Wiffleball Tournament" that grew into 60+ teams and was attended by at least a thousand. Finally I want to say thank you to all who came, whether to play ball or simply to enjoy a Sunday afternoon. I had the joy of seeing old friends, of making new friends, and of seeing the best of people at a time where most might find that hard. Thanks for all the kind words of support and all the good wishes. Thanks for making Sunday special for me and I hope that you had a special time as well. I look forward to seeing you next year at the Second Annual Take a Swing against Cancer Tournament. With prayers and hope I will be playing.

October 8, 2008
Basel, Switzerland Here We Come

After months of waiting, I finally heard I was accepted for treatment in Basel, Switzerland with the famous Dr. Mueller. Mark and I are leaving January 2 and will receive treatment on January 5. I think this is the answer to all my prayers. This treatment has proven to be successful for Carcinoid Patients who have exhausted all their treatment options here in the United States. I now feel like I have a chance. Thank you for all who have been praying for me and my family.

October 16, 2008
To my Running Angels ……R4R
Mark came home last night with tears in his eyes. He was so touched by your group and what you are doing for me and my passion to help others with Carcinoid Cancer. When I was diagnosed in May for the third time, Mark, my boys and I were just in complete shock and devastation. The original oncologist told Mark and I that this time it is life threatening and the fight would be tough. I had to reach deep down inside to stay positive and fight this for those that will be affected if I die—much like you all do when running and trying to finish those last few miles. I offered it up to the Lord and nothing but good has come out of that news I heard in May. What all of you are doing is proof of that. The hours of work and dedication you guys have given to this event are amazing. It is very difficult for me to sit back and let someone help. I love doing for others for my own selfish reasons…it makes me feel good. I see so much kindness and generosity coming from my cancer. I see the world differently now. I live amongst some true angels. Two little words, Thank You, just don't seem to show you how much you are appreciated. I don't know how to thank you, except guarantee you that I will pay it forward. You give me more of reason to fight even harder. I cannot let your hard work be for nothing. I am fighting for my family, my friends and this wonderful community. You are my "Running Angels."

October 19, 2008
My Garage Sale Divas
I am so sorry I could not attend this fabulous event on Saturday, the cancer was just getting in the way today. I did however send my better half and my power boys to fill in for me. It was really hard for me to stay because everyone knows my two favorite ways to spend a Saturday is at a sale and a party. In all seriousness, I heard from all my family and friends who were there to spend all their cash and find a bargain, that it was amazing. Cars where lined up like the parkway at rush hour filled with crazies trying to catch a deal.

    Cindy, I can only say thank you a hundred million times and it would not show how much I appreciate all your organizing and hard work. Janet, Jen and you too Daryl (I won't call you my Diva) you are all so amazing. I have learned that there are people in your life who come and go and touch you in different ways. You four are those kind of people to me and my family. You spent weeks preparing for this garage sale like ToysRus must prepare for the Christmas season, never expecting anything in return. You only did it because you care and are wonderful, kind and generous people. As I have learned, time is the most precious thing we have. Every one of you have your own families, full-time jobs, and can think of several better ways to spend all the hours you put into this event. Yet you gave your time to me and my recovery. I told Mark on Friday evening that I did not care if we only made fifty cents on Saturday because the gift of time you all gave me was more than any dollar amount. Once again "thank you" is just not enough.

This uplift could not come at a better time. Thursday I was speaking to one of my doctors about an insurance issue and he decided to turn to the "dark side." He had to confirm to me that no treatment I receive is a 100% guarantee and that I am terminal. As I tried to turn the conversation, he began to reiterate that any treatment, chemo-embolization (which I am getting now), sandostatain injection's (receive now also) or the European treatment will not be a guaranteed cure. They are just a glimmer of hope to keep me alive a little longer and sometimes that does not even happen. He continued to stay on the "dark side" and told me more and more about nothing is for sure and blah, blah, blah. Well his attitude became infectious to me like H1N1 and I started turning to the "dark side." Then on Friday I dropped off Logan at soccer practice and a saw sheds full of the "bright side." I saw my garage sale divas busting butt in the freezing cold. I saw old friends and new friends helping set up. I saw a few of my Running Angels passing out fliers. I saw tons of tables and was told they were donated by my dear friend and great chiropractor, Dr. Viola Valletta. I was told that my boys' 1st grade teacher and dear friend also, Julie Thompson-Volpe, has been making beautiful sun bracelets for weeks and was spending her Saturday afternoon selling them at the sale. The fields where full of people some strangers setting up for Saturday's grand sale. All I could do is put my face in my hands and thank God for all you.

I was invigorated with hope, feeling the urge to jump in my car, drive to UPMC hospital and lasso my doctor. I wanted to bring him to those fields and show him what believing in the impossible can do. But

I did not want to have the police that were there directing traffic to have to arrest me. However, it would of probably been free publicity for the event on Saturday. I am so lucky and blessed.

Thank you everyone again!!!

October 21, 2008
The night before torture

My house is full of people tonight. My mother and sister-in-law Sue are staying with us because tomorrow I enter into the hospital for my third chemo-emoboliztion of the liver. This time we decided to change up some things. Instead of Sue coming to the hospital with me and staying the two nights while I scream in agony, Mark is going to be my chemo partner. The past treatments Mark has been the daytime buddy, when things are just getting started, and Sue tagged in for night duty. It worked out great for me because she is on top of everything yet stays calm under the hours of me crying in pain. However, for Mark it is torment for him to be at home in a quiet house not able to help me get through the hell experts say will kill the blood flow to the tumors.

I am worried about this change because he gets so overwhelmed and hysterical when he sees me in pain. As much as I am flattered by his love for me, his outburst of distress when I am vomiting and screaming in pain does nothing to help me relax. I have managed to keep him at a small distance the last two visits; by telling him the boys need him at home. However, this time I don't have it in me to fight the battle with him. I did make him swear to me he will be my support and not a spaz. I know he has it in him. He has proven that he has been able to keep peace and serenity by taking great care of me when I have come home from the last two treatments. So I am giving him a chance to take a big boy pill and venture into the abyss of the night after chemo is directly inject into my liver filling it with poison. Please keep him in your prayers.

Until next post,
Sunny

November 3, 2008
Update

It's been eleven whole days and counting since my large chemo treatment. It's been a rough and long eleven days for us. I swear chemo-embolization is the cruelest form of punishment you can receive. Filling my small organ with an enormous amount of poison to kill softball size tumors is suppose to save my life but the pain that I endured is more like a slow and torturous death. Not to mention the inability to keep anything down and then double the pain when it's coming up just adds to the misery. Every time I GET through it I feel like I accomplished the world.

I know the suspense is killing most of you…pardon the pun. The $1,000,000 question in my emails and phone calls is: "How did Mark do?" I am happy to report he was wonderful. This time around, besides the intense pain, I got extremely sick to my stomach. The first two nights in the hospital were nothing but him holding a pink plastic "S" shape shallow bin while I upchucked my entire stomach. In between the extras of my entire digestive system he managed to help me get through the surges of extreme pain. I don't know what ZEN class he took but I am giving him a big fat "A+." He stayed calm even after buzzing the nurse several times for help and getting no response. Or, when the young girl reached across me to take the tray of grossly smelling uneaten meatloaf and accidentally elbowed me right in the very spot of my back that has a four centimeter tumor. This caused me to literally rip my hair out in agony. Then he bit his tongue when she flipped the tray right on me and left the mess in my bed for the MIA nurse to clean it up. Which, after about thirty minutes and General Mark sending out numerous SOS's, he finally cleaned up himself.

There was a time in the hospital where I was at the end of my control. I looked into his worried eyes and asked, "Is this all worth it?" With a more compassionate face then I have ever seen on him he quietly whispered, "definitely" ! I came home on Sunday to see that I was sunned by my dear friend Laura Caruso. If you are not familiar with the "You Got Sunned Crusade" see below. My whole yard was filled with smiling suns and my empowering quotes all written on the back. That just reminded me that I have such an amazing army pulling for me. When I got to the door I was hugged by my boys and it made those days and the days to come ALL WORTH IT. Mark looked at me and quietly said again, "definitely" .

Wednesday, November 12, 2008
Enjoy!

I would like to share a poem with you. It was emailed to me by my dear friend Carrie. I changed it a little to fit my feelings. This is a good daily affirmation. Tape it to your mirror so that every morning you can review it.

> Life is too short to go to bed with regrets.
> So love the people who treat you right.
> Love the ones who don't just because you can.
> Believe everything happens for a reason.
> Find the reason and follow through with what you need to do.
> If you get a second chance, grab it with both hands.
> If it changes your life, let it.
> Hug Long.
> Laugh Loudly.
> Pray Often.
> Kiss Slowly.
> Forgive Quickly.
> God has never promised life would be easy.
> He just promised it would be well worth it.
> Trust in Him and everything will work out.
>
> God is giving us a chance to live this way.

November 14, 2008
It's Spreading

Now that I got your attention, the awareness about Carciniod Cancer and how it is one of the most misdiagnosed cancer in the United States is growing. Today I was interviewed by Sheldom Ingram from our ABC local news affiliate. My story is going to be the main outreach story of tomorrow's news. I truly hope it touches the right people. Raising awareness of this rare cancer and staying alive long enough to make a difference is my main mission now. I feel like God is carrying me through this whole voyage of cancer. It is all moving so fast; I must just go with it and hang on.

November 16, 2008
R4R... RA (Running Angels)
WOW is all I can say. It is amazing how eight people (okay we will say 10 because of Mark and Mike G) come together in 6 weeks and pulled an event off that takes others a year to plan. What else is astonishing to me is how God brought each one of you with such different talents and personalities together to accomplish one goal. He knew what he was doing and you all worked so well together. I am not sure you all realize how you touched so many people. Yes, my family is so grateful for all that has been done for us in such a respectful way. I cannot begin to even express our gratitude in words. I can only show you in my actions and fight this horrible cancer. However, you have not just made a difference in for my family, but in this entire community. I saw friends laughing, strangers hugging strangers, groups of people cheering others to the finish line and when the last runners came around the field the cheers could be heard from miles away. I had two gentlemen, who I remember seeing a few months ago in a screaming match at the baseball fields, come up to me together and say, "this was amazing." It was the first time they spoke in months. This community was strengthened by your work. The people who live here now know that they live in a community that comes together in times of need.

When Joe called me about two months ago and asked me if he could do this for our family I knew it was going to be a huge success. The passion in his voice was so intense and determined. Then he rattled off the names of his rat pack and I knew it would not fail. I have so much respect for all you and knew that God had his hand on this event. Joe told me that other organizations that have pulled off a 5k like this kept telling him that it's impossible to plan with such limited time. Well I think he proved them wrong. I am so proud of each of you and can call you all my dear friends. I will tell you though Mark is going to miss your Wednesday night meetings and the food that goes with it.

On behalf of Mark, my family, myself and the community THANK YOU. The power behind those two little words is more then you can know. It did not matter if only $1 was raised, what you gave to all of us is priceless. You may call yourselves "Run for a Reason," but you are truly "Running Angels."

We are each angels with only one wing; and we can only fly by embracing one another. ~Luciano de Crescenzo

Sunday, December 7, 2008
No Place Like Home!

I have always been proud of three things: my family I was born into, where I grew up and where I am now. Last night strengthened my convictions. I walked into the basement of the church I was baptized in, made my first communion in, my confirmation in, married in and spent eight years eating school lunches in, to be greeted by a large crowd of people who have touched my life one time or another. Of course my amazing family was there as always, but I was hugged by old school mates, old teachers, some who babysat me and others I babysat for, my first coaches, my first boss, parents of old school mates, my brothers and sisters old friends, college friends, old neighbors, new friends, new neighbors, and even my old girl scout leaders. They were all there to show me support. I felt so safe to be home. Greenfield and the people who grew up there are one of a kind. "Once a Greenfielder always a Greenfielder, no matter how long you've been gone."

There are no words to express my gratitude to all who attended the dance last evening. I can only say how proud I am to be raised in such an outstanding community. As I always say the two little words "Thank You" does not seem sufficient enough. I will guarantee all who have supported me in the past months I will keep fighting to beat this disease and then pay it forward.

Dara Pegher and Ellen McCarthy, you are both very special people. The time you have spent planning this event for my family means more to me then any dollar amount. You have both been through cancer with family members and really do know what we are going through. I truly appreciate your respect and kindness.

In less then one month from now I will be in a hospital in Switzerland receiving my first treatment. These events made it possible me to receive this treatment. Of course I pray that this is my miracle, but I truly believe there is a reason for this all to happen to me. Every event confirms my faith.

Chapter 3:
Prepare for Overseas

"If my mind can conceive it, and my heart can believe it, I know I can achieve it."~Jesse Jackson

December 10, 2008
Count Down!
Twenty-two days and counting, until Mark and I kiss our boys goodbye and head off to save my life. I try so hard not to deeply think about this trip and treatment because I don't want to chicken out. But last night I could not sleep and my mind started pondering about this whole experimental thing. With so much regret I have to admit, I am scared. What am I doing? I must be crazy to fly halfway across the world to receive some experimental drug that I don't even know will save me. What am I doing to my family? I am putting them in complete financial distress, not to mention the emotional effect it will have on them.

This whole "life with cancer thing" seems like a long dream. Sometimes a nightmare…mostly a dream with crazy twists and turns. In the beginning, I felt like I was having an outer body experience and looking into my life from afar. I wanted to ask someone to just shake me and wake me up. Several times I would ask Mark if this is really happening to us? He would just shake his head yes in his zombie way. We were both just going through the motions like robots.

But now, after the shock is gone, I know that if I control all I can to beat this cancer God will take care of what I cannot control. Letting go of control is the most difficult part of this whole journey. Like most having a sense of authority with your life gives us a safe and empowering feeling. I have learned, very quickly, that trying to dominate the uncontrollable gives you a feeling of hopelessness.

As the thoughts of failure were wondering through my head, I reached over and tried to wake Mark, hoping he could say something that would give me conviction about my decision to pursue foreign treatment. Instead he grunted and rolled the other way. I then realized that although I have an enormous amount of help standing on the outside of the rink ready to tag in for a few minutes so I can take a breather, most of the battle I need to fight on my own. Well not all alone, but with God at my side. I realized last night that God is truly the only one that has complete control. So I then decided to get up out of my bed and quickly tiptoe past my sleeping boys' rooms to the kitchen. There I ate a big plate of Christmas cookies and my mind went from doubting my existence to thinking I was fat.

December 13, 2008
News from the Swiss!
Today I received an email from the University Hospital Basel. They confirmed my treatment days and time I need to be at the hospital the morning of January 5th. They are ready and waiting for me.

December 15, 2008
KDKA Interview
Sometimes I ask my husband to pinch me and wake me up. I cannot believe how everything is falling into place. Okay, I still have cancer but my life has so much meaning now. Today I was interviewed live by Marty Griffin from KDKA radio. He was so helpful in getting the word out about the rarities of carcinoid cancer and the treatments available. He reminded me that it is not about ME anymore. It is about all those who are fighting cancer. When I was told in May that my carcinoid cancer had returned and had metastasized to the liver and bones all I

could think about was my boys, Mark, my mother, my friends, my brothers and sisters, and the rest of my family. My heart ached for them. I was not afraid of what was to come for me because I knew with God's help I could get through this adventure. But the pain that my loved ones will go through watching me suffer is what I could not handle.

A few days after digesting my fate with cancer I was sitting in the waiting room at Hillman Cancer Center waiting for the oncologist that agreed to take my case. I was then smacked with a sense of awareness. Everyone sitting in this huge room was affected by some kind of cancer. This is not just my journey, this was a journey with all those fighting cancer with me. I am not the only one that has been told that my life was being threatened and will probably die a very painful death sooner then expected. I am not the only mother, wife, daughter, aunt, sister, friend, etc. sitting there with fear in her eyes grasping a spouse's hand because you are afraid it might be the last time you will be able to hold it. Sure everyone had a different kind of cancer and everyone in that room was at a different stage, but they were fighting just like me. That is when I stopped feeling sorry for my situation and decided to do something about it. Each and every patient sitting in that room has someone who loves them. Some were holding a hand of a supporter like me, some were sitting with their children, some were with a friend, but everyone of them was loved and loved someone. I realized that in order to fight this cancer I needed to be fighting it for others and not just for myself. Maybe it was how I was raised or just another annoying personality trait of mine but I have trouble doing things just for myself. I have to have a purpose for it.

So I decided to fight my disease for others and that is where it has been going since that day in the cancer waiting room. Everyone who knows me well knows that when I become passionate about something I cannot quit until it is done perfectly. That is the one personality trait that completely drives my husband insane. Perfect in this case means cured. As I was talking to Marty, it came to me that when I changed my attitude, and offered my cancer up, everything around me started to fall in place. Even on that very day, just minutes after my conversation, the new doctor I was waiting hours to see, seemed more positive then any other I had seen before.

I was determined not to let this doctor go in the direction of negativity, even if it was reality. As he entered the room he started shaking his head side to side and then added in a "wow" as he read my reports. If my memory serves correct, I believe I stopped him in his tracks and I told him to get on with the bad news and give me some solutions.

While Marty was introducing me, he used words like amazing and unbelievable to describe the way I was fighting this enemy. I don't see it that way. I am not any more fantastic than any other cancer patient fighting for their life. I just find a way to fight this disease for others as well as myself. To let down someone else is just not an option for me. It may seem awesome, but it is truly just a choice I made to win this battle. That choice can be made by anyone going through a difficult time. Get through it by having others depend on you. However, you must have hope and faith in order to even begin that process.

I am not positive all the time. There are times when I just want to break down and curse the world around me. In fact I have even had some times when the pain was so intense or I was so tired that I didn't want to fight anymore. But I know that will only move me a step backwards. I call it the "dark side" (got it from watching those boring Star Wars movies with my boys). When my boys or I start feeling sorry for ourselves because of our circumstances, we tell ourselves over and over again not to go into the "dark side." Every day before my boys walk out the door to go to school I tell them to make good choices. They of course mock me and repeat what I say in a sarcastic tone. They do this imitating because to them they are just words I say over and over again. Although to me it is my life because every day I must choose between fighting or giving up. Hopefully, through my choice to fight, my boys will learn what it means when I say make good choices.

The interview with Marty Griffin today just reaffirmed my determination to make a difference while I fight for my life. I have this need to show that there can be life after a cancer diagnosis. Sometimes it can even be better than before.

December 23, 2008
The GOOD in CANCER
It is two days before Christmas and I feel like a child. I am so excited to spend this holiday with my family. Every year is wonderful with three boys but for some reason this one is more sensational than ever before. This is the GOOD in CANCER. It helps you look at the good times

as if they are the best days of your life. You begin to see life in its simplest form. You are able to truly appreciate the smallest things, like pulling out that baby's first Christmas ornament or wrapping that one gift your child cannot wait to open Christmas morning. I see many people rushing around and feeling stressed about this amazing time of year. I almost feel sorry for them because they don't have cancer. They are unable to look at the world like life is coming to an end. They can't live like they are dying. Cancer makes me the person I am and for that I am grateful. That is why I believe that God knows what he is doing.

When I had my lung removed four years ago because of Carcinoid Cancer, I got out of the hospital Christmas Eve and was so sick. It was snowy, gray, and cold. I somehow managed to arrange under the half decorated tree the few gifts that I had purchased for the boys the day before I entered the hospital for the surgery. The next morning I could hardly make it down the steps to watch them open those gifts. They were excited but something was missing as they tore off the paper. Joy was overcome by fear…the fear of losing their mom. Then a few hours later, my brother came and took the boys for the day to Grandma's so that they can spend a "normal" Christmas with their Aunts, Uncles, and cousins. Mark slept most of the day from exhaustion of spending three weeks with me at the hospital. I just sat in our brown leather chair alone in the living room staring at a floor of red and green torn paper. I was unable to move…paralyzed with horror. I had no idea what would be next. Yet I knew that this was not a Hallmark Christmas.

That Christmas changed my whole outlook on the season. As I look back now I received my best present ever that year. I unwrapped the gift of reality. I became aware that this season is about HOPE. My eyes were opened and I was able to see clearly. Every Christmas after that has been more wonderful than any before.

Merry Christmas everyone and thank you for all your help this season.

Tuesday, December 30, 2008
Three Days and Counting

I am leaving in three days to Basel, Switzerland for this "experimental" treatment. I have to say the fear of the unknown is eating at me. I could not sleep last night so I decided to write down all the things I needed to get done before I go. I always feel that when you are overwhelmed if you write it all down and organize a way to get it done, it makes the anxiety go away. Well, after making my list of really unimportant things in the big the picture of it all, I still felt nervous. I then realized I am not nervous about leaving the boys or getting my house organized for people to stay here. Let's face it, they will have a great time with my family. I think the true feelings come from the treatment itself. I started going to the "Dark Side" (referred to in an earlier blog). My mind raced with questions like: What if this treatment does not work? What if I am too sick to come home when scheduled? What if I miss Nolan's birthday on Jan. 14th? What if Mark cannot handle seeing me so sick and he has no one to help him? What if the doctors don't know what they are doing? When I get home what is next? What if I don't have enough money to go back for another treatment? What if the boys get sick here at home and I am not there? What if the boys feel sad when I am gone and don't want to tell anyone? And on and on my mind raced.

I hardly ever get this way. I truly have felt lucky to have this option of treatment. So I decided to forego the anxiety and take my own advice. I tell everyone who starts the "what if" mind games that we have no control on what could happen until it happens. I am offering my "what ifs" up to God. I am going to get on the plane, enjoy the time with my husband and focus on getting better. Of course I am also going to bring my camera, even if I can only take pictures from my hospital room window. It is closer than a lot of photographers get to the beauty of Switzerland. So this is how I will get my sleep for the next few days.

Please continue to keep me, but mostly my family in your prayers. I really think that they need them more then I. I always say that it is harder for the ones who love the cancer patient than the patient themselves.

Thank you everyone who will be helping my family out while I am gone. The meals, the rides for the boys and all the support is a huge blessing.

I am planning on blogging during my trip so check back. See you all soon!

Thanks,
Sunny

Chapter 4:
Basel, Switzerland

"Fear of failure must never be a reason not to try something."

Saturday, January 3, 2009
We Made It

We made it to Basel, Switzerland. It was a rough trip for me, being sick. We had three flights—Pittsburgh to Philadelphia, Philadelphia to Germany, and Germany to Basel, Switzerland. The first was on a small commuter plane and went very quickly. I was struggling a bit because of lung issues or lack of a lung and the air pressure on the plane. Take off and landing are horribly painful and I feel like I cannot catch my breath. My bones where the tumors are were starting to bother me, but not anything more than a normal bad day. Mark suggested on the eight hour flight to Germany that we upgrade to business class. He often flies business class for work and I thought he was just being spoiled. The cost would be about $2000 more per person and of course I was my thrifty self and declined. BIG MISTAKE! It was a real hard flight. Mark and I sat alone but the two seats we had where very tight. I got really sick to my stomach, was in tremendous pain, and of course, the higher the altitude we went, the more difficult it was for me to breathe. However, I pulled through. We were about an hour late landing in Germany but the Basel flight waited for us. They did not wait for our luggage, though, so we arrived at the Hilton with not one suitcase.

It was a few months ago that I decided to try this treatment. At first, when my research came up with this treatment everyone thought I was absolutely nuts. My doctors followed up on the research and told me there is about a 40% or less chance that this will work. By work, they mean just slow the growth. The chance of shrinkage is less then 10%. I was told that the cost of the treatment may not outweigh the benefits. However, they gave me no other options but to let the cancer take its toll and get my affairs in order. I just could not accept that there was a chance to prolong my life and it was not worth taking. You cannot put a dollar sign on life or your family. Get my affairs in order for what? To prepare my family to be motherless. That is not an option…quitting is not an option at all.

After a few weeks of pestering my doctors and showing them that this treatment was just not a whim that I pulled out of nowhere, they jumped abroad. Since then the support has been amazing. My doctors have rallied around me to make this trip possible. I cannot believe I am actually here. It seems like I am dreaming.

Originally, the hospital in Basel told us that we would be put on a waiting list, and probably get in the spring of 2009. I was fine with that because that gave us time to prepare and get the money together. However, my doctors felt that spring would be too late and I would be too ill to make the trip or even receive the treatment if I did make the trip. I then was introduced to Dr. Raizman here in Pittsburgh. Dr. Raizman is a gastrologist who is suffering from carcinoid cancer as well. He then went to bat for me with the Swiss doctors. He basically begged them to accept me ASAP. So with help and much prayer we got accepted for January 5th. I heard the news on October 7th and everything fell into place after that.

Please keep praying and I will make it through.

(continued)
Mark is sleeping, not sure how he can do that in an exciting new country. He is probably tired from trying to talk with a European accent all day. It is hilarious to hear him try to put a French accent on his mumble jumble language he speaks. I actually understand him better now. I am going to grab my camera and hit a museum. I figure I will get inspired before I go into the hospital.

Thank you everyone who helped me get here. Thanks mom and my sisters for watching and loving the boys while I am gone.

Sunday, January 4, 2009
Almost Time!

We had a wonderful day in Basel. It is such a beautiful and spiritual city. We spent the day with our friend Pete who drove from Holland to show us the European ropes. He is so wonderful to be around when you are stressed and anxious. He has such calmness about him. It was great for Mark to have a confidant and for me to have an artist buddy to pal around with. We walked the city, went to a few museums and ate at a quaint Swiss cafe. I had no clue what I ate because Pete, who speaks several different languages, ordered for us in German. But I took a few bites and it filled me up. Mark however garbaged it all down and is now telling me his stomach is upset. He will just never learn.

Of course I photographed the whole day so that I can capture this moment for the boys. We decided to take a tram to the hospital so that tomorrow morning we would know where we were going. I hate to be stressed and late for anything even if it is to receive some unknown poison. It is about a ten-minute tram ride from our hotel. Perfect for Mark to run back and forth while I am there.

As soon as I went through the revolving doors, it was like being at one of the hospitals at home. I don't know what I was expecting, but I felt the same pit in my stomach I do every time I go into the one of the monopolies of UPMC. The smell was the same, the people moving in and out had the same scared and tired look on their faces, the same information desk, and the airy feeling or sadness was the same. I did not even give Mark and Pete a chance to come through the doors when I ran out. It was like I would lose my freedom a day early if I stayed to look around.

It was cold out and I was not feeling my best, but I was not ready to rush back to the room to get ready for dinner. We decided to take a ferry ride across the Rhine River to see the other side of Basel. We again walked the cobblestone streets, watched a few Frenchmen play bocce and enjoyed some children playing in a dilapidated playground. Every place I turned, people had smiles on their faces. It did not matter to them that the weather was below freezing, or that the bocce balls were old with weathering paint or that the playground had rusty, squeaky and quite dangerous equipment for their preschool age children to play on. In the United States that playground would have yellow caution tape on it with a sign that said, "Demolition Soon" on it. I actually felt ashamed when Pete made the comment that the play set we have in our back yard was three times the size of the city playground here in Basel. Yet the children, snuggled up in their winter coats, were so happy. I was so bewildered by the fact that everyone was content and satisfied. At that time, I realized that I was meant to be here at this exact time in my life.

Yes, I am trying to get a miracle drug that will put me and others with Carcinoid Cancer in remission, but I have received so much more from this experience. Pete has been hounding us since the boys were born to come to Europe. He is always telling us how Americans are so spoiled and dissatisfied. When he comes to visit us in Pittsburgh I love to sit for hours and listen to him tell us about each country and the customs. But the time was never right for a visit because I believe I was never ready to appreciate it until now. It goes back to my earlier blog "The GOOD in CANCER." This is one more experience I would not have if I did not have Cancer. I would not have the opportunity to realize that we live in an amazingly blessed country. I learned that the material things I think my children must have mean nothing. My 2500 square foot home would be a mansion here. Each one of my children have their own room filled with clothes and toys. We have two SUV's with leather seats and three rows so that the boys each have their own space. Yet I am here fighting to live. I see so clear now. I see what life is all about and I hope it is not too late to take what I have learned and share it with all those I love. It is not about all the stuff we Americans try to accumulate. It's not about having the best of material things. It's about happiness and health. It's about being satisfied with what we need and not want for the new of everything.

Pete had to leave to prepare for an opera he is conducting at the end of the week so we said our goodbyes. I don't know what we would have done without all his help and support. His free spirit and zest for life is just what we needed. Not to mention what seeing him did for Mark.

We had dinner and that experience I will save for another blog. After today I am now completely primed to go tomorrow. I feel confident that I will make it through and back to Pittsburgh before January 14th (Nolan's Birthday). Just one more goal I will set. Please keep the praying and the good vibes coming. I (or Mark) will keep you all updated in the next few days.

Thank you Pete for coming to our rescue. Teaching us how to communicate with the locals and the money exchange lesson was huge. But just being a great friend to both of us is more then we could ask for.

With all my love and my new sight,
Sunny

Monday, January 5, 2009
Not Just Any Manic Monday…or Mark Pinch hits

Monday, January 5, 2009
Mark Tries Again This Time With Actual Blog

Monday, January 5, 2009
Mark Take Three

Well this filling in for Sunny on the blog I am embarrassed to say is a lot harder than I would have thought. If you have already wasted time trying to delve into the other two attempts, skip it, its just titles. She has done a tremendous job at sharing her thoughts and conveying her emotions with this so I am trying to not disappoint you all over the next couple of days. Unfortunately, there are no WIFI capabilities at the hospital so you are all stuck with me until Wednesday when she should be discharged. Unlike, the fake Dukes of Hazard (Coy and Vance) and the scab Steelers of '87, I will try to be as close to the real thing as possible. After all of the effort that went into the fundraising, the months of planning, and two sleepiness nights in Switzerland, today in some way seemed almost anticlimactic.

We arrived via taxi for her 9:30 AM appointment (yes, even world famous doctors apparently go at a slower pace over here) and except for the hundred or so bicycles chained to racks right outside the main entrance and the cluster of smoking doctors huddled outside the front revolving doors it all seemed familiar in a way. Inside we had a little trouble finding ZIMMER 4-2, as apparently all of the "lifts" didn't actually go past ZIMMER 2. The nice man at the INFOMEER desk spoke no English, but he did manage to point us to the proper bank of red "lifts" and we proceeded up to the fourth floor. You would think nuclear medicine would be a fairly translatable word, but ah…no such luck. There was no lobby, no registration cubicle or booth, not even a waiting area (although since ESPN is a four letter word that they haven't apparently learned yet over here what did that matter). Sunny being Sunny, she just started knocking and opening up doors and asking —"Ingles?" After interrupting a few minor operations, a nurse's coffee break, and stumbling into the supply room, we once again were blessed with the universal language of pointing and were shown the proper area. After being buzzed in we walked through two huge sliding glass doors and waiting for us on the other side was her nurse Pierre.

Pierre walked us down the short hall and into her room. Never asked for ID. Never asked for paperwork. Never put one of those little ID bracelets on—quite disarming in a way after our previous experiences at Hillman where you are herded like sheep from one station to the next. The room actually looked familiar in a way as well. Two beds (she would be sharing her room with a nice older American woman who was also undergoing her first treatment), no privacy divider, two TVS (three US Channels each), two phones, two radios, and a tray by the wall stocked with bottled water, tea bags, and such. Private sink, right by the lead wall, and two fresh from IKEA chairs which I was afraid to sit on, not quite sure if they would pass the Carney Fat-A#$ test. Pierre was great. He spoke ok English, did a great job in explaining how the next few days would work and never rushed us once. Since she had to order her meals for the next several days he did his best to translate the German menu into English so Sunny could pick her options. He explained that during the first 24 hours Sunny would be like that song by the Firm "Radioactive" and that I could not stay with her. When I did visit I couldn't be closer than 2 meters (thank God for the lead wall I needed to be behind because after having mistakenly tipped the cabbie a $5 franc coin instead of a $2 franc coin, I am seriously questioning my conversion skills). However, on Tuesday we could actually go outside and walk the hospital grounds. Wednesday if all goes well she could be possibly discharged, but not recommend to leave the country for a while. He was very matter of fact, but in a way that wasn't rude, it was reassuring—like a routine. Before the doctor came in I stowed her personal stuff in her closet (in Europe its bring your own robe, gown, and footsies party at hospitals). Another way they keep the cost down.

The doctor's style was even more calming, he joked with us, he never rushed us once through our questions and I could see a noticeable change in Sunny's demeanor from anxiety to one of peace. He explained that the biggest side effect would be nausea and that although there would be pain as well it would be nothing like the chemo-immobilization treatments she had received back in the states. She even made him laugh as he went to personally put her IV line (first for an Amino Acid drip which protects the kidneys, and then ultimately the treatment) by telling him the pressure was on because back home nurses did that. After having failed miserably on getting it into her left arm, I am proud to say he did it pain free in her right. He wished her well, said he would see her downstairs in an hour and left us to be.

For the next hour we talked, laughed about Pierre's ascot for his sore throat and his constant coughing into his arm which he kept apologizing for (but after all I guess when your work admits toxic radiation what's a little bug to make you call off sick), we prayed, and then it was time for her to go downstairs to meet the doctor for her treatment. From the moment we stumbled into that area until that point, I swear couldn't have been more than 45 minutes. The efficiency was amazing.

She called me as soon she got back up to her room. She was extremely nauseous and needed some crackers or something to eat. The hospital roast beef and surprise yogurt/cheese blend of the day wasn't cutting it. Knowing Sunny though she was probably calculating the calories and grams of fat in the meal and that is what made her sick to her stomach. I hopped the 11 Tram (the orange one) hit up a quaint little bakery for two croissants (one for her and one for her new roomie who was also done with treatment) made my first trip to the local supermarket (THE COOP, and apparently Advantage Card discounts have geographic restrictions) and fifteen minutes later dropped off Goldfish crackers, fancy European Breakfast bars bought on sale of course (in case she asks later how much) and blew her a kiss. I wasn't allowed to stay for more than a minute…Pierre was outside rearranging his neckwear and gargling Ricola's…but let me reassure you all that under the circumstances she looked great. She was sitting up, talking to her new roomie, and watching some real bad old American TV. (I Love Lucy, I think) But after having seen her come out of the chemo-immobilization process bruised, battered, shivering, dry-throat and IV tubes to the max, this was a pleasant surprise and I think an answer to prayers. I am in by no way trying to diminish at all what she is going through—I just answer the question How's Sunny Doing?-—I am not living it…but from my eyes she looked beautiful. The difference was like putting a dog down via euthanization and what Micheal Vick's boys did to those pit bulls. That was how much physically more relaxed she seemed.

Basel is a great city and the people have been friendly and helpful (not enough Black 'n Gold but I am working on teaching the locals how to say Roethlisberger with a Yunzer accent). But I know Sunny can't wait to get back to our kids, our fat dog, family and friends. Your thoughts and prayers are what have helped her get this far, and I know you all are very much in ours as well. This has been an incredible journey and I can honestly say I am blessed with an amazing, resilient wife who just will not let this beat her. Every minute of every day since her relapse she has been a true inspiration to me and to all those who are around her. Now she is in a Swiss hospital bed, inspiring the woman next to her. I don't know where she gets her feistiness and spunk but I know that is why I love her. Please continue to pray and I know she can't wait to see you all back in Da Burgh. Keep the faith, go Steelers, and I know she is thinking of you all.

Mark

Tuesday, January 6, 2009
The Day After

Proud to say that after reading the blog from yesterday, Sunny has allowed me to continue to substitute for her on the blog. First off let me answer the obvious question—How's Sunny Doing? She is actually here with me at the hotel taking a shower although she won't be discharged till tomorrow. That's right. We are allowed to leave the hospital even though she is still a patient. I can't imagine trying this back at Montifore or Shadyside. I think the bells and whistles go off when she walked ten feet from her room back in the States. She is very nauseous, although she hasn't gotten sick since I have been with her since mid-morning. She has a bad headache (and for once, not due to her annoying husband or loud kids) and is in discomfort. But the fact that we walked around, called home to yell at the kids (just kidding of course, Grandma was already doing that) went to The COOP (Sunny had to check to ensure I really did buy those European breakfast bars on sale yesterday), caught the 11 Tram (that's right the orange one) rode for six or seven minutes, walked two blocks in a light snow back here to the Hilton and she didn't have to sit to rest once has been an amazing answer to prayer and a true indicator of her CAN DO personality.

Last night was a long one for both of us. It snowed, but not much. Just enough back home that Jon Burnett and his weather cronies would have had us out stocking up on milk, bread, salt etc. as if a "major snow event" was coming. It was pretty though. It hit me after 9:00 PM when I called her room only to get a male voice telling me "NEIN…Not after nine-try back in the morning"—what reality was? Reality was that Sunny was in a hospital, after having undergone a new kind of treatment for the first time, with nurses who were kind (although she calls the one NURSE LURCH because of his mannerisms) who may or may not understand what she is saying to them, with no real TV, in pain and discomfort, with a roomie who she didn't want to wake up as she was vomiting, with her main support (me) ten minutes by train away in case of emergency, no ID (the passports are here with me), no ID bracelet with emergency contact info, no way to get a hold of me if something happened. It was nerve-wracking the rest of the night for me, but she told me this morning it was a long anxious night for her. She had to get a full body scan late in the afternoon and when Pierre took her down to the abyss of the hospital, down a dark hallway (felt like a moment from One Flew Over The Cuckoo's Nest) she felt like she was following Igor to the laboratory. The machine was loud and intimidating big she told me, but continuing along with the theme of the week, the girl tech spoke good English, was kind and understanding, and Sunny was back in her room in 20 minutes.

She has to get two more scans in the morning early Wednesday and then will be discharged. I can't tell you how good it will be to have her cramped back into this room with me. Sunny being Sunny I am sure her positive attitude and the reaction so far to the treatment will have us on the plane back to the states in time for a late night pepperoni roll at Somma's (just kidding, we won't need milk yet). I am in awe of how well she is doing, and can clearly see prayers continued to be answered. God she is so tough in a gentle kind of way. She is not scared of what this treatment can do to her she is only worried about me being alone without her. After one day and night with her roomie she has managed to make an impression on her too. The woman told me when Sunny was getting dressed that Sunny had gotten her through the night. She was so glad Sunny was there. I saw that on both nightstands next to each hospital bed were their Bibles. The roomie said, "we each read our Bibles together."

While I am typing this (of course I just deleted half of this accidentally somehow so this is the second try from this point on) she is resting comfortably two feet from me (heck with that meter conversion stuff) and my buddy Peter called. Having someone to show us the lay of the town ahead of time was a real Godsend for Sunny and I. Having that someone be one of your best friends from high school who lives on this side of the pond, has been to our house in Plum for the holidays makes it even better. It was great to finally get to his side of the world (although I didn't think it would ever take cancer for it too happen). Sunny really enjoys his company because photographers and musicians go together like Beam and Coke Light.

We really miss you all, especially our kids and family and dear friends, and can't wait to drive through that old tunnel and see the prettiest cityscape in the world laid out in front of us. Keep us in your thoughts and prayers as you all are in ours and if Sunny is OK with this entry I will try it again later today or in the morning.

Mark

Wednesday, January 7, 2009
Sunny Days at the Hilton

Well this should be my last entry into Sunny's blog. She checked out of the "Hosspital" around 11:00AM this morning after getting two more scans (pictures of the dye which show all of the lesions/tumors and where the radiation is taking too) skipping another fortified breakfast of Swiss Mush with sides of fruit and juice, talking with her new friend/roomie and then finally speaking with the doctor. Let me answer the $1,000,000 question-How's Sunny Doing? The doctor indicated that the scans while also being used as the base for a second treatment confirmed that the Y90 was working in that it took to all of the tumors. Thus she was "invited back" for a second round of fun in Basel on March 16th. The doctor also indicated that the hell that is called Chemo-immobilization had worked, as the big lesion in the liver had no dye attaching to it, which indicates no blood flow at this time. That gave her a much needed boost of positive ammo to leave the hospital. She had another sleepless night due to intense nausea, a very sick patient in the room next door, and the discomfort that was being caused by the Y90. She indicated she felt like she had a bad hangover as she laid down for a nap here in the room-which I am happy to say she is still enjoying. A bad hangover like feeling for up to a week is a common side effect for the treatment. This is the first time I have really felt a connection with what she was experiencing because as some of you know the word hangover does exist in my vocabulary. So with a fresh packet of Burger King Fries which she nibbled on a few (that's right Booger Fling... and let me tell you a whopper with cheese never tasted that good back on RT 286) and an old episode of 1990 Judge Judy to entertain her she nodded off.

When I went downstairs of the hospital with her to get her first scan this morning I discovered why there is no need for a waiting room—you don't wait. She was scheduled for 8:15 and she was in there promptly at 8:15. I sat in IKEA's latest line of funky blue hospital plastic chair with an American Cowboy next to me (another patient for the treatment I learned) boots, leather vest, the hat and all and the tech seemed surprised when she told me "25 minutes...you take lift back to room...ya" and I told her I would just chill there. She gave me her cute little wave and off she went with such confidence and strength. I wish I had just half of her guts.

Coming back here on St Patrick's Day will be a bit different from the old days of too much fun in Market Square. But I imagine green strudel, pastries, cheeses, priscouito, and chocolates taste the same on either side of the pond. Sunny and I will have to learn how say "Baked Potatoes, Green Beer, and Stew" in German in the next two months. Maybe Uncle Tommy already knows how? I will "ring" him when we get back.

It is another Pittsburgh like day outside, gray, dreary, no hint of the sun...except for the one sleeping a few feet from me. The temperature is -4C which I think is in the low 20's but we already know how that conversion thing and I get along. The Europeans keep biking even in snowstorms, which is pretty funny to see...a six foot man in a business overcoat clutching his "bag" slip sliding through the snow while trying to stay in the appropriate bike lane. That's another thing we noticed...even the bike lanes are marked two directions and are in better shape than anything PennDot ever put a backhoe into. If we were to fundraise over here the R4R crew would be out of luck—there just aren't any runners. Smokers, lots of bicyclists, smokers, pushy TRAM riders, smokers, and dogs. Dogs in restaurants, dogs on the trams, dogs in the room next door...and these aren't little foofoo American dogs, Sunny and I have seen about 10 breeds of huskies, ST. Bernards, labs, and collies, but not one being carried or with a goofy little doggie sweater. Sorry cat lovers, these behemoths must snack on them. Also learned a couple of valuable lessons today—McDonald's is the universal panhandling spot, the pigeons that used to live in Market Square have crossed the pond and continued to breed, you must weigh your bananas and put the price label on them before getting to the register at THE COOP or you risk getting called "stupid Americana..." and the yellow Alarme Zimmer Wetz sign is apparently used in lieu of street salt. Don't ask. Sunny just woke up by the way and said the first thing she wants when she gets back is a Primanti's sandwich (only because Somma's kitchen will be closed).

We are more than halfway through this leg of her journey, the treatment and the hospital are behind us and I think we are both really missing Da Burgh and you all at this moment. Keep us in your thoughts and prayers and I assure you Sunny and I think about you all constantly. We look forward to seeing you all soon. She is an amazing woman and I cannot put into words how much she means to me—saying she completes me would be stealing a line but also an understatement. As I sit here finishing this post I cannot help but look over at her laying there sick as all hell yet still smiling. She says she is the blessed one but we all know that each of us are blessed to have her in our lives. When I met my wife I had no idea what she would be teaching me about life. She was a skinny, pretty little college student waitressing to pay her way through school. I was a spoiled college kid waitering because I screwed up in college and needed to prove to my parents I was not the slacker they thought I was. After introductions from our resteraunt manager I joked with her and called her chicken legs. She looked at me and said, "You have potential but I can see you don't care about that." She had drive and ambition even at twenty years old. She knew exactly where she wanted her life to go. She was not working for some spending money at the local bar or new designer clothes like many college kids. She had a plan. She would pick the busiest shifts so she could make the most money in the shortest amount of time. Of course those where the shifts that interrupted my partying so I did not work with her for a few weeks. Then I realized I had to know this chick so I started picking up shifts that she would work. She had a way of wooing the customers and leaving at the end of each night with a huge stack of bills. She would have a line of drunks waiting for her section because she let them think they may have a chance. Yet her focus was only on her plan and if that meant be nice to a few idiots for a larger tip she did that. Focus and goals was the woman I had to marry. She changed my life.

Thanks for letting me play Sunny the last couple of days and I know you all will join me in welcoming her back to this page tomorrow.

Much Love to home,
Mark

Wednesday, January 7, 2009
Another Milestone was Reached!
I cannot believe I am done with the first round of treatments in Basel. While I guess by the way I feel I can believe I went through something. I am feeling pretty yucky and sick. Nothing like the three long doses of chemo-immobilization but I am not ready to hit the slopes. I am sick to my stomach, dizzy, very hot then extreme chills, and headaches, pain in every spot a tumor was detected and extreme fatigued…all completely normal and good to have according to Dr. Mueller. He told me that the more side effects you have the better the treatment is working. So I say, "BRING IT ON." I can handle it if it means my boys will have a healthy mom. That is correct; the doctor that actually took care of me was the genius who discovered this treatment. I was completely surprised when he came into my hospital room and introduced himself. He was very kind and completely concerned about all my worries. He asked me about pain and taking pain meds. And I told him I try hard not to take them. He explained that cancer of the bones is extremely painful (no shit I felt like saying) and relief of that pain helps me to relax which in turn will help the therapy eat the tumors. He explained how stress feeds on the tumors and that I need to free myself from any possible stress. Easy right? I of course thought, *and then take this horrible monster out of me, and then I will relax.* We talked about the seriousness of my cancer and he agreed that I needed to be in Switzerland ASAP. He talked to me for a good 30 minutes and when he left I felt like he was my doctor from the beginning. He was very humble considering he is saving lives on a daily basis.

I am so blessed to be out of the "Twilight Zone." A kind and efficient Twilight Zone but nonetheless the strangest episode I had ever seen. I think Mark described it well in his posts but the nights were even stranger. An experience I will write about when I am not so fatigued. I am confident that I will be okay to fly home on Saturday and let me tell you looking forward to it. I am signing out for now and will fill everyone in more tomorrow.

Thank you everyone who cares enough to read my boring posts. I am so blessed to have so many angels supporting me.

Hugs and good wishes,
Sunny

January 7, 2009
To my boys

I promised you another post tomorrow but I just had to write something to my boys. I am not sure if I will press the publish button because I don't want them to know I am a blubbering mess right now. When I have time to think about this whole situation I can only imagine how scared and overwhelmed they must feel. A few months ago, we as a family were in Disney World riding amazing rides and relaxing by the pool at one of the most magical resorts. Our life seemed perfect in their eyes. Although I was having horrific back pain they were unaware that anything was wrong. We were together and loving each other. We were the "Hallmark" family with the picture perfect life.

Now their mom is half way across the world fighting for her life against a disease that has no cure. We as adults, can understand that life can change in a blink of an eye, but children are supposed to be sheltered from those changes. I wish I could shelter them from this whole cancer life. I have no answer on how to do that right now. I wish I could take a big cozy warm blanket, wrap it around all three of them and hold them tight. I remember when they were all babies and Mark was traveling or working long hours. The boys and I were like a team. At night when we were home alone and they would awaken with a nightmare, I would get our favorite fuzzy Steelers blanket, plop it in the dryer for about ten minutes so it was warm and then the four of us would snuggle up on our big leather couch with one of their favorite books. They use to fight over which one got to sit on my lap, turn the pages or pick the book. In the end I was always able to help them feel safe and protected. I don't know how to do that now.

To my boys:

I must say I miss you three so much. I cannot wait to receive each one of your emails every morning. I am so proud of you all and how well you are handling me being sick. I know you are scared. I want to promise you at this very moment I will do whatever I can to help you feel safe again. I will fight this cancer with all I have. If that is not enough remember that everything I have showed you will help you throughout your life. Be strong until I get home and can wrap that warm blanket of love around you.

I love you more than life itself,
Mom

January 8, 2009
Hilton Stay!

Today was quite uneventful. I am feeling about the same as yesterday. But like I stated earlier, the worse I feel the better the treatment is working. So as I lay in the tiny Hilton room feeling like I have a horrible hangover from college days I am hopeful. I have complete faith that this is working. I can actually feel each and every cancerous tumor swell. Doctor Sommer's (Dr. Mueller's sidekick) explained to me that the tumors will swell first because the radiation and yittium 90 (the cocktail mixed with the radiation) enters the tumors. When that begins to happen it causes significant pain and nausea, but in time will eat away the tumors. So I have the pain and sickness. I am guessing that means it is working. No not guessing, believing it is working.

After sleeping for about 12 hours Mark thought I needed to get some fresh air. So we went to a little cafe that was like a kitchen of someone's home. It actually reminded me of my grandmother's kitchen.

The front door had a big welcome sign on it, but no restaurant sign or even open sign. The only way to tell it may be a café was the small chalk board with the special menu written on it (in German) on the sidewalk next to the steps that led to the door and a small metal table with two chairs and a pretty pink table cloth with a vase of flowers holding in down. The food seemed to take hours, but that is normal here. Hoda, the waitress, brought me a bowl full of some kind of oatmeal looking mush. I tried to eat and did get a few bites down but it was rough. So I forced Mark to finish the bowl when she was not looking because I did not want to insult her choose of "comfort food." I felt a little better but could barely keep my eyes open and had no appetite. We left. I sucked it up went for a walk around this beautiful city with my cute hubby, because I knew he did not want to go back to the hotel and watch me sleep.

On a lighter note, Mark is definitely making havoc over here. So far he has been yelled at by a German airline stewardess for stacking his tray wrong, pushed off a curb for walking to slow, harassed by a pan handler and told to "fuck* off, called a stupid Americano at the local grocery store for not weighing a banana and holding up the line up, got in a little heated Steelers vs. Patriots disagreement at the hotel bar when I sent him down for a glass of ice and not to mention being afraid to enter the swimsuit optional swimming pool. Mark is Mark wherever he goes.

Later that day
I took a break from this post to lie down and when I got back up I received an email from home. The email had two heartwarming articles in the *Plum Advanced Leader*. One was my son Austen's basketball team, "Plum Storm." They are doing "Points for Sunny" fundraiser (please see home page for details). When Steve Fuhrer, the coach, told me about it I was really touched and thought it was a great idea to inspire my son to play his best. But being over here sick and reading that article it hit me how much this makes this fight all worth it. It is not about the money that will be raised. It's about the support and kindness that the Plum community has given to our family. I always say that it feels so good to give to others and to show your support for others going through a tough time. Cancer is our tough time. I never knew, until now, what it feels like to receive that support and kindness because I have had a very blessed life. I can tell you it feels good and

safe. I feel safe because my boys are living in a community of love and kindness. Safe that my son Austen is being coached by a man with a heart the size of the community. Safe that when I am away receiving treatments my home is full of family and friends that are loving my children like I would. Thanks Steve and Ellen for giving us that feeling of safety.

The other article was about the upcoming concert on January 9 at the Plum High School by "Backseat Love Story." Justin Dillon, a member of the band, teaches Nolan guitar and Austen and Logan drums. He has been a real inspiration to my boys not to mention a great escape from what they are going through. He is an amazing teen with such great values. I was in complete shock when his mother Lisa told me that Justin and his band members wanted to do this for me. I was dropping off Nolan at lessons and I went back to the car and had a good cry. I don't do that often because I refuse to give in to the negative side of cancer, but this cry was a proud cry. I was so proud of these Plum High School students. I don't care if not one cent is raised; the support they are showing for me is worth a million. One more "GOOD IN CANCER." Thank you Backseat LoveStory, Havannah Drive and Mandy K. I hope you all can make it to the concert. I will be there in my heart.

Well I was expecting this to be a short post, but I really had a ton to say.

Thanks Mom and my sister Judy for staying with the boys. I know that is it hard work and that juggling their busy schedule is crazy. Thanks to the rest of my brothers and sisters for being their chauffeurs and for helping Judy and Mom. Thanks to all who are bringing the delicious meals I been hearing about. Thanks to Sharon Mitolo, Colleen Caffas and Jim Nolan for riding the boys to all their sporting events. I really do appreciate it all.

Friday, January 9, 2009
We Are Coming Home!

Yes, I am okay to fly home. I got the okay today from Dr. Mueller. I am still sick to my stomach and in some pain but I need to get back to US ground. Before the trip I was told January 10th would be the soonest I would be able to fly home. Well tomorrow is Jan. 10th and I am on my way. The Swiss have been great, but there is no place like home. So boys open your arms because I need some big hugs.

※※

Friday, January 9, 2009
I am jumping in to help Sunny expand this last post entry from over here on this side of the pond. Although it meant pulling me away from the European version of *Animals Do the Funniest Things* I will try to stay focused. It's only been a week over here but it seems like a seismic shift in my life, my relationship with Sunny, and quite frankly my perspective on the world in general (although I am lobbying for ESPN to go international the day I get back...I miss that little ditty-na na naht...na na naht so much). I have learned through this part of Sunny's journey, that being back home with a support group, where familiar things are often overlooked or worse, sources of whining and complaining, am ultimately the best place to undergo and fight something like Sunny is fighting. This has been hard on her but she has tried to be a trooper and go out for a few hours each of the past three days. It may have been a short jaunt out on a clock, but it was yet another example of her standing up to this disease, looking it in the jaw, and then giving it the old "Sunnysmackdown" as only she can.

Although we have had a good week here all in all and the early prospects for this treatment working for her, I can't help but think how much easier it would be to fight this back home in Da Burgh or Baltimore, or Minnesota, or even Cleveland. There are a number of clinics in each of these cities and cancer centers which should be frankly embarrassed that 3 of the 7 patients here in Basel this week beginning their treatment were from the United States. For every Sunny and the other lucky two, imagine how many back home never can get on that plane, or have this disease diagnosed because of the lack of money to properly educate the medical community. Its Ridiculous with a capital R, and no offense to the Swiss care which she received here which was tremendous, but it isn't like the stories you read about in the *Post Gazette* where a family comes from "NOWHERESVILLE INDIA to seek care for sick child"...America is supposedly the most advanced nation in the world, with the brightest minds, the best technology, the leading drug companies, it can't be money, because from what I am reading here its getting tight everywhere. What is the reason? I now know a little how those families which come to Pittsburgh from other countries must feel, and recognizing how "international" our little town isn't, how much harder if must be for them. The difference is we can do something about this…I know Sunny has made that choice, and after being here, good bread, kind panhandlers, friendly sauna nudists, aromatic cheeses, ice cold $10 budweisers, three English speaking stations on our tele at all times, warm Coke lights, friendly supermarket "customeers" and all, I will help her harder now than ever to bring this back to the states. Basel is a town that should be visited for its culture, its art, and its beauty not as a "last resort option for desperate American cancer patients."

I know that you all have been praying, helping with our kids, and the fundraising, and I want to assure you that this has been a big step in Sunny's treatment. She will beat this because she never fails at anything. She is a winner in every sense of the word. All 110 or so pounds of her is a fighter. I am amazed at how Fucking tough she is yet so beautiful and fragile looking. She is an inspiration to me every time I look in her big blue/green eyes. This whole time not once has she asked, "Why me?" I have seen her scream in pain, catch herself from passing out and vomiting repeated only to see her then say, "lets not waste our time here and go do something." I know that I have said this before but I truly have no idea where she comes from. When you look at my wife, before she speaks that is, you see a tiny pretty little Irish girl. Never would you expect this tough superhero of a woman. What impresses me the most is she has no idea she is anything special. She thinks we are all like her. She is clueless how special she is. I am so thankful she is married to me.

Mark

Chapter 5:
"Babies We're Coming Home"

"A house is made of walls and beams; a home is built with love and dreams."

January 12, 2009
Back!!!
I am ¼ of the way through this Swiss journey and safe at home. I had all intentions on posting Sunday morning but I slept through the morning and Sunday afternoon I could not take myself away from the boys. I know I was only gone for nine days but going through what I went through emotionally and physically in those nine days made me feel so separated from everything here at home.

The flight home was uneventful and actually relaxing. I did get sick on the plane a few times, but nothing that I could say was devastating, at least not for me. I am sure the others sitting near me may disagree. Going through customs in DC was stressful, but I think it was Mark's frustration that made it more stressful. He was like OJ running from one station to the next while I stood in one line holding my puke bag (sorry for being so graphic) and took my time. I was too sick to care what happen and was radioactive so I knew I was going to set off the alarms anyways. I had a letter that I received from the doctor to let security know that I am not a terrorist and just "Light Bright Girl." Mark was stressed to the max and jumped from line to line because, "this line is shorter, Sun." I just stood in one line and waited. Guess who was waiting on the other side of customs for her travel buddy?

When we pulled in the driveway at home, Nolan was waiting outside with arms open. He always listens. Sorry Austen and Logan. Of course when I got through the doors there were two suitcases sitting right by the stairs. They were not Mark's or mine because ours were MIA again. Yes my dear mother and sister were packed and ready to hit the road even though it was past midnight. They looked like they were through some kind of treatment themselves; Carney boys' treatment I guess. Actually I may have looked better (not to compete). Not sure what my three boys put them through but they were exhausted and completely looked whipped. To think I took the hardest and most difficult boy with me. Mark, I mean for all who don't know him.

Nonetheless, I am home and for the first day actually kept some food down. I feel so confident that this treatment is going to work. I am determined to do whatever it takes to fight this horrible disease for me and for others. I was reading Mark's last post (the one he finished for me) and I was surprised it finally hit him that this and other cancer treatments need to be available here in the US. I knew that he understands that I have become so passionate about that, but I don't think he understood what I was feeling until he actually stood by my side and went through this treatment with me in Switzerland. Although, I have been through so many treatments in the past he has always had distraction and a way out. This time it was just him and I. No children, no work, no family to lean on, no late nights to run out too, no friends to shoot darts with or play cards with, no clients to call back, no ESPN, no American TV. Just Him, Me and the Cancer. He may be beginning to understand why I am so fervent about helping others receive this treatment. Mark has not been able to quite understand my need to be so concerned about others with Carciniod Cancer or giving them the blessing of knowledge that I have received. He gets annoyed that I will stay up until all hours of the night and answer emails from people with carcinoid cancer asking questions about my treatments. He feels that I need to take care of myself first and then when I get in remission I can go on my crusade (deep down hoping I found some other passion by then). In all fairness to him, I would probably feel the same way if I were the spouse watching my other half slip away and feeling so ill more often then not. The only way to explain it is that I know what it is like to suffer from this cancer. I know what this cancer and lack of knowledge can do to someone with it. I, unfortunately, know how this monster can consume one that is afflicted with it. Not to mention the destruction it does to their families and finances. I don't want to see anyone else have to go through it for years like I have. I know what it does to my body. I know what it does to my self-esteem (yes I had more confidence before I had cancer), I know the pain my boys feel when they see me so sick. I know what it does to a marriage. I know what it can do to your life. Fighting to bring this treatment to the US is the only control I have over this disaster. For once Mark finally gets it. Once again, "The Good In Cancer."

This week will be a slow recovery, but by next week I plan on being back at life. Dr. Sommers explained that I will feel pretty run down and hung-over. But by next week I should be okay. Of course, he does not know me well enough to know that I will be X-ing off the days and holding him to that prediction. Maybe Dr. Gamblin can fill him in on my persistence.

I try to end each post by expressing my gratitude for some blessing I have had. Well I think today God deserves my thankfulness. Thank you Lord Jesus for all my gifts and for letting me go through this trial. I know I will be blessed for it.

January 14, 2009
The Power of Attitude

Our lives are not determined by what happens to us, but how we react to what happens; not by what life brings to us, but by the attitude we bring to life. A positive attitude causes a chain reaction of positive thoughts, events, and outcomes. It is a catalyst…a spark that creates extraordinary results.

January 15, 2009
Nolan's Birthday

Before you begin reading today's blog I want to explain that this is a more personal story and not much about my cancer. So if you are trying to overcome boredom on this below zero degree day read on. Not sure it will help but it will kill some time. If you are hoping for my cancer story look for future posts.

My goal when in Switzerland was to return by January 14th, Nolan's 10th birthday. To some that may seem like such a small goal but to me it was a milestone. In May when I was told that my cancer had spread to the liver and bones in the back of my mind I thought that would not see any of my boys turn a year older. With much hope and more prayers I was able to celebrate Austen turning 12, Logan turning 11 and now Nolan turning 10. It is common for mothers to reminisce on their child's birthday about the very day they were born. It is one of those memories a mother will never forget. So like the emotional mother I am that is what I did yesterday at 6 am while I watched him sleep. I thought about my life 10 years ago and how I would never guessed I would be fighting for it now. Even though I had already fought carcinoid of the ovaries, I believed the cancer chapter of my life was completely behind me. I worked out every day and ate all the right things. I took every possible vitamin I could take. Did whatever I could do to be healthy then. I was so happy then… just did not know it.

    I can tell you detail by detail the day I found out that I was pregnant with Nolan. It was a spring Saturday and Mark had a group of friends over to help build a deck in our little city home. Austen was a little over a year and Logan was 4 months old. I was feeling exhausted and under the weather for about a week and just could not figure out what was wrong. I remember opening the bathroom cabinet and seeing a pregnancy test that I used when trying to conceive with Austen. I thought, "what the heck," maybe it is the Immaculate Conception. Mark was traveling a ton and when he was in Pittsburgh he was working 16-hour days trying to make up for our lost income when I decided to stay home after Austen was born. I don't even remember holding his hand let alone anything else. Not to mention I was told 2 years earlier that my chances of having a child were slim to none and I had already beat the odds twice. Call it woman intuition or "just in case" syndrome, but the test was positive. I remember just sitting done on the bathroom floor in complete shock. Hearing all the commotion from the open window coming from Mark and all his boys outside (include our two babies). I think I sat there for over an hour with all kinds of self-centered thoughts running through my head. Never once realizing what a blessing I was given.

    When I pulled myself together, forced to because I heard Mark yell for Austen to put down the nail gun, I walked done three flights of steps in our century old, very small, city home. I was in complete panic but needed to tell him immediately because why should I be the only one afraid and be carrying this burden alone. I opened the cellar door to the outside and looked around at all the disappointed looks on his friends' faces. I know they were thinking, "here she comes to spoil the fun." Each and every one them single and carefree. I looked beyond Mark and beyond the six foot wooden fence, we put in our yard to keep Austen from playing in the street (which by the way he managed to climb by age three), and saw Mark's brand new red convertible he purchased six months earlier. It was a gift to himself because he tripled his sales goal that year and worked his butt off to do so. I closed my eyes to imagine a minivan in its place. Then I recalled the deal Mark and I made before we got married to never buy a minivan when we have kids. Of course I was a bit bitter about that little red car because I gave up my very successful sales career and his was career was booming while I was changing poopy diapers and wiping throw-up off my oversized t-shirts. He had a closet full of fine suits and great shoes and I had a laundry basket full of running shirts that I collected from all the exercise I did to lose the baby weight.

God where was my mind those days! I gave him the "finger come here sign" and heard all the sighs from the boys outside. Whispers were coming from all over the half built, unsafe deck my precious babies were sitting on. "The boys" were turning down the music, hiding the beer cans and pretending to work. Mark was so happy and so carefree then. He was 28, beginning a successful career, had great friends, had a wife that rarely nagged because she was so overwhelmed she did not know where to begin, two amazingly healthy boys (let me mention again they were "BOYS") and was in great shape (yes he would get up every morning at 6 am and hit the gym).

I dragged him upstairs and sat him down. At that time sheer panic went across his face…the last few years had been to many talks like this. I was diagnosed with cancer first, then remission, then cancer was back, then told I would never have children, then remission, then pregnant, then quitting my job, then pregnant again, then my father passed away… all in less then two years. The fear in his face was priceless I thought. So I waited at least three or four minutes for effect before I actually spoke.

Then, I began by yelling at him, something to the nature of how we never plan anything, we just jump and don't look, how I can't handle what I have and how his life has gotten better and I am my mother (sorry mom I only wish I could be as amazing as you). I continued by saying that I did not go to college for this and that he needs to pitch in. He just stared at me like I was an alien. So I spilled it out like a bag of beans. To my surprise he jumped up and down in pure delight. Screaming and howling YA YA!!! Lifting me up in the air and spinning me around like a rag doll. He was thrilled even when I dropped the mini-van bomb. He kissed me several times and then yelled out the window to his friends. I on the other hand felt trapped and so jealous of him.

It took me a few more days to realize that this was once again a gift from God. The first three years after Nolan was born was a blur of crying babies, colic, ear infections, Barney and Elmo, yes a minivan, changing diapers, bottles, pinkies, blankies, potty training, first day of preschool three years in a row, play-dates, home remodeling, and just to make things more adventurous a move, me starting a business and a few promotions for Mark. I look back on that spring day and with such disgrace of myself. Nolan is such a joy to our family. There is never a day that goes by that he does not make me smile and feel loved. Through my trials of cancer Nolan is the one that brings the light to my heart. From the moment he wakes up in the morning to the moment he falls asleep he brings the sunshine to our home. How could I have every thought this wasn't planned? Nolan was God's plan for us. So January 14, 1999, was not my plan, but God's.

God knew what my future held and he gave me each of my boys for different reasons. Austen is my rock and as some say my clone. He's strong, a fighter, a perfectionist and self disciplined. Not only does he look like me, he has my personality all over. When I look at him I see what others see in me. He carries my good and bad qualities. He can be hard at times…cold and unforgiving just like me. Nonetheless, he is the anchor of the three boys. Logan is my compassionate and sensitive child. He is stubborn and strong-willed. He always wants what is fair for everyone and will fight until he wins. When I need anything, Logan is the one I call on. He is a deep thinker with an amazing mind. I truly believe he feels others' pain. And the birthday boy is the joy. He always has a smile on his face and is very quick-witted. He is laid back and carefree. He is the first to hug me everyday…not because he needs a hug but because he knows I need one. Nolan is the giver that will take something for himself and give to someone else so he can see them smile. He has an amazing "can do" attitude and will try at something until he gets it right.

All of these qualities that my boys possess are signs that God knew what he was giving me. They are what I fight for everyday. They are what I get out of bed for in pain everyday. They are what keeps me going.

So what I have learned is we can plan and plan our lives, but if it is not what God has planned for us it is not the right plan. God is the one who determines our future. We just need to trust in him and the blessing will come.

Thank you Nolan for being the joy of my life. Thank you for all your strength and positive attitude you bring to our family. Happy Birthday my dear baby. You know that you will always be our baby.

※※

Friday, January 16, 2009
Back Home in the Arctic Zone
It's been a week since I have had the pleasure to jump on to Sunny's blog and pinch-hit. As always let me answer the billion dollar question—How's Sunny doing? She had a painful night last night—(no it wasn't a Mark snore fest —although she did mention once or twice in the last week that apparently my feet and "mild " Swiss cheese have a remarkably rancid resemblance) it was the worst period yet for the pain. She has been nauseous all week and not able to eat much at all (in true Sunny fashion, even though her lack of appetite this week would starve Posh Spice, I did manage to get reprimanded for buying yogurt with 180 calories instead of the "light" lo-cal variety—God bless her) but that seems secondary right now because she is in a lot of pain, especially in her back, shoulders, and I guess throughout her bones. She had numbness in her left arm as well yesterday morning, which I don't recall her complaining about before, but she insists has been there.

I think the hardest part for her to deal with however, has been being cooped up. It really started two weeks ago this coming Monday when she had the treatment in Basel. She was in the hospital for the next couple of days and although she was able to roam freely around town on Tuesday afternoon there, she was back in the room Tuesday evening. Sparsely decorated would be an understatement but she made do. Then being stuck in the Hilton for the most part in the room until we flew back on Saturday. And then of course back here to the deep freeze which has really kept her in the house for the balance of the week. She managed to see Mall Cop with me and the boys today (I think she thought that I said "mall stop" but she was a trooper nonetheless). However she was completely out of it. She even accused some woman in line of stealing her purse, which was on her shoulder. I guess that is what she means when she claims to me that the pain meds make her a horrible person.

After almost a week back here I know I am finally feeling as if I am home again. Watching the Steelers last Sunday was a real treat for both of us after having watched Judge Judy's 90's reruns, Sally Jesse Raphael with her red glasses and English Dart World Championships for the previous week. (yes, Americans may be the country of couch potatoes, but if we had the sparse European television options they have over there I guess we would be more fit too). I want to thank everyone who has made meals for us since this journey began last year, but never did food taste so good as the meatloaves, pasta, pork, and desserts and all did this week. I know you haven't lived until you have had veal sausage links and Coke Light without ice by the Rheine in the snow, but somehow, someway, that seems all like a rapidly receding memory. Thanks again for all of you out there; you have no idea how much that means to us.

I guess now that I have had enough time to sort through everything we experienced and really let it sink in, I will share the top ten things that I learned from our excursion to Basel—

10. A Whopper meal really isn't worth $15 in any country paid with any type of currency

9. ESPN really needs to go international

8. We really didn't think Basel would be the warm part of our winter

7. Tennis shoes aren't a staple over there and I guess they wouldn't be here either if they cost $169 for a pair of Converse Chuck Taylor's—glue on glitter or not...

6. Global warming is real if the shortage of ice in Swiss beverages is any indication

5. Free train passes are fine and handy, but a garage kept SUV is just a "smidge" more convenient

4. Bikes are really four season transportation modes-snow be damned

3. You can argue the Steelers vs. the rest of the NFL anywhere in the world…

2. Learn the appropriate German or French comeback for "stupid American" before going to the checkout line with unpriced fruit

1. The Rocky mountain high may bring us Coors Light, but after flying over the Alps, they should make an extra Alps high beer because damn those are some impressive peaks.

Thanks once again for all of your prayers and support and for continuing to indulge me by reading my incessant ravings whenever Sunny asks me to fill in. I always knew that all of those "academic red-shirt" years at Pitt majoring in English-Creative Writing would be put to use. Wished it was under different circumstances obviously but we play the hands we are dealt while praying for that royal flush. We look forward to catching up with all of you in person over the next couple of weeks.

Mark

Chapter 6: "Pain"

"If you suffer, thank God! — it is a sure sign that you are alive."~Elbert Hubbard

Monday, January 19, 2009
Stronger and Stronger!!!

"That which does not kill us makes us stronger."

I am feeling stronger and stronger everyday. Of course I am impatient and lay in bed with frustration. The doctor told me that in two weeks I will feel closer to "myself." Well today is two weeks from treatment but I don't know what "myself" feels like. I have been sick for so long and in pain for longer that I cannot remember what I should feel like. Did he mean closer to my OLD self before this round of cancer? Or how I felt before I came to Switzerland? Nonetheless, I don't feel either way or its two weeks today. So I guess I need to wait and trust in the treatment.

Today I was frustrated that I could not spend sometime outside with the boys. I woke up this morning and struggled with pain…it was even difficult to get out of bed. I went to open the drapes to bring some sunshine in and saw the beautiful snow filling my back yard. I then noticed Austen's snowboard and a half built snowman outside. A sick feeling come to my stomach and it was not from the treatment this time. It was the half built snowman. I am the one that builds snowmen with my kids. I would spend hours outside just to get the largest and the best dressed snowman on our kid filled street. Mark, he is clueless when it comes to the free joys of a kid's life. I am not sure if he even had a childhood sometimes because he has no idea what real good old fashion fun is without spending a dime on all that fancy equipment. Things like snowmen, or stickball, or what you can do with a huge box or old tire are just not his thing. So when I saw the poor attempt by the boys alone, my heart froze like their little red noses outside.

I tapped on the window to get their attention and gave them a thumb's up for the attempt. Austen seemed really frustrated so he would not even look my way. He grabbed his snow board and off he went, embarrassed that I even saw his creation. Logan was in the process of actually stomping on the little body of snow that they called a man. And my sweet Nolan gives me a big wave and mouths for to me to come out. I open the window just a crack and could feel the coldness hit my only lung. I yell out to them to get Dad to help only to find out that was Dad's help. So I blew a kiss and slammed the window shut.

All I could do at that point is slope down with my back against the wall and my head under the window and sob. I hate this cancer shit. It's not about the stupid snowman that will not decorate our yard this snowfall. It's about what the battle and what it is doing to my family. They are trying but things will never be the same. I will never be able to build a snowman again. I will never be able to stand outside in the cold again. If I knew this last winter, I would have built a hundred snowmen and filled the yard with them. I would have taken a thousand photos so that they remember me doing that with them. This cancer robbed me of the opportunity to do it again.

I felt defeated when I looked at the half built snowman. I should be out there with them, I want to be their mom. In fact I remember just a few years ago building a whole snowmen family with them and them begging me to build one more, "Just one mom and no other girl snowmen." After all they are called men, mom," they yelled. I don't want them to be let done or to have the mom that is always sick. I want them to be proud of me...not sympathetic. The only way for them to feel that way is for me to fight this cancer with everything I got. I don't want to learn to live with it. I want to be rid of it.

I was angry at myself because I never taught my boys to ski and I will probably never ski again. It has always been one of those things that I had planned to teach them next year. I did take them one time by myself when they were about 4, 3 and 2. But I got overwhelmed and believe we just made snowballs. Then we packed up the minivan and went home. I am not being a downer or losing faith that my cancer will go in remission, but I know that the tumors and the treatment has done some damage to my bones and lungs. Reality is, I will not be able to be as active as I used to be.

While I looked outside this morning I pledged to myself to never say next year when it comes to showing the boys something. I am confident and hopeful that I will be healthy again, but I will live like everyday is my last day. I will get up every morning and thank God first. Then I will live the day as if I will never have that day again. I will hug the boys everyday (even if my 12 year old pushes away) and teach them something knew... big or small. I will accomplish one task everyday even if it's a bad day. I will never let a snowman go half built again.

Mothers need to live for their children. They need to know that they will never be ten years and five days old again. It should not take me getting cancer for the third time to realize that. Saying "later" to my boys because I am folding clothes or running the sweeper should no longer happen. Everyday I devote to them, not because of guilt but because it is what God wants mothers to do.

Wednesday, January 21, 2009
Keeping on Keepin On

Well let me lead off with the trillion dollar question-How's Sunny doing? I wish I could say fine and dandy but yesterday and last night were extremely painful for her. The treatment from Basel is definitely working its way through her bones and that has rekindled a lot of the pain she had earlier. The intensity of the pain was what struck me the most. That special type of pain that causes someone to temporarily lose their grip on reality. I think I managed to somehow not bring a basket of laundry upstairs the proper way—although through clenched teeth and all she managed to "set" me and the boys straight…apparently the boys and I did not do such a great job of putting a certain seat down—and whoops you guessed it—we had an impromptu instructional course on that at 10:00 as well, and then we managed to squeeze into our busy evening, a brief but stern lecture on "the proper way to enter a room quietly so your slippers don't make such a f#$%#%#%n racket—this one was rated PG-13 so only I attended. Anyways the point is that with all of the pain, Sunny wasn't herself(well except for that part about that certain seat that we don't put down—that one always seems to come up) and even with the pain meds she tossed and turned most of the night. There was a time when I even looked over and saw tears just drenching her pillow.

I was real happy for her a little after 1:00 am when she zonked for a couple of hours. She had trouble catching her breath for awhile in the evening and after fifteen years of marriage I knew it wasn't me taking it away, so we reached out to the doctors here at UPMC, and emailed our buddies in Basel. They all reassured her, that even though her husband lost 2 pounds and looks great, that it was actually the treatment working and instructed her to take her strongest pain pills, and if that didn't solve the problem to go to the ER and get a pain shot. Fortunately the ER wasn't needed last night but I know she is keeping all options open today.

So keep her in your prayers. I joke around but last night was really pretty tense around here. The boys don't like to hear mommy in pain and they most certainly did—Nolan even made her a "get well" card, which I know she loved. Austen and Logan kept their arguments to just below bloodshed which I also know she greatly appreciated. So please continue to keep us in your prayers as I know that is what really gets her through nights like last night.

I sent her a great email from the office yesterday that I got from my Weekly Bible Wisdom buddies, because it struck me as the perfect example of how she has tried to lead her life—it was living the JOY principle—Jesus first, Others second, Yourself last (much to my chagrin its not Jim Beam, Old Milwaukee, Yagermeister). It was a really poignant reminder to me that although she has been dealt a seemingly "bad hand" that she will press on because her priorities have and will continue to always be in the proper order—the JOY order. She did some cursing and yelling but she never once wanted to give up.

I would be extremely remiss if I didn't thank everyone for the wonderful spaghetti dinner. Thank God for pasta because as an Irishman I can only imagine what a "potato" dinner would be like——Potato and Beer, Potato with Cheese, Potato with Beer, Potato with pasta sauce…well you get the point…it wouldn't work. The wonderful folks who were the brains behind this(thanks Jen, Lori) to all of the friends and some new friends that I saw cooking, selling, hustling and bustling, (thanks Barb, now that I have seen you in action I know the kids are in good "large" hands) to all of the kids that were busy serving the salads, the pasta, and refilling drinks, to the face painters, the cookie bakers, and the candlestick makers(just kidding to make sure you were all still paying attention) Austen, Nolan, and I were very impressed. And of course, to all of you that came—it was a tremendous turnout, it was great to catch up with old friends even if for only a few minutes at a time with pasta sauce on my shirt (thank goodness Sunny had to stay home or I would have been scolded for being a slob big time) because without you, all of that hard work would have been pointless. It was a TREMENDOUS DAY and on behalf of the Carney's—thanks.

With all that Sunny went through in the past four days I forgot to mention that our furnace decided to stop working. After a cold night spent with a conked out furnace (the temp was actually in the low 40's inside with a wind chill of -59 every time Sunny walked by me because I was the one who had "my" furnace guy check and clean in late December-but that's for another day) after driving to Hampton with Austen's team beating Hampton, and then driving all the way back to eat hot pasta was fantastic and well timed. So thanks.

Mark

Thursday, January 22, 2009
It's a Hard Days Night

Well let me start off by saying it isn't by choice that I pinch-hit for Sunny today. She is in a lot of pain once again as the treatment from Basel works its way through the numerous tumors throughout her bones. It has been a stark reminder that although she is a trooper and will constantly fight the good fight, and always seems so strong and tough, that it is cancer she is living with. I wish I could trade places with her; however deep down I know that I would not be able to handle this all like she is. The pain she has suffered the past several days has affected even her most positive of spirits, and the feeling that the boys and I have is one of helplessness which is not something we are programmed to deal with. I am used to being able to provide solutions—if my stomach growls I feed it…if a light bulb goes out I change it…if my kids are killing each other I punish them. Her pain is such that even with the meds…even with tedious arranging and then rearranging of pillows, even with heating pads microwaved, and then nuked again one at a time, I know I can't do enough to alleviate her pain. It's frustrating as hell not being able to ease the pain your better half is going through, and yet I can't let her or the boys see anything other than a positive attitude. I have thanked you all numerous times in the past for your prayers and support, but if ever there was a time that his healing hands were needed its now. Sunny is finally asleep as I write this but I know it will only be a matter of time before the meds wear off and she wakes with a moan that I truly wish none of you ever have to hear.

She is such a trooper. We went to Nolan's basketball game tonight (he won a barnburner 16-5 4th grade game) and as I sat on the coach's bench I knew the pain was beating on her, but not defeating her. She smiled and cheered at each misjudged lay-up, at each clank off the rim, and each time Nolan was able to force a turnover. It meant more than anything for him to have her there. Her face looked pale as she forced her painful grin into a smile when Nolan made his foul shot. I kept looking over at her only to see someone that seemed so fragile…fragile like the finest piece of glass. God, I just wish I could do something to take this all away from her for just one day, but she would not let me carry that burden for her. She would take this a hundred times over before she would give it to anyone she loves. I cannot help but think that God has truly sent her to be our angel. She is here to teach us strength, kindness, perseverance and so much more. To many, attending a fourth grade basketball game seems like such an inconsequential event, but not to her when it's for her son.

I went to drop off her latest wonderdrug script at Walgreens; U2 was on in the car. If you have never heard the song "Sometimes You Can't Make it Alone" which Bono wrote for his dad as his father suffered from cancer, than you should get your hands on it or You Tube it. It's one of mine and Sunny's favorites and really strikes to the point of how much all of your support has meant to this family. When I got to Walgreens and the young pharmacist said "Hi Mr. Carney" I paused for a moment. Never in my life did I imagine myself being a regular at a pharmacy to the point where my ID was no longer needed and they knew my order before I got to the register. That was what Silky's and Somma's was for. It made me realize for a moment just how much our lives had changed in the past eight months. Sometimes I forget because of her strength.

The tenacity which she has fought this with is easy to overlook I think because I guess the best way to describe it is she usually makes it look so easy. Like Air Jordan hitting a clutch three, or Big Ben scrambling around and then completing a 65 yard touchdown to a scampering…hey where'd he go TD…Sunny has seemed to make living with Carcinoid Cancer natural. That's why this week has been both a well-timed reminder and so damn frustrating. I wish there was more that I could do. I know that is what she would say and feel if the roles were reversed.

I appreciate all of the kind feedback regarding my feeble attempts at filling in for Sunny on this blog and I promise you the next one will be its usual mix of updates on "How's Sunny Doing" and the my feeble attempts at sharing my twisted thoughts of life with cancer. Keep us in your prayers and I look forward to doing this again tomorrow because my wife is a fighter and I am happy to be the writer.

Sometimes You Can't Make It on Your Own
© 2005 U2

Lyrics
Tough, you think you've got the stuff
You're telling me and anyone
You're hard enough

You don't have to put up a fight
You don't have to always be right
Let me take some of the punches
For you tonight

Listen to me now
I need to let you know
You don't have to go it alone

And it's you when I look in the mirror
And it's you when I don't pick up the phone
Sometimes you can't make it on your own
We fight all the time
You and I, that's alright
We're the same soul
I don't need, I don't need to hear you say
That if we weren't so alike
You'd like me a whole lot more

Listen to me now
I need to let you know
You don't have to go it alone

And it's you when I look in the mirror
And it's you when I don't pick up the phone
Sometimes you can't make it on your own

I know that we don't talk
I'm sick of it all
Can - you - hear - me - when - I -
Sing, you're the reason I sing
You're the reason why the opera is in me

Where are we now?
I've got to let you know
A house still doesn't make a home
Don't leave me here alone…

And it's you when I look in the mirror
And it's you that makes it hard to let go
Sometimes you can't make it on your own
Sometimes you can't make it
The best you can do is to fake it
Sometimes you can't make it on your own
Every time I read the lyrics I can't help but think of HER spirit!!!!!

Sun,
I've got to let you know

A house still doesn't make a home
Don't leave me here alone…
I know you are hard enough
But let me take some of the punches for you…

Mark

Sunday, January 25, 2009
Sweet Child of Mine

First off, let me lead by apologizing for the lag in the blog. It is now Sunday evening and this seems like it has been a long forty eight hours. I get to pinch-hit because Sunny has been unfortunately living like the King of Pain. What a big change from just a week ago. Obviously the treatment is working because she literally screams and moans in pain for periods on end and although there are meds, heating pads, pillows, low-fat Tapioca pudding, more meds, OJ and bottled water (European style-no ice), showers, prayers, and more meds nothing really eases it especially at night until she simply conks out. I wait until I am sure she is zonked completely and then I can leave our snoring, gas-challenged dog alone on the couch and sneak up in beside her. The mornings have been the best times for her after an hour or so when she wakes up, but I can tell that sitting up, laying down, standing up, walking around…I am sure you have heard of a "man with no country"…she has sadly been "the woman with no comfortable position."

As emotionally draining as it has been to be her Lou Duva (that's a corner man for you non boxing fans) for the past four or five days, I can't even imagine how physically sapped and mentally drained she must feel right now. Fighting cancer is like riding the Thunderbolt at our favorite local yunzer park…you wait in line…you wait some more for that special ride up front in the lead car…you shoot out of the pavilion straight down into that ravine…come up…fly out of your seat losing your potato patch fries (or your low-fat Tapioca pudding) unintentionally crushing your partner…then its click…click…click…up that long hill pulled by the belt…waiting…anticipating…praying for a good day…and then you raise your arms because its a good rush and then up and down…up and down…up and down…except unlike a well designed roller coaster where you are supposed to enjoy both the ups and downs, you can't live like that.

In sales (my easy way to relate) you quickly realize that one of the keys to being successful is to not celebrate the highs too much and quickly put to the sides the downs. Cancer isn't like sales. You need to celebrate the up moments. You need to embrace them and hold on to them because it is exactly those moments that you draw upon when the downs come. Without rejoicing for the good days, the good hours, the good minutes…you got no shot of mentally pulling through those tough times…Sorry to go off on a little tangent there but my mind is racing with what to put in this and honestly my pudgy Irish fingers have trouble keeping up. I feel like I need to give you some of Sunny's inspirational tone to the post, but God it is so hard right now. I am sure if she could stand to sit in front of her computer she would have something to say like this.

Sunny had a few down moments this week. She wanted to give me some advice on how to live after she was "gone" (typical she even wanted to be in control of a post-Sunny world). I told her to forget about all of it because I never listened when she was right next to me so there was no shot in hell I would listen then. I don't bring this up to depress her when she reads this or for you to feel sorry for her. I want to tell you about the Sunny I know and how even with all of that pain she was going through on Saturday afternoon she sent me off to watch Nolan's basketball game (I got to work the scoreboard and clock and the horn…which is a whole other story but if you how quiet I like to be, it was a real cool thing). She then had her friend Sharon take her and Logan to watch Austen's game down the hill at Riverview. She cheered him on, cheered on all of his teammates (the Storm) argued with a few Fox Chapel parents who apparently didn't' realize that that damn redhead that kept scoring three's and stealing the ball was her little redhead. Apparently, these little rich sissy parents were cursing at her aggressive son. I pity them like I pitied the furnace guy last Saturday, like I pitied the doctor at UPMC seven months ago who told her he was not sure if there was any options for her. Some of the early inductees into Sunny's Hall of Fools. She was wupped physically (yes that's the medical term…check out wikipedia for yourself) and yet she just did what she always does….cheered on her son and "smacked down" anyone who did not do the same.

Although she was exhausted when I got home from Nolan's game (he won, unfortunately Bif and da Boys from across the river got the best of Ace's team) she was alert and excited. It was one of those "up" moments…it may have been only a couple of hours at a meaningless sixth grade boys basketball game but to Sunny it was another kernel to draw upon tomorrow when she starts back on the down track. When her friend Lisa called and told her she would be shooting the Plum girl's softball team this spring it picked her up so much. Sure it's a few shekels…but it's more than that…I know it's feeling like she is needed…like she is back in control of some part of her own life. Thanks to both Sharon for the ride to Riverview (and for not getting lost on the way to or fro) and to Lisa for giving her some more purpose.

There is one big difference between riding the Thunderbolt and to fighting cancer. The praying that I know my kids did the first time I rode with them (dear God please let me make it up this hill…please don't let me puke…please God…) doesn't quite merit or get the same attention from the Big Guy as all of the prayers that you all have been offering for us. Thanks. And rest assured that although this is a trying time the bigger picture is not forgotten. She will beat this. She is a fighter. I am her corner/cut man. You guys with all of the prayers are like those Philadelphians who followed Balboa in Rocky 2 and ran the race with him…through the streets…up the stairs…and we will all raise our arms triumphantly as one when she beats this. (and if you want to pick me up a Philly cheese steak on the way I promise you it won't go to waste)…

Thanks for indulging me as I wandered through this entry but there is so much I want to convey and share…remember and never forget…you are all in our thoughts and prayers and I can't tell you how much you all mean to us…Until next time she allows me to do this (although after all of the rollercoaster analogies she may want me examined first) be safe and God Bless…

Mark

Chapter 7:
The Ups

Attitudes are contagious. Are yours worth catching?

Tuesday, January 27, 2009
As many of you have read in Mark's previous posts it's been a rough week for my family. Today is the first day I am actually able to focus long enough to write. I think with the week I have had I really need to get it all out. I have been getting emails from so many asking Mark and I to continue to post and telling us how much they enjoy reading our thoughts. I want to express to all of you who follow my blog what writing this does for me (actually Mark too). This blog is my release. It helps me to express my feelings and thoughts about fighting cancer. Those whom I am very close with know that I have trouble talking about things that bother me. The blog gives me the opportunity to get all my worries out. So I thank all of you who read this for giving me this opportunity. It is just one more way you show your support.

    Like I stated earlier it's been a rough week for both the Carney family and the Jennings family (my brothers, sisters and mother…they are the ones I whine to). When I got home I felt sick and some pain. I kept on thinking it would get better as the days passed. That is NOT what happen…it continued to get worse and worse until it actual took over our life. Today it is still intense, but I think the new pain meds that the doctors put me on are finally helping me to function a little. Not to mention my mom moved in for a while (you always feel better when mommy is around). Anyways, the pain has been intolerable and just torture. The days were bad, but the kids were at school and Mark is working from home so I was able to hide it some. But the nights were just horrible for everyone. I felt like a baby (or maybe a man) screaming for some mercy from the pain. Mark and the boys would do anything just to give me some comfort. Rearranging my pillows, get my meds, help me walk around the house, bring me water, pray with me, hold my hand and putting a cold towel on my head. I know that it was as hard on them as it was on me and I am so thankful I have them.

Nonetheless, one more week has gone by in my journey of cancer. It is one more week closer to the end of the fight. A few days ago my end to the fight felt like death, but now that I am no longer insane with pain I know my end to the fight is remission. Yes, there was a day were the pain was so intense that I sat with Mark and told him what to do after I was gone. Of course I cannot completely give him full reign of our kids' life even when I'm gone. I told him how to do Christmas shopping for the boys. I let him know where I hide the Easter baskets, what to give the boys when they graduate from High School and College, who to give each piece of my jewelry too. I gave him instructions on how to treat his daughter-in-laws when the boys get married and I even told him where the safety deposit box is (got to move that now). If you read about liver and bone carcinoid cancer it tells you over and over again that towards the end of disease the pain is unbearable for weeks and that many patients need continuous morphine. When even the morphine would not work then I let the cancer take over. So of course the "dark side" got the best of me and my mind started wandering.

Not to mention that on Friday we got an answer to an email that we sent to the doctors in Switzerland asking if the pain I was feeling was normal. The Swiss doctors suggested we immediately go to our American oncologist and get scans done because I could be in a life threatening situation called tumor-lysis. I would explain it further but to my delight (after hours and hours at the Presby hospital and scan after scan, IV after IV) I was cleared. I was then told that I needed to take the stronger pain meds or be admitted for IV pain meds. I think with Mark's exhaustion he may have not minded if I stayed, a few out the hospital because once the get you in you cannot get out. I knew that if I received the IV pain meds I would never learn how to deal with the pain on my own …maybe never get home. So I gave them my scout's honor (girl scouts honor…may have had my fingers crossed a little) and they let me go home.

It has not got much better but I am finally able to blog a little (although I started this blog at 11 AM and God knows when I will finally post it). I am praying that everyday it gets better and better. I do know that I will continue to fight hard every single day. Some days I may have more to give than other days but I will give something everyday. Because cancer has helped me understand that if you don't like something change it; if you can't change it, then change the way the way you think about it. That, my friend, is another "Good in Cancer."

Thursday, January 29, 2009
Life Lessons

My friend Michele emailed me a list of life lessons today. As I read them I thought about ones that implied to me, ones I live by today and ones I need to work on. I have always loved little inspirational quotes and sayings. I think that comes from growing up with an Irish heritage. Below are my favorites:

1. Life isn't fair, but it's still good.

2. Cry with someone. It's more healing than crying alone.
   (One I need to work on. I hate for someone to see me cry.)

3. It's OK to get angry with God. He can take it.
   (Just keep believing in Him and put him first.)

4. It's OK to let your children see you cry.
   (But hopefully I laugh with them more.)

5. Don't compare your life to others'. You have no idea what their journey is all about.
   (Love this one. One my dad use to say.)

6. Get rid of anything that isn't useful, beautiful or joyful.
   (Ladies, I know at times our husbands may fit in this cate-

gory, but we really do need them. They are beautiful at times. Mine can be really joyful when he wants to be. I think this applies to things not people.)

7. Whatever doesn't kill you really does make you stronger.
   (That is what I have been told over and over again. I hope this one is true.)

8. When it comes to going after what you love in life, don't take no for an answer.
   (Love this one.)

9. Over prepare, and then go with the flow.
   (I prepare but I need to go with the flow more often.)

10. No one is in charge of your happiness except you.
    (So blame yourself when you are not happy…or change your circumstance to be happy.)

11. Always choose life.
    (This is my number one.)

12. What other people think of you is none of your business.
    (I always say if you like yourself anyone who matters will like you too…if they don't then pray for them.)

13. Time heals almost everything. Give time time.
    (I need to work on this one.)

14. However good or bad a situation is, it will change.

15. Your job won't take care of you when you are sick. Your friends will. Stay in touch.
    (I have learned this lesson. I have some of the best friends in the world. I am so blessed and lucky with so many amazing friends in my life. Thank you God.)

16. Believe in miracles.
    You gotta believe.

17. God loves you because of who God is, not because of anything you did or didn't do.

18. Don't audit life. Show up and make the most of it now.
(This is really hard to do when you are going through an adversity. Today so many are going through struggles…illness, lost of someone dear to them, family member ill, financial stress lost of job, etc… I try to find one thing good about my day (sometimes it's just a smile from my husband when I tell a dumb joke). But I still need to work on this one.)

19. Your children get only one childhood. Make it memorable.
(I hope mine forget about all they are going through at this time, yet learn something from it, and remember all the fun we have had as a family.)

20. All that truly matters in the end is that you loved.
(Another one my dad would say.)

21. If we all threw our problems in a pile and saw everyone else's, we'd grab ours back.
(This goes back to when I say we all have our own cancers. Except the cards you are dealt and learn to live the best life you can despite your problems.)

22. Envy is a waste of time. You already have all you need.
(Another thing my dad would say. As a little girl I use to think he would say this because he had so many kids and so little money but now I really believe it.)

23. The best is yet to come.
(We all know what God has waiting for us.)

24. No matter how you feel, get up, dress up and show up.
(This is my answer to everyone who says, "She does not look sick." Thanks for the Compliment but a shower, makeup and a nice outfit does wonders.)

25. Life isn't tied with a bow, but it's still a gift.
    (If it was tied with a bow it would be harder to open. Treasure it.)

It was time for me to get back positive Sunny and stop focusing on my pain. By the way it is getting a little better.

Monday, February 2, 2009
Superbowl Lessons!
First I must say way to go STEELERS!!!!

What fun it was to watch the Superbowl with my husband and boys! We were like the "before cancer" Carney family. Excited and stress free having fun together…forgetting about our journey. This was the very first Superbowl Mark was able to watch with our boys and we treasured every minute of it. Every year at this time Mark is out of town at a conference or traveling on business. The boys and I would end up going to some party that a friend or family member would invite us to and Mark would call in all through the game talking to the boys about different plays. It worked for us, but it was not like having him home. The boys enjoy watching football so much more with dad than with me. Well this year there was no conference, client or meeting more important than staying at home with his family. The boys and I really enjoyed it.

Throughout the day on several television stations they gave some amazing stories about the players and how their hard work, luck or perseverance got them to the world football championship today. Some of the stories talked about players and coach's strong faith in the Lord, their difficult childhood, the players' family or the wonderful things some have done for society today. It gave me such peace to know that many of these men seem to have it all yet still give back to others and still keep God number one in their lives. Nonetheless, some are struggling with their own personal problems too. Although all the stories were inspiring to me and my boys, one sticks out in our mind. This story actually brought tears to my 12-year-old's eyes and kept my 10-year-old in silence for a few minutes after it ran. And if any of you know my oldest and youngest, that in itself is amazing. Austen is one of the strongest emotional children I know and Nolan cannot keep quiet for more than a minute. Both are qualities I love about them.

Anyways, it was the story of Arizona's wide receiver Larry Fitzgerald. I am permitted to talk about his story here in the Carney household because even though he is not a Steeler, he is one of Mark's and the boys' favorite University of Pittsburgh players. Larry talked about how he was lucky as a child to have both parents. He was the oldest of two, had two amazing parents and one brother who was his best friend. He had no childhood hardships to talk about or did not grow up on the rough streets. He actually had a pretty charmed life with a father who loved the game of football and encourage Larry to fulfill his dream. His father is a sportswriter for the Minnesota Spokesman-Recorder. Today he was believed to be the first reporter to cover his own son in a Super Bowl.

When asked about his mother his eyes filled with tears. He said that she was the reason he was who he was today. She was his biggest fan and his rock. She always instilled in him the confidence and assurance that he could do anything as long as he was willing to work for it. He called her, "his cheerleader in sports and in life." But he has much regret because in college he became distant with her. Although his mother encouraged him tremendously in football she motivated him more in education and school. Stressing to him that school comes first and it's not ok to miss one day. Larry started doing just that, missing classes. He said his mother lectured him about remembering his roots and asked him to settle down. Like a normal young adult on his own for the first time he wanted to do it his way and he pulled away from her. Then just before going out to practice on April 9, he got a call from his dad saying there was a ticket waiting for him to fly home to Minneapolis. Larry Fitzgerald, Sr., never told his son why he needed to come home, but Fitzgerald knew it had to do with his mother because she had been battling breast cancer for several years.

He went to practice that day before the plane came for him because he knew that his tough mother would have his head if he missed because of her. "It was probably the toughest practice I had to go to," Fitzgerald told Elliot Wiley of ESPN. "Football wasn't important that day." Later that evening Larry got home to find his mother unable to communicate due to a cancer-induced coma. After battling breast cancer for seven and a half years, which spread to her lungs and brain, Carol Fitzgerald died the next day. "If somebody hasn't lost a parent you can't understand what its like," Fitzgerald said.

He made his father leave her voice on his home answering machine so that he and his brother can sometimes call home just to hear her.

His father was being interviewed split screen along side of Fitzgerald, Jr. and he chimed in by adding that before the death of his mother Larry was focused mainly on growth on the football field now he focuses on that and so much more, "Jr. uses this difficult loss to fuel his life. He looks so much like his mother," says Larry Sr. "He has her humility, her smile and her stubbornness." He wished he would have called Larry earlier to come home but explained that she refused him to do so. "She hated for her boys to miss even a day of school. By the time I got Larry back home she'd slipped into a coma. You make your decisions and you live with them, but it's still difficult."

After his mother's death and spending some time home with his family Fitzgerald returned to school to finish the second semester of his freshman year. Instead of being distracted by his hurt, Fitzgerald says he was inspired by his mother's death. The wide receiver said that because school was more important to her than any accomplishment he could achieve on the football field, in her honor he worked harder than he ever had during the last month of school to finish with a 3.3 grade point average.

On the football field, Fitzgerald takes with him his mom's example of courage, strength and never give up attitude. He wants to be the leader his mom would preach to him to be. "You can't have an off day or bad days when you're trying to be a leader," Fitzgerald said.

"Larry is a unique talent in the sense that I tried to raise him knowing there are things in your life that you can't control," Larry Fitzgerald, Sr. said. "When things happen, you have to keep your mind on the things you have to do. I've seen that since the funeral."

Fitzgerald says his mother Carol was a huge inspiration to his life both before her death and after. She pushed him to be the best at school and on the football field. However her main goal was to be the best person he could ever be. She taught him to have a good time in life and not to complain about the small problems.

Larry went on to say that he still has heart ache and regret about his mother's death and the fact that he did not get to say, "sorry," before she slipped into the coma. On the positive side, he says that his mother's battle with cancer makes it easier for him to work out. He says he compares unpleasant physical feelings incurred during workouts with the amount of pain his mother felt when fighting with cancer.

The reporter commented that his mother must be so proud of him and looking down on him. He shook his head and said, "I can win this

Superbowl, but I will never forgive myself for the argument I had with my mother about school." His father was also interviewed and told Larry that his mother loved him unconditionally. She forgave him after it happened and watched over him every day before she died. But she never gave up on him and knew that one day he would be someone the WORLD would admirer. Larry now goes to children centers and schools and lectures on listening to your parents. He said he tells every child he meets, "tell your parents you love them everyday." Fitzgerald is a Christian who donates not only money but time to many organizations that help families with teens as well as cancer research. Yet he lives with that guilt everyday.

I know that my boys were touched by that story because of our situation. Let's face it, there were so many more sensational stories told about other players. I am glad that they saw it. Not because I want them to show appreciation for Mark or I. But because I want them to know that we love them unconditionally and no matter what they do our love will never change. I want them to realize how lucky they are to have a father that coaches their teams and cancels a business trip to spend a Superbowl with them. I need them to know that I am their biggest cheerleader in whatever path they choose to take. I want them to see that disagreements may happen between us but they need to move on and not let them linger. They need to know that we as parents make our choices because we love them and want them to become good people…not because we are "mean" as they say.

After that story aired our family was silent for over ten minutes. The three of them would not look my way. I saw some tears being wiped and heard some sniffling sounds. I knew why and I did not need them to make any eye contact with me. Usually when we hear a story like that I end it with a comment or explanation to make sure the boys got the moral of the story. There was need for that this time. They defiantly got it.

Like I said, this by far was not the most sensational story of the night to many. There is the story of Aaron Smith and his son being diagnosed with cancer this season. The Kurt Warner's, Arizona's Quarterback, Cinderella story of his struggles throughout his career and how he did not give up until he made it. And while climbing to the top he managed to be a born again Christian and have seven children. And every Steeler fan knows Troy Polamaluo's story of how he puts his Lord Jesus Christ first everyday of his life…not to mention his generosity.

Let's not forget Mike Tomlin being the youngest coach in NFL history to win a Superbowl. The list goes on and on. But to our family Larry Fitzgerald's internal struggles touched us the most because of our own personal struggles we are going through. Yes, because somewhere in the back, hopefully very back, of my boys mind their precious minds, they know there is a chance that they too could lose their mother from cancer. But I hope they know that they are loved unconditionally today, tomorrow and always.

Wednesday, February 11, 2009
I Resign!
Today I Quit Being an Adult Mother with Cancer

I hereby officially tender my resignation as wife, mother, daughter, sister, aunt, friend, business owner, photographer and adult with cancer.

I have decided I would like to accept the responsibilities of a healthy fun loving child again.

I want to eat fast food with a large milkshake and not worry about the calories or if it's organic.

I want to roll down the biggest hill or jump in a mud puddle.

I want to run through a playground and play war in the woods.

I want to return to a time when life was simple and the biggest bill I had was the .50 I owed my brother for a bet I made with him or a race I lost. Sorry bros I know I never paid any of you. When all I would care about was who went first and who hit the homerun.

I want to be a little girl and wear a pink fur coat and a bikini to the local public pool and lay out in the sun with it all on, not worrying who thought what. Sorry again to my older brothers and sisters who were forced by Dad to take me to the pool dressed that way. I loved fashion even at 6.

I want to think the world is kind, fair and everyone around me is my friend. Where you make big decisions by doing ENE, Meannie, Mynnie, Mo or in Greenfield it was "My Mother Punched Your Mother Right in the Nose." You then stuck to that decision because it was what it was.

A time when I believed that everyone was honest and good, and that anything is possible.

I want to have my dad's arms hug me so tight and make me feel that I am safe because no one messes with the warden's daughter. I want to hear him whistle on the back porch for dinner and watch the whole Jennings' clan run home because in 10 minutes the kitchen door will be closed until dinner is over. I want to hear his crazy sayings and him tell me over and over again, "everything going to be alright."

I want to think that life goes on for eternity and I am invincible.

I want to wear my home made dress that my mother would make us at Easter time and not care that the whole family had matching dresses and ties because she got a good deal on the fabric.

I want to unwrap that doll house at Christmas time that I had ask for three years in a row and every year of waiting made it more special when I got it.

I don't want my day to consist of a sink full of dishes, five loads of stinky boys laundry, doctor bills, mountains of paperwork, depressing news, bad economy, client calls, chemo treatments, feeling sick to my stomach, broken down cars, doctor visits, blood work, prescription refills, gossip, illness, and missing loved ones gone.

I want to believe in the power of smiles, hugs, a kind word, truth, peace, dreams, the imagination, mankind, and hard work.

So…here's my cell phone, my computer, my car keys, my bills, my credit cards, my clients, my appointment book, my household chores and all my other responsibilities.

I am officially resigning from my position today as a wife, mother, business owner, friend, sister, aunt, and cancer patient. And I am taking the position of the little girl I was 30 years ago.

I promise Mark it will only be for one day or until you screw the house up.

I guarantee you though when I take the position back I will be very relaxed and ready to go again.

All who would like to join me…come on in to my life.

Thursday, February 12, 2009
I'm Doing Great!

A friend of mine yesterday told me that she loves to read my blogs. One complaint she had though is that I have not let anyone know how I've been feeling lately. I think I try to forget my cancer and just write sometimes. I really want everyone to think of me as same old Sunny, not Sunny with cancer. Cancer is what I am afflicted with but I don't want that to be what I am known for. I accepted that around me there will be whispers and quiet comments like, "that's the mom with terminal cancer." I am ok with that if you don't really know me well. However, what I really want are people to say things like, "that Sunny she's a mother, or a wife, or a photographer, or a business owner or just a nice person." So I guess I just assumed by my writing again that all would know I am doing better even though I don't always write about my cancer. But I will tell you now I am doing great.

The pain from my last treatment subsided to a tolerable level and I am back to my normal activities. Of course it is just in time for me to book my next trip and treatment. I will be leaving March 13th to arrive in Basel, Switzerland on March 14th. I will be admitted into the University Hospital Basel on March 16th for my second round of treatment. I must say I am very nervous this time because I know what to expect. That may not sound like it makes any sense but I really am not looking forward to repeating the last 4 weeks again.

With that said, I will go and appreciate the fact that I have this opportunity. I will make the best of the trip and enjoy some time with Mark. So for all those who are wondering I am feeling good and getting on board for round two?

February 14, 2009
Happy Valentine's Day!

Today is the day that we show our love for each other. I had always expected Valentine's Day to be a day for me. After all, I felt I was married to a man that was lucky to have me and had three wonderful boys that I took care of all year. This day was about spoiling me. Valentines Day is a woman's holiday and I am the only woman in this home. I blame Mark for that because believe it or not he is a hopeless romantic and loved to treat me right on this day. Yes, how greedy and conceited I was before cancer. I have decided to change today to a day of showing my love to others and not others showing their love for me. I think after eight months of kindness, love and generosity given to me I have had my share and can pass it onto those I love. So I bought a heart filled box of chocolate for the boys and Mark and wrote each one of them a love poem. Because as a woman that is what we really want over any expensive gift from our men.

Well, I learned that men really, really, don't care about Valentine's Day even if they are the focus of the day. The chocolates were eaten in the first 20 minutes and I just noticed that the poems are lying right where I had given them. But I know that they are absolutely positive I love them and that I will do everything for them.

I thought that the poem below is a great reminder of how we should live our life today and always:

<u>IF I HAD MY LIFE TO LIVE OVER - by Erma Bombeck</u>
(written after she found out she was dying from cancer)

I would have gone to bed when I was sick instead of pretending the earth would go into a holding pattern if I weren't there for the day.

I would have burned the pink candle sculpted like a rose before it melted in storage.

I would have talked less and listened more.

I would have invited friends over to dinner even if the carpet was stained, or the sofa faded.

I would have eaten the popcorn in the 'good' living room and worried much less about the dirt when someone wanted to light a fire in the fireplace.

I would have taken the time to listen to my grandfather ramble about his youth.

I would have shared more of the responsibility carried by my husband.

I would never have insisted the car windows be rolled up on a summer day because my hair had just been teased and sprayed.

I would have sat on the lawn with my grass stains.

I would have cried and laughed less while watching television and more while watching life.

I would never have bought anything just because it was practical, wouldn't show soil, or was guaranteed to last a lifetime. Instead of wishing away nine months of pregnancy, I'd have cherished every moment and realized that the wonderment growing inside me was the only chance in life to assist God in a miracle.

When my kids kissed me impetuously, I would never have said, 'Later. Now go get washed up for dinner.' There would have been more 'I love you's' More 'I'm sorry's.

But mostly, given another shot at life, I would seize every minute .look at it and really see it. live it and never give it back. STOP SWEAT-ING THE SMALL STUFF!!!

Don't worry about who doesn't like you, who has more, or who's doing what?

Instead, let's cherish the relationships we have with those who do love us.

So let's live without regret today and offer to the ones we love.

Saturday, February 14, 2009
The Sun Always Shines on Me

I read Sunny's blog from earlier today and I felt compelled to share with the world (or at least those 8 or 9 of you that still read her blog when you realize that I am stepping in with my two cents). She didn't ask me to pinch-hit or even write this one…in fact she is a little under the weather with some kind of bug (as she puts it but knowing deep down that it's the cancer taking its tool on her) and asleep right now. I guess you can say I am stealing into her blog like she stole my heart 18 years ago. She is wrong about men not caring about Valentine's Day because we do. I actually resent the holiday in a way because to me my Sunny deserves to have every day be Valentine's Day. Its not that flowers and chocolates and gifts aren't important, its just that for too many today is a chore or a pain in the you nowhere and if that's not a day whose intentions have backfired then our Pirates will win 100 games this year.

My philosophy regarding being with Sunny is that I "married up." Whenever we walk in to a restaurant, a party or some important event (alright it's more often a doctor's office or an athletic activity for one of the boys) I am proud that a stranger can look and ask "Why is she with him." Yes anyone can look at her and see beauty, but when she smiles and speaks you see the real amazing woman that I am with. Everyday I feel that I am not worthy to have her at my side. After all these years it still shocks me that she is my wife.

When we took our vows for richer or poorer, sickness and health…it probably never occurred to either of us just how true those words uttered in front of all those people and God were. My wife has always been my best friend, my biggest supporter, my motivation, and my inspiration. Without her fight against this disease she had already shown me that she is a special caring, giving person…so her comments about feeling the need to give are actually a little ridiculous but completely in line with how she truly is. She doesn't need to give me or the Carney boys anything today…she has been giving herself to us every day in every way. She never puts herself first. I can't say I have always acted the same back to her. That's what makes her Sunny and me the sidekick who gets the pleasure of sharing each day with her.

That's why Valentine's Day is not a true expression of love that Sunny deserves…I just think it sells my wife short. Everyday should be Valentine's Day for her (I know Hallmark and Pro-Flowers would love the idea) and then maybe she could realize how special she is to me. And how much I love her. And how this house would not be a home without her. Hope you all took care of your loved one today and I wish you all could be as blessed as I am to have a spouse like mine. Happy Valentine's Day Sunny. I love you.

Mark

Chapter 8: Say It

If it's been said once and made a difference in someone's life, why not repeat it over and over again?

A Week of Motivation
Since I published the post a while back about quotes and memorable sayings I have received several emails, letters, and even a beautiful plaque from my friends and family telling me their favorite sayings. This week's posts I want to focus on motivational quotes and sayings. I booked my trip to Switzerland on Friday for round two of the secret potion and I must say I am very apprehensive about doing this again. So I need the motivation more than anyone else.

Last week I received a wonderful letter from my cousin, Sandy. Not only is my immediate family large my Dad's family is even bigger. Growing up I had always been about family and was blessed with many cousins. My father's brothers and sisters were very close and got together often. Unfortunately, many of them passed away very young of heart issues. So slowly we began falling a little apart and Sunday dinners, holiday visits and summer barbecues became weddings and funerals. The amazing thing though is that I have heard from so many of them since I've been sick. It's like the years we have had apart has not changed anything. They are still one of my biggest supporters.

Sandy was a few years older but still very good to me. Her father and my father were brothers and I believe only a year or two apart. In her letter she commented back to the post about my dad and his crazy motivational sayings. She explained that her dad also loved to write sayings down and would say them to her and her sister all the time. As I get older, I realize that I was surrounded by so many wonderful role models in my life. I am sure it goes all the way back to my grandparents, Irish immigrants, who made an impact to their large family and both died in their 50's. One thing Sandy wrote to me in her letter was, "What great Dads we had. We are blessed with great parents and families. Their faith in God, their crazy humor, the Irish tempers and their love of family is a trait we have all carried in our lives and hopefully in our kids." Although our time with our Dads, Aunts and Uncles were short they are the foundation that we live on today. We have an Aunt and Uncle from my Dad's side still here and they both have been involved in every step of my recovery. They have planned and attended every fundraiser and often check on me. They are the only part left to the past and my father.

One of the quotes that Sandy sent me was one her father, my uncle, lived by. It goes like this:

I shall pass through this world but once. Any goodness I can do or any kindness I can show… let me not defer or neglect it. For I shall not pass this way again.

Today everyone who reads my blog and supports my battle please show your support by living today with goodness and kindness to others. Don't wait until tomorrow…start today. For we are only on this earth once.

I shall pass through this world but once. Any goodness I can do, or any kindness I can show…let me not defer or neglect it. For I shall not pass this way again.

February 16, 2009
The Storm

> *"Life isn't about waiting for the storm to pass, it's about learning to dance in the rain."*

I received this quote from one of my clients but now a friend. I photographed her beautiful wedding in April. Her family and she were just amazing and wonderful people. She is a catholic schoolteacher and has her students pray for me all the time. Once again I am so lucky to have such remarkable people pass through my life.

This quote is how I decided to fight this cancer. I am not going to wait for my remission and I am not going to anticipate my death. I am going to dance and live through my cancer. As many of you know from either reading my past posts or just talking to me I am going to find "the good in cancer." I am sure most of you are thinking, "The good in a disease that ends your life and takes away the quality of life you have when you are alive." But I will tell you that cancer changes your life. It humbles you, it helps you see what is really important, it let's you appreciate a day of feeling good or just having a small cold. Cancer gives you courage, it strengthens your love for others, it makes you cry at a sunset and laugh at bad jokes, it helps you hold on longer to a hug from your child, it let's you walk through a room with clothes and toys on the floor so you can get to the bed where your child is laying and lay with him and talk and it gives you a chance to dance when things aren't so perfect. It lets you run in the rain and jump in the mud puddles. Having cancer gives you an excuse when you act a little child-like or decide not to clean for a day. There is good in Cancer if you embrace it and dance with it.

Many of us are going through a storm. The loss of a loved one, financial issues, job loss, illness, disconnection with your child, bad marriage or relationship, anxiety, loneliness and the list can go on. God promises us that our struggles or storms will pass. He just doesn't tell us when. So you can choose to wait it out under a canopy or choose to make the best of it and dance in the storm. I am choosing today to dance in the rain. I am choosing to live the best I can considering my circumstances. Since I made this choice a while back I have lived healthier but never happier.

So once again I ask all those in my corner to live this day for the quote of the day.

"Life isn't about waiting for the storm to pass, it's about learning to dance in the rain."

February 17, 2009
Breathtaking

This photo will explain number 1 below.

A few weeks ago I forced myself to get up and spend the day going to the boys games. I will tell you it took everything I had and more to not stay in bed that day. When I got home after hours of basketball and soccer I found a gift by my front door. It was from my dear friend (great neighbor I must add) Karen. In the package was a beautiful plaque that read:

Life is not measured by the number of breaths that you take, but by the moments that take your breath away.

She added a kind note telling me that she read my blog about quotes and this is her favorite. There was more kindness written but I want to keep that near my heart. What she did not know amazingly enough, is that this was the one quote that got me through my carcinoid lung cancer and the removal of my lung a few years back.

Late last night I started to ponder on this quote. I wanted to make sure I could express the meaning of the words before I wrote on it. What I came up with is, it does not matter how many years you have in this world: we can live to be in the 100s or we could die as a child, but if we don't have breathtaking moments to ponder about we have not lived. I started to list some of the moments that have taken my breath away since the news in May. It took me hours to finish and I am positive I missed a few.

Some moments that have taken my breath away:

1. Sitting on the beach at sunset photographing step by step as the orange ball falls into the ocean. Hearing your family behind you ask, "what is she doing…why is she crying…is she sick…it's just a sunset?." Then turning to see them all running, playing, and laughing (I think at me…but they were laughing). Not a worry in the world. They were away from the cancer now…away from their home. We were together and safe. Mom was photographing and being goofy again.

2. Watching your son pitch a no-hitter, another score three goals in one game or another finally finish his rendition of "Smoke on the Water" on his guitar. Seeing your son hit a three pointer and then turning to me with a thumbs up knowing that I know it was for me. Listening to two of my boys comprise a song together one on guitar, the other on drums. Hearing them say to each other, "cool dude" as they struggle through the music.

3. Hearing my general doctor cry on the phone as she tells me my fate. Knowing her sincerity. Yet you knowing that you will beat it and she will diminish her guilt.

4. Coming home from the beauty shop with a ponytail in my hand and a short hair cut (thinking in a week I will not have

any hair). Having Mark touch my face and tell me I look beautiful.

5. Standing outside Logan's bedroom door hearing crying and listening to Austen telling his brothers that no matter what, he will be here for them and that mom will be okay. Then five minutes later breaking up the argument over a video game. The latter of the two was only physically breathtaking.

6. Waking up on a Saturday morning a few days after my first chemo-embolization treatment…hardly being able to get out of bed, hearing voices coming from my yard and looking out to see all my friends planting flowers and cutting hedges.

7. Having a cousin and his wife dedicate a whole evening of his night club to "getting sunned" or having my sons' teacher make hundreds of sun bracelets to show her support for my family.

8. Having friends do weeks and weeks of work for a massive yard sale or spaghetti dinner to raise money for my treatments.

9. Watching my husband and family spend four weeks planning the country's largest wiffle ball tournament to raise awareness for carcinoid cancer. Then seeing that morning truck loads of food, drinks and don't forget beer all donated for this event and two large tables full of baskets for a Chinese auction.

10. Having acquaintances and now dear friends plan a 5k in my honor to help raise awareness of Carcinoid cancer and money for my treatments. And then seeing hundreds show up to run the "Miles for Smiles for Sunny" in the rain.

11. Having a group of women get together and plan dinners for my family while I am going through treatments. Then

having them deliver a few days a week guaranteeing that no matter how bad I feel my kids will have a home cooked meal. Then having those same friends run from yard to yard placing suns on sticks in the grass to show support from me.

13. A group of teenagers getting a few bands together and having a concert to support me and my boys when I was in Switzerland. Or a group of teenage girls playing a powder puff game in the snow to also show support.

14. Having a lifelong friend and the community I grew up in spend weeks planning an oldies dance in my honor. Even a snow storm could not keep hundreds away.

15. Seeing tears in Mark's eyes when he looked at me a few days after my first chemo-embolization because I was dressed to nines to go to a wedding with him.

16. Having my son's basketball team, The Storm, dedicate every point they make to me. Let me tell you they are amazing to watch.

17. Having a sister-in-law sleep in the hospital with me during my chemo-embolizations…jumping up every time I cried in pain. Having a nephew take his whole summer home from college to move in with me and take care of my boys. Having a brother contact all his friends and clients to tell them about my fund. Having another nephew take my boys to a week long basketball camp and having to take them all over his college campus while he tried to pick up chicks. Having a sister take a whole week off of work without pay to spend at my home taking care of the boys while I was in Switzerland receiving treatments. Having brothers come running whenever I need the boys to go somewhere and I am just too sick to take them. Having a sister to call all hours of the night when I am in pain or just need to talk. Having a mother stay with me at my worse to just do whatever I need. Having another sister-in-law write hundreds of letters to

everyone she knows to tell them about my fight and my fund. Having her go shopping for my boys and bringing them bags of clothes because she knew that I had been unable to do that. It is another nephew going planning an event after event to support me. It is a 9-year-old niece having a lemon-aide stand for my fund. Or a five-year-old niece make me a hand painted heart with the words, "Keep Fighting, Aunt Sunny" on them.

18. Having my husband look at me with pride no matter how bad I feel or how horrible I look. Watching him organize the kids' activities and drop them from one to another without a complaint. Having him see past the hospital stays, the pain, the weathering in my face, the sleepless nights, the ugly PJ's and telling me that he would do whatever it takes to get me better.

19. Listening to the birds sing outside my window when I am too sick to get out bed. Having the birds outside my window because my neighbor put a bird feeder in her yard so that they would come for me.

20. Seeing the delight in my boys' eyes when I am able to cook them their favorite breakfast, after being in bed for days.

The list goes on and on but I may not finish it today. So I will continue to mention moments that take my breath away in other post. The point is we need to realize breathtaking moments when they are happening. We need to know that it is not about what kind of car we have, how nice are home is, the designer clothes we wear or how many toys we have. Sure those things are nice and I like them just as much as the other. But it is the little things that God is given us that are moments that take our breath away. It is the sunsets, the green grass, a thunderstorm or an act of kindness. It is our children getting along or them drawing a heart on a piece of paper that says they love you. It is seeing a miracle or a prayer answered.

So today take notice in the moments that take your breath away and feel free to email them to me. After all, you just spent 10 minutes of your time reading mine.

The quote to live by today is:

"Life is not measured by the number of breaths that you take, but by the moments that take your breath away."

February 17, 2009

I thought today I would combine a few quotes that don't need much explanation, but would be good for the day.

"If you always do what you always did, you will always get what you always got." My nephew, Justin, is one of the basketball coaches for CMU. I did not ask him where he heard this quote but I think it is something my dad may have told him. Where, when or from whom he heard it does not matter…what matters is that he lives by it. I must say he does. He told this quote to his players and with the record they had this year I think they got it. I decided to write this quote on the boys mirror this morning. Just thought they needed to see it before the start their day.

"If you think you can, you can. And if you think you can't, you're right."
This is one I have lived by my whole life. I needed to write this one because I must admit there are times where I just don't know if I can continue. However, I am not ready to give in. So I will just think can. The other day Mark repeated it me again. I was a little down about going back to Switzerland and told him I was not sure if I could go through it again. Well if I think I can't then that is exactly what will happen. I must believe in myself and trust in God.

"When the going gets tough, the tough get going."
My nephew, Ray said this to me early this week. Famous great one to inspire you to get going and be tough.

"To succeed, we must first believe that we can."
Another one my dad would to say. No explanation needed.

I hope these get you through the day.

February 19, 2009
Do You Feel Luck?

"I'm a great believer in luck and I find the harder I work, the more I have of it." —Thomas Jefferson

So many times we just wait for luck to fall our way. When we have money problems we buy a lottery ticket and keep our fingers crossed that our numbers come up. My friend Sharon and I do this all the time because we have the same "Lucky Numbers." Every time we decide to play we hold them tight and say, "this will pay for treatments. This ticket feels lucky." Sometimes I rubbed it and say, "medical bills be gone…this is a winner." It's fun but God tells us that He will bless us if we work for it and use the talents he has given us. When we are faced with an adversity many of us kneel and pray. Then we wait and wait for a miracle. Sometimes God's greatest gift is unanswered prayers. Sometimes God wants us to work for the miracle so we can reap the greater rewards of becoming stronger.

Trust me, I have always been a believer in luck, after all I am Irish. I have at times looked at others and said, "boy aren't they lucky. Everything falls their way." I have a few "Lucky Charms" I carry with me. I look for four leaf clovers in the grass (maybe not in the suburb's perfect lawns, but defiantly in my back yard…sorry neighbors), I pick up a penny when it is on the ground (only face up though), I have two lucky numbers, I throw salt over my shoulder when cooking with it and the list goes on and on. But what I have learned is that the harder I work for something the more I seem to get lucky.

When I was diagnosed in the past with cancer I put all my cards in the doctors' hands. I waited by the phone for them to call and tell me what to do. I took every drug and pill that they gave me and did no research on what I was taking. I trusted that they were doing all they could, and they were. I don't want to discount my doctors' efforts. My doctors have always been great but they are humans with many patients. I prayed and prayed for God to heal me and give me a miracle. And I waited and waited.

This time I decided to work to get better. I made up mind to be proactive and not put my life in the hands of overworked doctors. I will not accept that the doctors knew everything. That is why I went on my own to help them learn more about this cancer. I have spent hours, days and months doing research and talking to many experts about this cancer. I have devoted this journey to my full time job. I think my adjustments may have been because I was told there was no more to be done or because God was telling me to, "do it yourself." What ever the case may be, I will testify that my luck has changed since my attitude has changed. No, I am not cured or in remission, but I feel like I have some control over what I am doing to get better or extend my life. And if all this hard work is not enough I know that my boys and Mark can look back and be proud that I did all I could do and worked as hard as I could to stay alive.

When I uncovered the European treatment I was so discouraged about the cost and the financial situation we were facing. I was angry that Mark and I have worked so hard for everything we have and once again medical bills and this illness is going to take it all away. After all, we were still paying on the bills we had from the last round of cancer. We did everything we were told to do to make our lives comfortable financially and once again we walked down the road of medical bill disaster. Mark worked for years sixty plus hours a week and missed out on so much with the kids to give us the typical middle class life. What I did not realize is that we did work hard in the past and God will take care of us now. The blessing came in and we are plugging away. Does that mean it's been easy? No, but we have definitely been lucky or should I say "BLESSED." We still hate to go to the mailbox and see the envelopes with UPMC or University Hospital Basel on them but we put it all in perspective now and it seems to be okay. We work hard to get through them and we have been blessed as well. It's not what we planned our life to be like, but we know if we don't give up and work hard it will change.

I say this over and over again to the boys every time they say, "they never win," "it's too hard" or "I don't feel like it." I don't think they hear it but like me it will hit them one day when they are waiting and waiting for their luck to change.

So today being Friday don't wait for the weekend to rest. Work hard today and change your luck. For fun though, go buy that lottery ticket too.

> "I'm a great believer in luck and I find the harder I work, the more I have of it."

February 21, 2009
Look Out Satan!

LIVE YOU'RE LIFE IN SUCH A WAY
THAT WHEN YOUR FEET
HIT THE FLOOR IN THE MORNING
SATAN SHUDDERS AND SAYS
'OH SH**T, SHE'S AWAKE.

Thank you Momma B.

February 22, 2009
Be Better Not Bitter

Okay, I am sorry for the delay in posts. Thank you for all the emails, phone calls and cards. As much as I tried to hide the affects that this cancer takes on me it becomes difficult to do so with my fellow blog readers. Yes at times the lack of posts means I am a little under the weather, and I don't mean the 3 or more feet of snow we here in Pittsburgh have gotten in the past two weeks. Sometimes I try really hard to convince myself, and those around me, that I am not sick. I actually will say things aloud like I have a case of the flu or got hit with a virus when I feel sick to my stomach or fatigue. The best according to Mark is when the pain from the bone lesions flares up and I say that I pulled a muscle or two. As much as I am open and willing to talk about my cancer, I still have trouble accepting that I am afflicted with it. It's like I compartmentalize it and when my normal life is interrupted by my cancer life then I am faced with accepting it. I sometimes feel like I am Sunny the mom, wife, friend, aunt, sister, business owner and also the Sunny with cancer—like two different people in one life. I am not crazy or suffering from split personalities but I think that many cancer patients feel this way. We try to stuff the cancer side of us and not let it interfere with the normal side of us.

For the past few weeks I have been reminded that I have a serious life threatening cancer. It sucks. I have been trying to spend the time that I am up and able to get around with the boys. It's hard to keep a normal family life when the glue to the family is fighting cancer. So I realize that as hard as it is at times I must always put them first even before my own recovery. So on days when I feel like I cannot lift my head off the pillow, I get up. On days when the pain is so bad that I bite in a washcloth so they don't hear me scream, I force myself to put a smile on my face and go to their activities. I do homework with them, watch them play their sports, listen to them play their music and make everything that is important to them become important to me. Through doing that I have realized I probably would not fight this fight so hard if they were not part of my life. They inspire me to get up when I feel like I cannot.

With all that said I have decided to be inspired also by all the concerned emails, phone calls and letters I have gotten and post a week of inspirational quotes that have come with them. I did this a while back and it really picked me up and actually got me feeling better. The first one is as follows:

"The difficulties of life are intended to make us better not bitter."

This was found in a fortune cookie by my friend Karen. She emailed it to me the other day and said when she read it she thought of me. I am hoping because I am not bitter and she sees it is the way I try to get through my cancer journey.

My cancer has taken a toll on me physically to say the least. There are so many things in my life that I have taken for granted. The simple task of walking up stairs use to be a no brainer, in fact I use to run bleachers as a form of exercise. Now I get to the bottom, take a deep breath and struggle up. Even sleeping at times is a painful act. But what this cancer has taught me is far more valuable than any physical disability it has given me.

I have become more compassionate, more courageous, more patient, more loving, more humble and kinder because of this cancer. I have learned that people are amazing and I could not survive without their support. I have found strength in me that I never imagined I had deep inside. Without even knowing it I have taught my children what it means to never give up and if you work hard enough you can achieve whatever you want…even life. I have taught Mark that love is more powerful than any evil that you may come across. And that nothing you love is worth losing because it to hard to keep.

The changes in my life have been incredible since cancer has struck me. I have no time to be "Bitter." I am enjoying being "Better."

"The difficulties of life are intended to make us better not bitter."

February 22, 2009
Ask for Strength

"Don't ask for an easier life. Ask to be a stronger person."

How many times have you asked God to make your life easier? I know that for me it's been more than I want to admit. Even those who claim to be well educated Christians ask God to take away some of their obstacles or problems. However, some of God's greatest gifts to us our troubles that come our way. He is the most powerful of all powers so if it is his will he could give you a life without any adversities. He can change your life for the better in an instant. However that is not what He has promised us.

What he has promised us is that He will never leave our side when we turn to Him. He will carry us through times when we feel we can no longer walk. He will give us the strength we need to get through the impossible and make it possible. All we need to do is trust in him and ask him for strength. There is no need to ask him to make things easier, because if we have the strength given to us by God we can climb the highest mountain and fight the hardest fight.

Throughout my cancer adventure I could count hundreds of times when I did not think I could get through another day. Although, those seconds of thoughts have been changed quickly by the strength that I have asked God to give me. Every treatment, every scan, every nasty medicine, every injection I give myself, every pain I have, every medical bill I cannot pay and every time I hear one of my loved ones cry because of my cancer are times that I wish would just go away. However, I know that my trust in God is what gets me through them. And when those times come, I close my eyes and pray:

"God give me the strength to overcome this roadblock. Help me make what seems to be impossible become possible. Let me be an example to others by showing them the gifts that I have received from my cancer. Please Lord give me your strength."

"Don't ask for an easier life. Ask to be a stronger person."

Chapter 9:
Faith

"Seeing is not Believing…Believing is finally seeing God's miracles."

February 24, 2009
Answer to an Email
I need to get something off my chest. About a week ago I received an email from a woman who also has Carcinoid Cancer. She was diagnosed in 2007 with Carcinoid tumors of the abdomen. She has gone through surgeries and it has not spread anywhere else. In my eyes she is very blessed and lucky. Like me, she is frustrated with the lack of information and funding available for this rare and deadly form of cancer. In the tone of her email I am sure she is little upset with my blog as well. She expressed her concern that I am giving the wrong impression about the severity of the disease and basically discounting its effect on people. She feels that I am taking it way too lightly. She also stated that I need to know that my treatment in Switzerland is not a cure…just a chance to prolong a patient with Carcinoid Cancer's life, if it even can do that. She continued to lecture on saying that it is my obligation to let everyone know that we Carcinoid patients are suffering and that there is NO proven cure for this type of cancer. She seemed upset that most of my posts are upbeat and positive, showing that it is easy to live with this

cancer. Her email continued on to the "dark side," as I like to refer to, reminding me over and over again that there is no cure and death is the only way to end this cancer. I must add this is the second email I have gotten like this so I thought I would finally address it.

I must start by saying, "I don't believe I have ever led on in my blog that there is a cure for Carcinoid Cancer." Nor have I stated that my treatments in Europe are a cure for all patients with this horrible cancer. Also, I think that anyone who knows me well knows that I am suffering everyday, but knows that I will do whatever I can do to go on. I refuse to defend my positive outlook on the disease as much as I refuse to air out all my negative feelings on a blog. Today we cannot turn on the television, open a newspaper, answer the phone or even leave our home without seeing the depression of our economy and others suffering. Why do I want to add to that? There is not a day that goes by that I do not wish my cancer away or that I don't feel the effects of the cancer physically. I just choose not to feel it emotionally. I want to add it takes a lot of work and effort to stay upbeat and hopeful. This is how I have decided to help others through this disease.

In my blog, I have links to all the research sites that I found to be helpful for anyone wanting information about Carcinoid Cancer. I am not a physician and will not pretend to be, but what I do try to do in my blog is give people hope. I don't believe it is false hope…I believe it is hope that you can live your life in an affirmative way even with this terminal cancer. I also started the blog to keep everyone who is praying for and helping me through this journey informed on how I am doing. If my faith and upbeat attitude offends anyone please feel free to discontinue reading.

Many times I turn on the computer and think I am not sure I can be cheerful today. Then I get into my blog and the words just come out. When I finally press the "publish post" button I feel like a whole new person. I feel strong emotionally and I know that is what helps me fight. I refuse to give in to the fact that there is no cure. Maybe if I do I will be able to relax and just let the cancer take its course. But every single day I have to look into six beautiful blue eyes and tell them that Mom will be okay. So I will say to those who emailed me trying to break my spirit, I am quite aware that this cancer is life threatening and there is no cure…yet. However, I have faith in the Lord and believe that I am making a difference by showing others that life does not end when you are diagnosed with Carcinoid Cancer. It is just my choice to fight this way. So when I do look in to those six blue eyes I see them looking back at me with admiration and hope too.

Thanks for listening to my rant. I pray that all who are dealing with the effects of Carcinoid Cancer can find the strength not to give up. After all, we are all in this together and the fight is easier with numbers.

February 27, 2009
Answer to Emails: Take Two!

I must say I think I struck a nerve with all those who love me and other Carcinoid Cancer patients when I posted a few days ago about my two emails from the "dark side." Since that blog I received many emails and phone calls from my supporters telling me to keep plugging away and fighting. All I can say is thank you to all of you. I now know that I am not crazy looking on the bright side and I AM in touch with reality. So when I hear whispers behind my back like, "I don't think it hit her yet" or when I receive a "dark side" email I can be proud that I have gotten beyond the whole life or death thing and chosen to be happy with the circumstances I am dealt. I just can't help feeling sorry for those that can't do that with me. They waste so much time with the life they have left being down and miserable. None of us know when our number is up and thank God we don't. So I must ask why if you are given this gift of a day do you spend it bitter?

Thank you everyone for your kind words and inspiration. And to my fellow Carcinoid Posse keep fighting with me.

It's been a rough couple of days with the pain. I am not sure why it is getting more intense but I never can figure this disease out. Just when I am starting to feel great, and the weather breaks for me to start walking again, the pain comes back. It is by no means as bad as it was a few weeks ago but it is there and annoying. Actually, that is the way I should describe this cancer…VERY ANNOYING. Like the three year old that sits behind you on a plane and kicks your seat the whole flight. Or when your child begs and begs in a store for some junkie toy that you had no intention on buying that day. Annoying like when you're pre-teen continues to ask you, "WHY? WHY? WHY?", when you tell him he has to do his homework before he can go outside to shoot hoops. Or the older brother that pokes continuously in the back seat of the car until the younger one yells. Or the two people that sit next to you in the theater (like there is no other seat in the whole place) and talk the whole time. That is how annoying this cancer can be.

I am trying to ignore the pain and continue on with what I need to do, just like we ignore all of the above. But it seems to be getting worse and worse. My busy season for my business is just around the corner so I have a ton of preparation to get done. Not to mention I am just burned out from the whole cancer thing. Okay I am whining now. It's all done, I wiped my tears and I am back at the fight.

In two weeks, I will be on a plane for Switzerland again for round two. That means I am half way through my European treatments. It sounds like I am getting some kind of face lift or something. Although, after this year, a face lift or a least some botox may not be a bad idea for me. I have to admit I am not excited about this treatment at all. The first treatment in January I was a bit apprehensive but I embraced it as a trip away alone with my husband….sad, but true. With three boys and their crazy busy schedule I have to either go into the hospital or schedule a bizarre life saving treatment (before I get attack not life saving just a chance to prolong my life, I know) in Europe to spend any time with Mark. I am sure many parents can relate to this, but I advise you to just make a date…don't go to this extreme. I guess I did not realize how hard this treatment was really going to be. I kept on thinking, "Piece of Cake. I am tough and can handle anything." Well, it sure did shake me up. But I did get through it and I am ready again. Since I know what to expect I think the anxiety is a little higher than before. It's like the "been there, did that" thing. However, if Mark will put up with me again then off we go to the ALPS. I did make a promise to myself that I will return after all these treatments are over and Ski down at least one slope. Who knows maybe I'll get crazy and just leave the hospital and take a quick ride down the white stuff.

So keep us in your prayers on Friday, March 13th. We know, we know Friday the 13th, but we think that means lucky because after all we are not normal. We will be posting everyday and you don't want to miss "Pittsburgh Mark" trying to fit into to one of the Artiest City in the world. Just His comedic experiences are enough to read about. I must add he had been studying German so look out in the "COOP" (Swiss Giant Eagle or Publix) for he will not only weigh the bananas he may weigh the oranges too.

Saturday, February 28, 2009
Today is the Best Day of My Life

Today, when I awoke; I suddenly realized that this is the best day of my life…ever!

There were times when I wondered if I would make it to today; but I did! And because I did I'm going to celebrate!

Today, I'm going to celebrate what an unbelievable life I have had so far: the accomplishments, the many blessings, and, yes, even the hardships because they have served to make me stronger.

I will go through this day with my head held high, and a happy heart.

I will marvel at God's simple gifts: the morning dew, the sunrise, the clouds, the trees, the flowers, the birds, the sunset.

Today, I will share my excitement for life with other people. I'll make someone smile.

I'll go out of my way to perform an unexpected act of kindness for someone I don't even know.

Today, I'll give a sincere compliment to someone who seems down.

I'll tell a child how special they are, and I'll tell someone I love just how deeply I care for them and how much they mean to me.

Today is the day I quit worrying about what I don't have and start being grateful for all the wonderful things God has already given me.

I'll remember that to worry is just a waste of time because my faith in God and his Divine Plan ensures everything will be just fine.

And tonight, before I go to bed, I'll go outside and raise my eyes to the heavens.

I will stand in awe at the beauty of the stars and the moon, and I will praise my Lord for these magnificent treasures.

As the day ends and I lay my head down on my pillow, I will thank the Almighty for the best day of my life.

And I will sleep the sleep with peace, excited with expectation because I know tomorrow is going to be the best day of my life, ever!

I have been saving this post for awhile before I published it. I wanted to make sure I could follow through on all the above before I send it to everyone else. I have decided that since the last four days I have been physically rough on me I needed to have a day of giving, praising and joy. So I ask all who reads this to join in. I believe if we live today like this it will be the best day of our life.

March 1, 2009
Health over Wealth

Yesterday evening after my oldest son's basketball game I promised my middle son, Logan, I would spend some time with him. After all, we just drove for an hour, watched his brother's basketball game, and then drove home for another hour. Nolan, his younger brother, was spending time at his friend's house so Logan was absolutely bored. Although, they won't admit it, my boys are lost without each other and really have trouble entertaining themselves. To my surprise when we got home he asked if we could sit down together at the computer and read my blog. He said that hears many people talking about it and he had not read any of my posts since I was in Switzerland. I was in shock that he chose to read my boring blog as opposed to playing a game or something he can beat me at. However, I must admit I thought to myself, "he will get bored after the first one and then I am off the hook and can go to bed," I was exhausted. I could not believe it but he sat and read them with me for over an hour. Asking questions about the disease and we both shed a few tears. He questioned the treatments, how they really made me feel, the health care in the US, why we have to pay for my life and much more. He then asked if he could write one of my posts. How could I say no? So below is Logan's unedited blog. These are his own thoughts and feelings coming from an 11-year-old child whose mother is fighting cancer. I am not sure if the psychologist would agree that this is healthy for him to do but I know my child best and his eagerness was enough for me. So to those who disagree of our openness with our children about my cancer do not read any further. Your comments are not welcomed. But to those who want to see what it like in the eyes of a child having a mom with cancer read on. I think you will be surprised how resilient children really are.

> Hello. Today I will type my mom's blog instead of my mom or dad. I am so happy she trusts me doing this. What I don't get is why do they charge for people's health? My Dad works really hard so our family can have health insurance yet the insurance company does not cover everything my Mom needs to stay alive for us. Dr. should take what ever they can get from the insurance and then fix the patients with no extra costs. I mean if they want the patients to live then why do they profit from it. So what if it makes them rich. I think that everyone in the world will choose health over wealth. I know that God says that we should help people because it is the right thing to do, not because you want to make money from it. My family had to give up a lot to afford the treatments my mom is now going through. Having a mom with cancer is enough but having to pay for many medical bills is just plain cruel. My Dad and Mom are smart, educated and work really hard but they have to spend their money one keeping my mom alive. That is just wrong and one day I want to change it all for other families.
>
> My mom has been battling this cancer for 13 years off and on. We never really talked about it until she was diagnosed again this May. You can never tell that my mom fights cancer so strongly because she is so beautiful and quiet. I think she did not want anyone to know. She is still here, so that means she is winning. So anyways, GO MOM!!! If she was a boxer she would be number 1 because that girl can fight. I hope her blog is inspiring moms with cancer

not to give up. Sometimes my mom's back hurts within an hour. So I just hope she is ok. If I had three wishes they would be:

1. My mom will win her boxing match with cancer.

2. Everyone else in the world with cancer will win their boxing match.

3. My mom's medical bills would have never existed.

My mom has been making me feel special for as long as I could remember, so all I could say is that she does not deserve this thing. She has been to all my sporting and school events even if she was sick. One time she was so sick from chemo that she stayed in the car through my whole soccer game and watch from the car as she threw up in a bucket. She even has one day every year since I can remember, and I can remember very far back, which she dedicates just to me. She doesn't care where I would like to go as long as it makes me happy. We spend the whole day doing what I want to do instead of going to school. We call it our SPECIAL DAY… but what I can't forget is that she does it for my brothers too. There is one song that explains this and it goes like this, "She makes me happppy ." That is all I know of that song but I know it's true for my mom. I try to sing it to her all the time with "Hey There Sunshine" and "Mom I All-star" From The Sunny album by Logan Carney. Remember this album is not in stores. So do not call for the album; call to wish my mom good luck in her boxing match.

Every morning when my brothers and I leave for the bus my mom shouts, "Make good choices." My mom makes good choices everyday by fighting this thing. She makes good choice because she wants to be around with us when the going gets tough for us. Because no one is as tough as her and we need her in out corner. My Mom can get really mad and then I say look out world or cancer.

I am so proud of my mom for fighting this boxing match and winning so far. I know that she will not quit like Rocky Balboa na na na na na na na NA NA NA NA NA na naaaaaaa. She never quits anything including giving in on my punishments. Sometimes I wish she would at least give in on that. Anyways, I just love her and I am proud that she is my mom.

Before I finish my mom's blog I would like to say thank you to everyone who has been to the fundraisers, dropped dinners off (which are delicious by the way), and prayed for my mom. It means more to us than you can imagine. Like my mom has always taught us I will pay it forward one day. So all I would like to say is that thank you and peace out.

Logan Carney

March 4, 2009
Spiritual Experience

We all need to take the lead sometimes. Yet we all need someone else to take the lead sometimes too.

I have to share with you this experience that a woman named Melinda Jennings emailed to a friend of mine who sent it my way. It is very moving and beautiful. I just had to blog it. I hope you enjoy it like I did. It goes like this:

I had this experience that I wanted to share with you.

Lately I have contemplated the role that women or "Sisters" have in each other's lives. I feel that women need each other. As I was driving up to Atlanta one day I noticed two birds flying together. Of course I was on the freeway speeding along and the glimpse of these birds was fleeting, but a lasting impression imprinted upon my mind. One bird was leading doing the hard work, breaking the wind so its friend would have an easier time. Then in that quick instant I watched as they changed places or changed roles. The transition was flawless and beautiful. I thought how we, like the birds, often need to change places – either we need to take a breather from the hard winds of life or we feel it is our turn to step up and break the winds of life so our friend will have a smoother path. I know that those birds did this instinctively – the Lord wired them this way – they help and serve each other and I believe that the tenderness and compassion that we have as women make us the same way. The Lord has wired us to want to serve and lend a listening ear to each other. I also believe that, just as the birds, if we are always in front breaking those winds eventually we will wear out and won't be able to go on anymore. I know that it is OK to take the back seat and let a friend take over for a while. Knowing that their turn will come again, but that a person needs time to replenish the soul so when it is their time to take the lead they will be strong enough to do so.

I believe that each one of us is an "angel" to a friend sometime in life. Times of crisis come and the Lord sends these special angels into our path to break the hurricane winds that blow. The Lord knows each of us as individuals and sends help when we need it. I also know that we need to be close to the spirit and be listening to the still small voice so when we have a friend who is struggling we will be in tune to be there for them. I loved the talk at October conference time by Jeffery R. Holland, where he says, *"My beloved brothers and sisters, I testify of angels, both the heavenly and the mortal kind. In doing so I am testifying that God never leaves us alone, never leaves us unaided in the challenges that we face. "[N]or will he, so long as time shall last, or the earth shall stand, or there shall be one man [or woman or child] upon the face thereof to be saved." On occasions, global or personal, we may feel we are distanced from God, shut out from heaven, lost, alone in dark and dreary places. Often enough that distress can be of our own making, but even then the Father of us all is watching and assisting. And always there are those angels who come and go all around us, seen and unseen, known and unknown, mortal and immortal."* I thank those women who were sent from the Lord during those difficult times in my life. They lessened those harsh winds and were angels in carrying me so I did not feel so alone. What a blessing it is to be a woman today. Reach out and help a friend today and if it is your time to follow allow that friend to reach out to you. Both are enriched with the spirit of friendship and love.

I truly love this story. But I must add that people need each other not just women. I have been blessed with so many angels. My angels are women, men and children. My angels deliver dinners for my family, send me an encouraging note or email, call me to see how I am, help me with my boys, pray for me, run for me, plan events for me, or sometimes just give me hug. For so long I have always wanted to be the lead bird. I never wanted anyone to pass by me and lead. But since this round of cancer I have let others take the wind. As hard as that was, and I don't think I will ever get use to it, it has allowed me to focus on fighting this disease. Thank you to all my angels or birds.

Chapter 10: Preparing

March 9, 2009
5 Days and Counting Slowly!
Last night, I started writing a whole different post about leaving for Switzerland. It was about how I am ready to go and fight the fight. How I am not afraid and am ready to give it my all. I put in a few quotes and made it totally inspirational. But then I reread it and thought this is all bullshit. Sorry!

I am scared to death. I don't want to go on Friday. I am hoping that my doctor calls me and says, "Hey Sunny, we made a huge mistake. You don't have cancer. Cancel the trip." I would even settle for, "We found a new treatment. No pain. No nausea. No Swiss hospital. Here in Pittsburgh." But we all know the chances of that are slim. Even with all my positive thinking and wishful dreaming it just cannot happen. So like all my posts, this is as honest as the rest. I am not looking forward to leaving on Friday the 13th. The answer to the number one question being asked to me this past week, "are you ready?" is a big fat, "NO." Mark is actually the calm one and is looking forward to our trip. He said he loved the time we spent with each other alone. I think he's been hitting my pain meds or something. I cannot even think about any of it. I actually threw away all the clothes, perfume and lotions that I wore the last trip because I just could not bear to have any memories around me.

The smell of the lotions and perfumes and the sight of the clothing had to many frightful memories.

I know it's because I now know what to expect. To relive the past nine weeks again is just an agonizing thought to me. It is not the trip that stresses me out, it's what happens when I get home. It's the vomiting, fatigue, enormous amount of pain and all the rest that is to come. It's my boys having to see me suffering and my husband's total exhaustion. It's me not having control of the situation and having to rely on others for help. Anyone who has been through cancer and the treatments that go with it can totally relate to what I am saying. I hate to seem like the only one who has been there. I just have to be honest and tell you I am not ready to do this again. BUT I WILL AND I WILL DO IT WITH ALL I GOT.

I have run through all the words to get my mind to change. The "go get them attitude" words like, "you can do it, it will pass, you got through it once, keep fighting and so on." I will continue to do that until it's all over. I will continue to think positive and offer it up to God. I will not quit! But I have to be honest and tell you that I am not ready. So please continue to keep me in your prayers.

March 10, 2009
Courage

"Courage is not the lack of fear but the ability to face it."

I received this quote from my nephew, Ray-Ray, after he read my whining post yesterday. Apparently, I said it to him one time so now he is passing it back to me when I need it. He definitely does not lack courage. He has been fighting juvenile diabetes since age 11…he is now 38. That's right I have a nephew the same age as me. I remember the day he was diagnosed and the sadness in my sister's eyes (his mom) when she found out. I can tell you exactly where I was and who I was with when I heard the news. I was with my niece who ironically was the same age too (passed away since) and we where sitting on the back porch of our family home waiting for my sister to tell us what was wrong with him. We just got back from a family vacation with the whole crew at Hilton Head South Carolina and Ray-Ray (now goes by just Ray) was sick through the whole trip. The three of us were inseparable growing up. Christy and I were happy about that; Ray-Ray was forced to play with us girls. But we had a bond that was like siblings or more. We argued at times but mostly we were like the three musketers or maybe more like the show, "Threes Company." We always had each others back. Christy passed away a few years ago with complications for cancer treatments. Ray and I were with her up until the very end. She is really who taught me to fight. So it's no wonder he cheers me on now.

It was great to read that quote again. It is so true. He helped me realize that it's fine to have fear but to have courage you must face that fear. To go even further, I know that if I face that fear it no longer is a fear. It then becomes a challenge or a goal to reach. Once that challenge is met or that goal is reached it's on to another one. Wow that's deep. On a lighter note it's similar to the Bungee Jumping experience. The whole way up your feet shake, your stomach turns, you look down and think about turning around (which of course you can't because you're being watched by all who dared you to do it). Then you get on the ledge and the cord is wrapped around your ankles and all you can do is pray and fall. After it's done you realize that you accomplished something that most would never think of trying. You may never want to do it again but you did it, it's over and your fear is now courage.

So I have decided to turn this fear of the treatment and the fear of the agonizing weeks ahead, into courage. I will do what I need to do and nine weeks from Friday the 13th I will have reached another goal. I will be half way to the end…half way to remission. And one step closer to getting this treatment to the United States for my entire Carcinoid posse.

Thanks Ray-Ray (which I will always call you) for the return of motivation. Thanks to everyone for the encouraging words to strengthen my courage. Thanks to all who have sent cards, called, texted and emailed me their thoughts and prayers this week. Mostly thanks for believing in me when I lost a little faith in myself.

"Courage is not the lack of fear but the ability to face it."

Another "Good in Cancer."

March 12, 2009
Continuation to Breathtaking

> *"Life is not measured by the number of breaths that you take, but by the moments that take your breath away."*

As promised I am continuing to add to February 19th's post titled "Breathtaking." Please go back and read it so you understand this post.

Some more moments that have taken my breath away since my relapse.

19. Being asked to come to my boys' school yesterday (thinking it was to help set up for an art show) and greeted with an enormous bouquet of flowers, an inspiring note and donation to the fund by my sons' principal, Gail Yamnitzky. The note was quite beautiful and explained that the children and art teacher, Ms. Ruane, decided to dedicate the art show to me.

20. Being escorted into a hallway filled with 1000 glittering hanging suns and rainbows all with messages on them from the students, parents and staff to me. Some of those messages quoting sayings that I have been saying throughout my whole cancer journey.

21. Seeing one larger rainbow with three suns hanging from it….the larger one with a note from Mark and each of the smaller ones with a note from each one of my boys.

22. Seeing my photographic work hanging in that hallway and replicated drawings of each photograph by my son's 6th grade class. I could have stayed and stared at them for hours.

23. Knowing that my children's art teacher spent months planning and working with the children for this event and hours the night before hanging each every sun just to inspire me to continue this fight.

24. Walking into the "teacher's lounge" to a beautiful meal paid for by the staff at Pivik Elementary (that's right, not the

district or our tax $s) with a table decorated with sunflowers and suns.

25. Hearing Nolan play his first concert that night at the art show. Seeing him smile from ear to ear because the piece he had practiced for hours and hours each day for 3 months was done perfectly.

26. Knowing that while I am thousands of miles away trying to save my life, my boys are going to school full of amazing people who care about them and love them.

I cannot tell you how amazing yesterday was for me. I am still in complete awe at the most wonderful school, Pivik Elementary, my sons are blessed to go to. To have a public school in America show their students that life is about caring for others, as well as teaching them how to achieve in their education is beyond what any parent can ask for. Today's teachers and school administrators have so much pressure to meet the marks. It is very difficult for them to have time to teach the rights and wrongs…how to be a good, caring person. Pivik manages to balance it all. They educate in a way that is just not seen in America today. You never really realize how wonderful people around you are until you have to overcome a difficult adversity. But once you do realize the wonderfulness that surrounds you it becomes "breathtaking."

"Life is not measured by the number of breaths that you take, but by the moments that take your breath away."

Forgot to add to please keep my family in your prayers. We are off to Switzerland for round two of treatment in just a few hours. My boys will be here with my family but I know their hearts will be with us. Thank you all for your support and help during this time.

Chapter 11:
Off to Switzerland

"In Switzerland they had brotherly love, five hundred years of democracy and peace, and what did they produce? The cuckoo clock!"

March 14, 2009
We Are Here!
We made it to Basel. I must say the trip was not that bad. Besides a few mistakes the travel agent made it was fine. There was a brief moment in Philadelphia while getting ready to board to Germany that the angry Sunny started to come out and someone got a "Sunny Smack down." It's not very often (I'm sure Mark will disagree) that she arises but when she does there is absolutely no control. What I cannot tolerate is rude and whinny people. Especially when I am paying the same cost to fly to Basel as I would to fly my whole family to Disney World 13 times. But I must say with a few deep breaths, counting to ten and walking away, shedding a few pissed off tears (different from true sad tears) and then lashing out at Mark for everyone else's rudeness I managed to stay in control…okay maybe not. It felt good though to finally get pissed off. I am sure Mark will like to post about that story later.

But I must say I did really well compared to the last trip. Of course I have pain, after all I have cancer in my bones and liver, but it was manageable this time. I did not get sick to my stomach either. I hate to get my hopes up but I am really expecting good news on Monday when they do my scans at Hospital Basel.

It is hard to believe just nine months ago I was told "no options." It is a true miracle right in front of our eyes. I want to just stand on the top of the Alps or Pennsylvania Ave (my street) and yell to everyone "CAN'T YOU SEE THE MIRACLES!" We need to all open our eyes and see the amazing things that are happening around us. The doom and gloom of the economy is not what is important. Sure we are all scared about our jobs or our family's future but as all that depressing news continues miracles are happen everyday. Good things ARE happening. Stay positive and strong and open your eyes to the good. See that God is in every day.

Okay I just got down off my soapbox. I was only writing to tell you we made it. Mark is sleeping right now and I just read about two museums that we missed the last time we were here. Knowing that is not Mark's thing I am going to grab my camera and go on my own. So before I enter into the "twilight zone" on Monday I am off to hit what I missed the last time.

March 15, 2009
Selection Sunday

Well I know back home today is Selection Sunday—a day in which college basketball fans across America find out if and where their favorite college teams will be playing in the big dance known as March Madness. Over here in Basel surprisingly there not much attention being paid to the whole concept-Selection Sunday. Instead we will be letting Sunny choose what museum she wants to go off to AGAIN and then me trying to keep up with her tiny ass as she dashes off. After a rather painful evening (especially at dinner…where a hair in your salad is a hair in your salad no matter what country you are in…and "Couch potato's" isn't a stuffed baked potato but more like globs of cheese and ham in a dish of whipped potato's) left her feeling hungry, nauseous, and a bit cranky (before I even started to snore) she is up and about today ready to go like always. We are soon off on the number two train for Basel's Modern Art museum and to sneek a peek at a Picasso or two…etc. I am wishing I was sitting in my Steelers' chair at home watching ESPN but I would not dare say that to her because she is so excited about teaching me some culture. She keeps going on and on about this museum is a once and a lifetime opportunity to see a real Monet or Picasso. Love her sales pitch of "once and a lifetime." She is good but not that good.

    I am glad she is in better spirits today because yesterday was hard for her. Back pain…fatigue…it seemed like nothing would ease her pain. Yet she was again a trooper and really did not complain. We are back at our favorite Swiss Hilton, with the main difference being this time we were able to upgrade to the Executive Floor, which actually has smaller rooms, but a great lounge down the hall with complimentary food and beverages. (I think it might have been Sunny's way of keeping me close by when the need for a Jim Beam and Coke Light called). As soon as Sunny walked in the lobby yesterday she was greeted with big hellos and hugs by the same Swiss troops that took care of us here at the Hilton a few months back. They remembered her like most remember her. Sunny has a way of making everyone feel special and not even realizing she does it, even when she is going through one of the scariest times of her life. The bartender came out and shook my hand but squeezed Sunny with a big European hug. She remembers his name was Mark (ok she better remember that) and she asked him if he was still keeping up with his art. She smiled at him and asked, "How many pieces have you sold since I've been gone?" God, she is so amazing and caring. We were escorted to the penthouse floor and Sunny questioned the price to the bellhop (typical Sunny). He told her that the upgrade was on the house.

    There is actually one less channel now for us to watch on the tele…they took off our beloved Vintage American movie channel which was kind enough to run the Eastwood/Eddie Murphy marathon last trip…oh well…at least we still have Judge Judy and Rickie Lake from the early 90's to pass by the evenings.

    As I sit in front of the open window to write this (it is a beautiful 60 degrees Fahrenheit) I can hear the sirens of a Swiss police car wailing off in the distance like an old Bond movie. With the rustling of the trains going by I am thankful that we have the opportunity to be here again to help Sunny continue her treatments against the Carcinoid Disease. Although we are both more comfortable this time here, I know we both miss being home a hell of a lot more as well. Maybe it's because we have "had been there…done that" or maybe it's because we know how tough our kids are trying to be back home with out us or her I should say. But this will be an even longer week than last…and I can't tell you how much I am looking forward to just getting back. Austen's hoop team lost a tough game yesterday and it hurt knowing he felt bad because I wasn't there to help coach…Logan has two soccer games this weekend and I hope he continues to do well…and Nolan…well I want to thank Nolan and one of his teacher's Janet DeMarco for a special project that Nolan came up with where he handwrote a letter for Sunny to open each day of our trip here…its only Sunday but it has really touched her.

I will have to jump back on this again later today because she is impatiently standing next to me…camera ready…arms folded…ready to go and tackle the museums. As much as I am not looking forward to wondering around the unknown I am so happy to spend this day with her. She is so excited and her smile is just so beautiful right now. Once again I don't know how she has so much courage and strength but I am proud she is mine.

Keep us in your prayers as you are in ours…and until later…Danka Shane (or something like that)

Mark

March 15, 2009
Few Hours and Counting!

In just 15 minutes I will be entering the Swiss hospital I renamed "The Twilight Zone." I am over the anxiety and now just plain ready to go. I figure the faster I get it over with the better I will feel in the long run. Cliché I know, but that seems to be what is getting me through this all…a bunch of clichés. I think Mark and I walked all over the city of Basel nine times yesterday. I wanted to push myself hard so that I will be exhausted when I go into the hospital tomorrow. Just some strange theory I have…the more tired I am the less I suffer. We saw every museum except one that we found out about after it closed…Basel is considered the city of museums. I even talked Mark into going to the "World's Largest Doll Museum." I think he enjoyed it or at least pretended.

I am now leaving to take a train to the hospital. I will first get a scan to see how the first treatment took. I am sitting here reliving the last treatment just to prepare myself. It wasn't that bad I keep saying. Off I go and I will leave you with Mark for updates.

※※

March 16, 2009
New Moon on Monday

Well it's hard to believe but I managed to screw up this post entry thing once again. I know a lot of you have been waiting for an update. I somehow managed to delete my earlier entry and in a moment of frustration almost chucked this little laptop into the Rheine River. It is now past dinnertime over here, and I just spoke with Sunny for probably the last time today. Today was treatment Monday and I am honestly not quite sure if everything we heard was accurate or positive. She went over this morning at 10:00 and on one hand it was reassuring to know our way around (no kicking in on closed door meetings or feeling as wandering lost through the Hospital like a sassy American woman and her stupid American guide…) but in some ways knowing the pain and nausea that awaited her was hard enough.

When we got there, Nurse Martin was waiting for her and like the entry to the Hilton he greeted her with a big hug. He too remembers her from a few months ago and when she asked him if he greets all his patients this grand he said, "Especially the kind ones." She got a big smile her face as she cutely blushed. He read the menu options… (Although the egg quiche thing with plums didn't go over so well tonight she later confessed) and then Dr. Doogie (whoops I mean Dr. Nicholas) came in and we got the process rolling. They were so efficient in recalling last time she had had excessive nausea and they had already ordered the latest Superdrug in the war against nauseous side effects and would really help. Well lets just say that the Superdrug was almost upchucked back onto me when she took it which caused nurse Martin to kid "you have to take it for it to work" and for nurse Pierre to tap-tap-tap nervously in the room behind, as if he would have to clean up her mess. That's how my little Sunny shows her nerves. She keeps a smile on her face but her stomach is always a mess.

When she went down to the twilight-zone basement for the treatment I said my goodbyes. I feel so lonely when I leave her here to fight by herself. She gave me a quick wave and off she went. She had the beautiful smile on her face but in her eyes there were tears of fear. I think she thought I did not see them but those big eyes are hard to miss. I want to share with you what she told me it was like. Picture an olds James Bond movie where he has to transport some old uranium or a really old Get Smart where 99 has to protect the secret serum and that is what its like. The room is lead lined, the doctor dressed in space protected gear enters a code on the wall and opens a drawer…then another code opens a platinum silver case, and then another one, and then out comes the $20,000 dose of orange radiation in a test tube. Homer Simpson sure would feel at home.

I think she was fine at that point but when Dr. Mueller came in later and told her to expect the same amount of pain and discomfort as last time, she got a little anxious. She called me and tried to sound so strong and tough but after knowing her better than anyone else I could tell it was all to calm me down. It's been a long day and it has been great to have my friend from Holland here for the next 24 hours. He brought her an enormous bouquet of flowers that was given to him at his performance the night before. Sunny was so honored that he drove them here from Holland just for her.

I want to close tonight with three quotes that Sunny has written in the cover of her Bible that sits on the night stand by the side of the bed she slept in last night. When I read them I felt like she was right next to me saying them in her confident voice so I thought I would share them with you:

> *"Let us live with urgency. Let us exploit the opportunity of life. Let us not drift. Let us live intentionally. We must not trifle our lives away."*
> —Raymond Ortlund

> *"Outlook determines outcome and attitude determines action."*
> —Warren Wiersbe

> *"I've never seen a monument erected to a pessimist."*
> —Paul Harvey

Until we do this again…thanks for all of your support, thoughts, and prayers.

Mark

March 17, 2009
Tuesday's Almost Gone

Tuesday…the day after the treatment. Sunny actually had a pretty good day. She looks great and felt a lot better than she did last time. Don't get me wrong, its still not a walk in the park (especially like we saw on Sunday…older couples walking by the river with cross-country ski-poles…no snow…no skis) she had a pretty bad headache and sharp pain in the liver at times, but the nausea seems to be under control considering…and once again we left the hospittaal to go back to the Hilton for five or six hours. It was nice having her back at the hotel and will be even better to have her with back home.

Pete went back to Amsterdam but Sunny was able to see him this afternoon before he had to drive back. He surprised her with another beautiful bouquet of flowers (I know, I know …why didn't I already have flowers there? Lets just say I wasn't going to dare figure out to price that at the COOP after the whole banana incident last trip) both at the hospital and here at the Hilton. What made it a really nice gesture was that they were from his performance Sunday night and as conductor tradition dictates he give them to the best performer at that show…to Pete that was her. Sunny was really touched and relieved that he "hadn't spent a fortune on them." It was really great to hang out with him while Sunny was out of pocket yesterday.

We really look forward to being back Saturday and as always please keep us in your thoughts and prayers as you are all in ours.

Mark

March 18, 2009
Results

Well they let me out of the "Twilight Zone" and back to the Hilton. Although I received the best care I could have possibly asked for, it is still a strange place to be. I guess I am just use to the American hospital. By no means is it worse or better just different. I will say though the kindness, efficiency, and compassion that the nurses, technicians and doctors have here is amazing. They were very good to me and genuinely caring. Not over worked or frustrated...just relaxed and patient.

I know that so many of you are waiting for the results of the scans and I have every intention in going into all the details...just not now. After spending the night at the hospital with no English stations on the telle and finishing every book I brought (thanks Kate Austin for the great book), I had much time to go over and over the results and scenarios in my head. They are complicated and I have decided to come home and sit down in front of six beautiful blue eyes and talk to them first. I want my boys to know everything in simple terms before I go into the medical jumble. Whatever the results are they are just preliminary and many more scans, a recommendation to a doctor in Iowa and a few new monthly treatments will follow. There is hope always hope and I will never give in to this cancer.

I am doing good, but very weak and tired so I will leave the blogging to Mark for now (please read below). Thank you all for the amazing care you are giving to my boys. I don't know why I am so lucky to have so many amazing people in my life that love and care for my boys. Thank you for the dinners and for all the rides to their activities. Thanks to their teachers for the amazing kindness they are showing them while I am gone. They are doing okay but they have expressed missing us and worry. But they are just such amazingly strong and resilient boys.

Boys: Mom is doing great and much better than last time so no need to worry at all. Enjoy your time with Grandma and stay focused on what you can control. I will stay focused on what I can control here and be home real soon. I love you so much. MOM

March 18, 2009
Over the Hump Day
Well another St. Patrick's day has come and gone. Sorry for the short blog entry yesterday (and no it wasn't due to an affinity for green beer on the 17th of March...in fact the only green we have seen over here is the green buildings...be green and recycle...etc...even the Irish bars were kind of tame compared to the energy of Market Square...unless the 70 year old Swiss/Irish guy singing off-key karaoke in front of a

crowd of ten or so old enough to have helped Paddie himself chase the snakes out themselves). I did not want to waste anytime that I had with Sunny on the computer. For me its torture to have to bring her back to the Twilight Zone and come back to this empty room. So I wasn't out gallivanting through the green streets of Basel…or out buying "milk" or getting "gas" I crashed and then woke up and crashed the computer. Stupid Americana…

It's Wednesday evening here at Hilton Basel…and the end of another glorious day as the temps went all the way up to 16 Celsius…take that Pittsburgh…you only hit 68 Fahrenheit today…and the sun was out. Our Sunny came back here—the hospitaal portion of our European adventure over. She had several more scans done this morning down in the Twilight Zone, and I think it's fair to say that the results were mixed. There definitely has been positive news in that nothing has grown (stabilized is how Dr. Doogie put it) but there hasn't been shrinkage like they had ultimately hoped for. Because there was no shrinkage yet, she was not asked to come back in 2 to 3 months liked planned but will return again in August for 3rd treatment. We will monitor things back home with blood work, CT scan, eventually an Octreotide scan, and as a bonus prize potentially the opportunity to go to Iowa or Nebraska (all I know is its Big 10 or Big 12 country) to visit the states top carcinoid doctor. She does not want me to go into anymore details because it is too complicated to put into words right now. I know that she was hoping to explain the results better in Medical terms after she sits the boys down and talks to them.

To change the subject a little to sports I understand that not only are the Penguins on a possible playoff role, but my Pitt Panthers (best 7 years of my life) are a number one seed in the madness of March. I hope they have a long run, not just for selfish reasons but with all of the pain Sunny will be going through when she gets back, it is real nice distraction/break from reality for the boys and I…just like the Steelers run to the Super Bowl when we got back in January. Watching Euro Sports Live with extended coverage of some kind of game where they bounce a soft soccer ball, pass to teammates like football, bounce like basketball, hit like rugby, and throw the ball into a soccer like goal, indoors in a hockey rink where Germany was up 22-16 on Denmark I wonder if they have any clue to the therapeutic powers of group sports bandwagon jumping.

Speaking of the tele, Sunny has just finished taking another long shower to ease some of the pain in lower back and liver…and now is sitting behind me entranced with what Judge Judy's verdict will be. I should have taped this episode back in the states, gone down to the executive lounge, bet a few drug-selling Novartis schmucks a few francs and paid for dinner. However, even she couldn't sit through the back to back Rikki Lake and Sally Jesse Raphael marathon…its no wonder they think Americans are stupid over here because on the tele is that…Paris Hilton's British Best Friend reality series, the head of AIG and our brilliant congressmen arguing over bonuses and suicides on three networks, the Simpson's in German…Nein Bart Nein…and Two and a Half Men in French…although I think Pierre may feel it is about two guys and a midget…

After we checked out around 11:30 this morning (we had to wait for Dr. Doogie to drop off the note giving Sunny permission to trip the security gates) we came back to the Hilton and then she wanted to go right back out. She is amazing. After several disappointing attempts to find "cool" culture here (the doll museum was interesting, but stuffy, and I felt a bit out of place as everyone else had kids with them or wore dentures except for Sunny and I) I had finally scoped out the museum of fine art which was hosting a Picasso exhibit, had Van Gogh, had Maltese, and seemed to be the real deal. It was fantastic. Besides the aforementioned masters and all of their naked bosom, dangling genteel, group hugs/orgies, there were paintings from the 15th century on and some of the most beautifully preserved nativity scene, stage of the passions, and Virgin and child art you can imagine. Sunny was a trooper as she went to each of the three floors (we went backwards against the flow of the floors unknowingly…drawing stupid Americana stares and extra special observation room the museum's Barney Fife security team). When she felt dizzy we would sit and rest. When we saw a bummy…we sit and rest and laugh about what our boys would have to comment on that painting. She made it through in about 2 hours, feeling a little dizzy at times but not wanting to stop at all. Once again, tough as nails.

We came back here to Hilton Basel and made a quick change of coats, I put my shorts back on, and we walked a half a block to a new place we stumbled over on the way to the museum…the Steak House. We were drawn to it because the menu posted outside referred to a Philly Cheesesteak and other US OPTIONS. We were all about US OPTIONS at this point. In we went. Turns the menu had no English, but I know the ingredients in a Philly Cheesesteak, hoped they were universal, and was surprised when Sunny also ordered the same. However, I don't think she had even one bite. The place actually had two TVS on, like some kind of pathetic attempt to be a sports pub, but alas…no ESPN, it was cross-country skiing in a city outside of Vienna where they brought snow into the city streets, like Detroit's or Cleveland's old Formula 1 races, and then had an urban ski competition …sorry…nice try klumpters but you are missing the point of sports television altogether…The sandwiches were very good, they tasted like home, but the bottom of the bun was a bit soppy and I had to use knife and fork or risk having another one of those Stupid Americana with cheese on his sweater" moment. Sunny just pushed hers aside and waited while I ate both of them.

We made it back here around 4:30 and Sunny was definitely out of it, a bit woozy, and tired. I made a few calls back home, let her rest for a couple of hours then dove into this. We managed to confirm that the boys will be able to go watch the Steelers-Plum hoop game Thursday night (thanks HOOPS JJ) and we confirmed that they hadn't locked Grandma out or tied her up (thanks boys). We are now one day closer to driving back through those beautiful tunnels, and into that wonderful cracked, chipping driveway we call home. Can't wait.

Please continue to keep Sunny in your prayers as she is tired, has a fair amount of pain in her back and liver and that she will rest well tonight. We will continue to think about and pray for you back home and look forward to cheering on those mighty Pitt Panthers from my own lumpy couch, with the bad-breathed weight challenged dog and all on Sunday afternoon.

Mark

March 19, 2009
Another Day!

Today was a day of emotions. I am not sure if it was the morning phone call from my boys and them telling me they really miss me. Maybe it's knowing that I actually made it through the treatment and can hear their beautiful voices. Or it could be that I feel so blessed be in this beautiful city receiving a treatment that many other carcinoid cancer patients don't even know about. Or it might just be that I am living a dream and I have discovered that I have more courage than I ever thought I could find in me. Or maybe it's just that I am amazed at what Mark and I have gone through in the last nine months and I cannot believe how much our relationship has grown in just this little bit of time. I am thinking that I am so emotional today because of all the above…this glorious day is just overwhelming me.

Wherever the emotions are coming from, I am feeling pretty good considering what I have been through in the past week or so. The doctors here in Switzerland told me to go back to the hotel and rest for 3 to 5 days. Rest! How can anyone rest when you are sitting in a small hotel room watching reruns from the 90's of Judge Judy, Riki Lake and Sally. However I was able to turn on MTV for a few hours in the middle of the night last night and caught some show starring the rapper "Flavor Fav" or something. He had some big clock around his neck and was picking woman to live with him. Quite, entertaining to say the least until my laughing woke up Mark and he asked me to turn that crap off. I must say I was a little depressed for some type of American TV but agree it was crap.

I think the doctors once again, where taken back that we have decided to head home on Saturday as well. They thought that maybe we were rushing things. But I know that I cannot rest until I am home with my family and friends. I am in some pain and quite nauseous but I feel better than I did the first time. I know that once these drugs start going through my body and organs things will get worse, so I want to be home in my own bed when that starts. All and all though I am feeling pretty good…it's like a bad hangover.

I even managed to take a few hours out and about in the Market Place. Mark was the one that seemed exhausted and I teased him a little when he asked me if he could take a rest. I am not sure if he was really tired or just being a little over protective of me and faking it. Whatever the case, I gave him 5 minutes on a bench then tugged him around some more. I bargained a little with some Swiss's vender to bring home some trinkets for the boys and then went into the famous chocolate store. I must tell you that Swiss chocolate is good but outrageously expensive and no bargaining allowed in that red carpet store. However I did reach deep down into my pocket and bought some for my angel helpers at home.

I have now hit the wall and don't think I can leave the bed now. It's that good tired feeling, like you accomplished something and now can rest feeling. As I lay here in the low European bed I cannot help but relive the moment nine months ago when my original oncologist told me he predicts I had about six months left of life. He firmly told us that there where no more options available for my cancer and to go home and get my life in order. No options...right. Here I am and I see so many options for me. I am not sure what is in the future but I know that whatever He has for me I am ready. Until tomorrow.

March 20, 2009
TGIF

Well it's Friday finally....our last day in beautiful Basel, Switzerland. It has been a nice couple of days since Sunny has left the hospital in that we have been able to spend a lot of quality time with each other (its easy when there are no distractions from things like ESPN or Survivor, work, her business, phone calls, etc). I actually feel at peace because like Bono sings we are "ONE"...one stupid Americana couple going the wrong way through a world famous museum....one cancer fighting couple that won't back down...one couple who has placed this all in God's hands and knows that through him all things are possible. It's been a while since we have been "One." Over the years and battles with this horrible disease our marriage has taken a rough road. I never realized that we were falling apart until recently when we became "One" again.

I know that she saw the destruction that this cancer had done to us...ME. But I just took her for granted because she made this fight her own and made it look so easy. It finally hit me the night after the first oncologist told us that this was the worse scenario and he had no options for us. She was cold to me that night and very distant. I had time to think because she was handling this on her own. I realized that I have not been the best husband and my life of fun was really not fun. It had hurt her and turned her to stone. My life without my family concerns in mind was not the man she married, nor was it the man I like to look at in the mirror. She had that fire in her blue-green eyes that I've seen so many times before....the "I'll show you" fire look. Sunny as strong as ever looked at me and gave me the out. As serious as I ever saw my baby she said, "You need to either leave 100% or be here for 100%. It's your choice but you need to make it now. I cannot be distracted with your single life. I have a huge war to win and you can be in my army or not." I knew then that I could not live without her and my life would be empty without her love. It's like Bono's words, "A house doesn't make a home...don't leave me here alone."

Sunny's pain today has been constant but not as strong as the last time. Her nausea has come and gone but she has continued to want to go out and do things and not to be cooped up here at Hilton Basel. We went to the zoo today....36 acres. Actually the perfect size to walk through in 90 minutes and I got to take some more videos while she got some amazing pictures. We learned just a few days ago that this little escape was a mere two train stops away from our hotel here, although in the other direction that we have been accustomed to. So we hopped on the number 8, went past a few Pizzeria's with Take Away service (that's for to-go food not irate customers) another wonderful centuries old church and after a quick two block walk we were in the zoo. It's a little chilly but the sun is out and so is the other "Sun." I know that she was not her best but she never complained once, even when she had to turn in an alley to vomit. This is why I am so in love with her she just pushes on. I have never once heard her ask why this is happening to her or question the why she has gotten this cancer. She pushes her self until there is no more to give and never wallows in self-pity. Something I have never seen before in anyone I have ever known.

The zoo was actually the cleanest place we have seen so far in Switzerland. No graffiti, no litter, no smoking, and a wonderful soup and salad bar that for some reason Sunny didn't want to try. We went through the Viviarium and saw lots of cool fish, penguins, and alas no real sharks. We got real close to rhinos, a snow leopard, a tiger, pelicans, and flamingos. We dodged a diving Swiss vulture or something which scared the Swiss cheese right out of us, we got to see little Swiss children scream, carry on and then not listen as their frustrated parents try to get them under control (apparently the whole Dr. Spock "we should just talk to our children and understand why they are beating each other with sticks as they walk by turtles" speech may have been a gross mistake in child rearing). Sunny and I just shook are heads and said in English, "Why don't the take the sticks away." Then the coup de grace was we got to see the papa boar sneak up from behind and "jump" on the mama boar, like a dog in heat on an unsuspecting leg. We both laughed not because we are immature nature prudes, but because we envisioned what our three boys would have said or done at that special moment in time.

After catching the train back to the main station outside Hilton Basel, we tried to find a place to sit down and enjoy lunch. We walked around the corner to a pizzeria we had spied on the train, only to discover that they close at 2:00 and reopen at 6:00. I must admit, this has been fairly common around here, this 3 or 4 hour siesta time that restaurants take every day obviously needs some "you can rest when your dead" attitude from Sunny. Kind of defeats the purpose of the long lunch or the multi-martini business luncheon….sorry last call guys it's almost 2:00…. PM that is. So we went back to a place that is as warm to Sunny's heart as Somma's is to mine…Starbuck's. We had a 40 franc lunch consisting of bottled water (no gas), two blueberry muffins, a pasta salad, and some kind of ham on bagel sandwich that Sunny actually enjoyed immensely.

We are back resting…Sunny is watching her Jeremy Kyle hour (he's like a cross between Jerry Springer and Oprah with a Benny Hill accent)…and I am waiting for CBSSPORTS.COM to be able to watch the basketball on the laptop. It even has real honest to goodness American commercials. By the way the slightly effeminate lad won Paris Hilton's British Best Friend last night in case anyone was wondering. Apparently beat out the aspiring singer and the former stripper. Sunny informed me of that after I begged her to turn the TV crap off. Now you see why I sit in front of a Dell and watch a small, fuzzy screen with in and out audio and thank God that technology can let me watch Pitt play tonight at 7:55 PM Basel time.

We are going to head back over to the train station in a little bit because Sunny still has a few chutzkys to buy. She is feeling confident and is fresh off a multi-lingual bartering beat down yesterday afternoon at the Market Platz, saving 10 francs on some items at a poor artisan's stand because he, like me, cannot figure out the money conversion rate as quickly as she can. She is the best. With all of the pain, dizziness, and everything she's been through this week, she still goes store to store, finds the best sales and then picks out the perfect gift for those loved ones back home. She is the one with the cancer, and yet I am embarrassed to say I am the one whining about back pain from walking all across town with her trying to keep up to my little shopping Swiss Sunny. Ever little trinket she buys is for someone else. She says things like, "I could see so and so with this on" or "so and so would love this because it's her favorite color." That's my girl…always trying to make others happy. She even picked up some famous artist brushes for our inspiring artist/bartender at the Hilton.

After we hit the station stores, we are going to catch the 11 train to the river so that she can get a picture of the sunset. It's a beautiful scene with all of the old architecture, the church towers, and the reflections off of the water and she'll be damned if she misses it again. She's been watching it from her hospital bed and cannot live Basel without taking of picture of it. She promised me if I go with her we will stop for a beer and sushi or veal sausage warts or a weenie in a bun or something. However I know that if I tell her I am too tired to go she will do it by herself…and I am not going to let that ever happen. She is stuck with me forever now.

Then we come back to pack. The longest day of the trip is tomorrow. The return back to the States. Philly will never look so beautiful and neither will the Parkway or the tunnels in our wonderful hometown of Pittsburgh. We miss our boys, we miss our family and friends but we are almost back. Please keep Sunny in your thoughts and prayers especially tomorrow during the travel back home as we will continue to keep all of you in our thoughts and prayers. Thanks to everyone who helped out with Casa de Carney and with those crazy Carney boys of ours this week.

Thanks,
Mark

Chapter 11:
Home Sweet Home

"When you're safe at home you wish you were having an adventure; when you're having an adventure you wish you were safe at home"
—*Thornton Wilder*

March 22, 2009
We Are Back!
After 22 hours of traveling we are finally home. I must say I feel like I've been through a tough battle, but the war is not over. It was a difficult day of traveling. First and foremost, I woke up Saturday feeling like I had one of those college hangovers that I so don't want to relive. You know the one where you take one foot and place it on the ground from the bed to make the room stop spinning. The thing that is so devastating about that feeling is that I did not even get to enjoy the party from the night before. I could barely get out of the hard Hilton cot (that's what Americans refer to as luxury bed in Europe) and as soon as I did the room was spinning even more. The pain was immense and the vomiting began. I manage to hit Mark awake to tell him I was going to the lounge to try to put something in my stomach and take those amazing Swiss pills that they hospital gave me that will make me a new woman and ready to travel. Mark later found me and was back to his normal

travel anxiety struck self. I was really too sick to comfort his fear of missing the plane or what ever else he was rambling on about so I put my hand to his mouth and gave him that, "Shut the F#*k up" look. That did not work though, he is impossible to shut up.

We get ourselves together and I go to check out just to see the entire lobby filled with jewelry artists and buyers in long lines ready to check in. This week in Basel the "World's Largest Watch and Jewelry Exhibit" was starting. The rumor around the Hilton was that many famous designers, Hollywood stars and world-renowned collectors were all checking in on Saturday. We were even told that Paris Hilton called for a suite at the last minute and the Hilton had no rooms to give her. But at this point I could care less who was waiting or checking in…I was getting out of there and home to the boys. So I poked my way to the front of the line, pretended that I had no idea what I was doing and was back up to the room to retrieve Mark in 10 minutes. I just kept on saying, "English?" and holding my hands up like I had no idea what was going on. Frank, the front desk manager saw me across the counter and gave me a wink. He knew exactly what I was doing. Mark was down at the lobby earlier and told me that the wait was over an hour so when I got back to the room so quickly he gave me a high five and off we went to catch a taxi to the airport.

Check in at the airport was also frustrating because our travel agency booked us the wrong setting and we had to work that all out, which I had to leave up to anxiety wrecked Mark because he knew some German and could communicate better. So we finally made it from Basel to Germany and loaded our plane to Philadelphia when I realized we had one of the oldest and most uncomfortable planes still flying. So the tears start flowing and Mark begs me to just stop. The pain was so intense and Mark was driving me crazy because he would not calm down I just had to pull myself together. So I accepted my fate for the nine hours in the air and the German Stewards named Helga started passing out drinks. Mark decided to flirt with the German Stewards and she played right along. After tempting him with two of her strongest Bloody Mary's by saying, "are you man enough to drink the drink I make?" she managed to spill a whole container of OJ completely down me from head to seat. We had eight hours and 45 minutes on this plane and another five hours of traveling after that so I must say I was not happy. When I stood up to wipe my ass up the people in the seats around me all gave out a universal, "oh no." I was completely soaked down to my undies. Mark and the stewards both looked scared and had a worried and panicked look in their eyes. I have only seen that look a few times in Mark and it was usually because of some kind of news with my health. But it defiantly changed my attitude. I grab the steward's hand to stop her from touching my areas I did not want to be touched, looked her in the eyes and told her that it's okay. She continued to apologize in German and actually looked like she too was going to cry. But at that point I realized in the last nine months I had been through so much and overcome so much some OJ in my hair, bra and panties is nothing.

Mark just looked at me and smiled. I know he thought I was going to just deck her or was hoping I would control myself and just "the sunny tell off smack down" as he calls it. But all I could do was laugh. I was completely soaked down to my lacey's with some lovely smelling OJ and all I could do is laugh. The others around me started helping clean up the mess while I stood there and laughed. I will tell you I had more Europeans touching me than the women in the 15th century paintings of orgies we had seen a few days earlier in the museum. After getting three blankets to put on the wet seat I sat down and Mark said, "I am proud of you, you didn't do a Sunny Nutty on her."

The flight was fine but I must tell you if I don't hear another language for the rest of my life it will be too soon. I know finally now what it is like for a foreigner to come to our beautiful country and not know what the hell everyone around you is saying. I was in pain and sick to my stomach but I got through it.

We arrived in Philadelphia only for me to be stopped and hauled away by a customs police officer walking by me because his battery packed radar machine was going crazy. The radioactive therapy I received in Switzerland sets off all the warnings when going through detectors. This time I had a double does of the magic stuff so the custom police pulled me away. I had a note from Dr. Mueller but that was not enough for them. Mark had a look of terror on his face again, so I was more worried about him having a heartache than I was about anything they could do to me. They did not let him come with me so you can imagine what he was acting like. I was taken in a curtain room and yes searched. First with the magic wand and when that went crazy it was the inevitable…a strip search. While the female officer lifted my shirt I began to explain my whole story. Within 20 minutes of intense questioning I had all those big gruffy officers in tears. They where so kind to me once they discovered I was not a terrorist and just a mom trying to fight this horrible cancer. The one that pulled me aside, young good looking man in his twenties, began telling me about his mom and how she had just past away a month ago from cancer. He explained that when she was diagnosed she just gave up. He told me how hurt he was that she did not even try to fight it. Wiping his tears he then gave me a hug and told me to keep on going for my boys. The officer then called for us to have in escort to our next terminal and when I finally hooked up with Mark again he could not help but shake his head in disbelief as I rolled by him in a golfcart like thing with three young hunky uniform men laughing with me. They told him to jump on the motorized cart and off to the next flight we went. At that time, I knew that the whole day was meant to go the way it went. God knew exactly what He was doing once again. He puts people in your space for them to make a difference to you and you make a change in them.

Our flight from Philadelphia to Pittsburgh was delayed of course. But I was so exhausted and so overwhelmed I did not even begin to care. After several calls from the boys wondering when I was going to be home or asking me how much longer until I can get on the plane we finally boarded to our last destination. It was such a peaceful flight. Mark and I had a whole row to ourselves I feel asleep and awoke to the captain say, "Welcome to Pittsburgh" and the rest is history.

Yesterday I was very sick and in pain but at true peace. Even though I could not make it out of bed I was home and under me I could hear my family rumbling and living. That is all I really needed at that point. I know that everyone is waiting to hear the results from the scans in Basel but I will save that until tomorrow. We are still working things out and contemplating our next option.

Thank you everyone for all your prayers and support. Thanks mom and my family for watching those wild boys. Thanks for also having them miss me.

March 24, 2009
The Results!

I am sorry for the delay on the results. I think my family and close friends are ready to beat it out of me. I have mastered avoidance of bad news. I just feel that sometimes if you ignore the negative the positive will soon take over. Well, it's been over a week since the doctors in Switzerland spoke to me and I now can see the positive in all I am doing. The scans where not great but they were not bad. I realized its all how you look at it.

Good news first…they showed no growth in any of the existing tumors. They showed stability. However there are a few new small tumors that have popped up…one in the liver (very small) and several in the bones. They unfortunately were not visible with the first treatment so the doctor strongly feels that they have only had one round of the magically Y90.

Bad news…there was no shrinkage, which is not what I and the doctors in Switzerland were hoping for. Because there is no shrinkage and new lesions have appeared Dr. Mueller wants to wait and see for a while before trying any more Swiss treatments. So I was not invited back for round three at this time. He is thinking that in about three months things will look better. I must say I was speechless last Monday and was glad I was isolated on the "twilight zone." I had time to just think with no one around me. It was just me and the white walls planning out my next move. I did not even let Mark in on all the results until the next day. I needed to digest it before could spit it out to him. Not to mention he was alone in a strange country.

The Swiss doctor explained to me that stability is not bad news. It prolongs my life for a year or more. He said he has had patients that have stayed stable for over 10 years. Of course, he added that they were not as metastasized as me but he also doesn't know me like I do. He went into the fact that nine months ago looking at my scans I would have had no chance without this treatment. He said that in January (my first treatment), I looked so much worse and the cancer was taking a toll. He was wonderful at pumping me up. He wants me to see a world renowned doctor in Iowa and continue to follow my progress with scans. I was given some suggestions on diet and exercise. He also suggested an additional monthly treatment administrated at Hilman. That treatment will be covered by insurance, YA. Then if all goes well return in August for more treatments.

So it's the waiting game. In the mean time, I have a lot of living to do. I have decided to restart my nonprofit division of Sunny's Photos. That is where I donate my time to families who have been struck by cancer and give them the gift of portraits. I did this for many years but when I had my relapse in May I just could not get myself up to doing it again. So I am now motivated to begin that. I actually think I need to do it to heal myself through this cancer. I am going to continue my ongoing treatments and new diet. But mostly, I am going to enjoy every day with my family. I am going to live in the moment and not worry about what is to come. I have decided in order to fight this battle I must do six things everyday:

1. Pray and thank God
2. Tell my four boys that I love them
3. Make someone smile
4. Laugh
5. Cry
6. Laugh until I cry

I feel blessed that I have the gift of knowing how precious life is. It is unfortunate that it took three battles with cancer to finally get the importances of living a simple life. I am going to continue to fight and enjoy my stability. I will thank God every day for the blessings he is giving me.

March 26, 2009
The Magic Question!

I have been getting a ton of emails wonder how I am feeling. I guess I can say I am feeling pretty good and that is why I have not wanted to talk about it. I don't want to jinx anything. I've been cautious at what I have been doing, especially alone. I know that the time is coming soon when the treatment takes effect and I am waiting like a child waits for Christmas except not with excitement. I am not sure I want to unwrap this gift. After the last treatment I felt okay the first week, about what I feel now, and then it all hit me. The nausea and pain began like the 4th of July fireworks. Yesterday I looked back at my posts from January, some I did not publish because they where just too personal, to figure out when the hell started. It was really hard to relive that month when reading about it. But it looked like it was about two weeks after the treatment that I started spiraling down to horrid abyss.

I've been catching up on all my work and photography projects for clients. I also started back up my nonprofit division again and scheduled one family for portraits already…for the last week in April because the agony should be gone by then. So if anyone knows of any families that are going through the cancer journey please refer them my way. They can go to my photo website, and email me through there. I am hoping to expand this large enough that my photography colleagues will pitch in and volunteer with me. I would love to grow this division and be able to give cancer families the gift of memories. Cancer changes the lives of so many. When struck with this disease, no matter what kind or what stage, you start to have two lives….the before cancer life and the cancer life. Some are even blessed with the after or cured cancer life. I cannot tell you how many times my boys will remember an event from the past and then end the story with, "that was before the cancer." Now they even go as far as saying, "that was the lung cancer time" or "remember before the first time you were sick when we…" I am sure those who have gone through this journey and are reading this are shaking their heads with complete understanding of what I am talking about.

I want to record the happy times of the cancer journey for people—the times when you see life and your family so much clearer. When suffering from cancer you go through so many down times and those are not what a cancer patient or their families want to remember. However, when going through this trial you have many good and fun times. You and your family live your life endlessly and that is what I want to document for others. I want them to be able to look back at the happy times that cancer gives. Hey, another "GOOD IN CANCER." My list is growing.

To answer the big email question, "I am hanging and fighting." Please keep praying for me. Keep prayers strong next week when the treatment makes it to my bones. I know that the more pain I have the better the treatment is working. At least that's the story I am sticking to.

Chapter 12:
It's Back

March 27, 2009
Walk Into the Sun!

> *"If you walk towards the Sun the shadows will always follow behind you!"*

I love this quote. I spent the evening last night at my son's chorus concert with my girlfriend Karen. I was telling her that people have always commented to me that I don't show my true emotions about having this cancer. I told her how I have people tell me that I can cry more and don't need to put up a front to help others think that I am fine. I expressed to her that I really don't feel sorry for myself and am going to live my life looking forward and not be bitter about the cards I have been dealt. And I will say again "I am not sad and do not feel hopeless." Yes there are times that I cry, who would not if they were going through what I am going through. But I have decided to wipe the tears quickly and get back to enjoying life. She then told me this quote that she had engraved in her High School graduation ring.

> *"If you walk towards the Sun the shadows will always follow behind you!"*

I had never heard her quote before but I think that I am going to steal that from her and use it as my new quote. If you keep walking to the positive, the beauty of the sunshine, all negative will fall behind you…or the shadows. We need to believe that the best is yet to come and that life is full of good things. Enjoy the heat of the sun on your face and don't turn around to look at the abyss of the shadows. Everyone knows that when you stand in a shadow you feel cold and dark. You tend to slump down or wrap your arms around yourself to stay warm and protected.

There is no way you cannot feel great and energized when you stand in the sun. Doctors even suggest that you try to get at least 10 minutes of sun a day to boost your happiness. God even put vitamins in the sun that help with depression and anxiety. You can spread your arms and feel the happiness hitting your body. It is impossible to feel bitter or depressed when you are walking towards the beauty of the sun. When you believe that hope is just up ahead and the doom and gloom are behind you all you can do is smile and have peace. I got my nickname "Sunshine", later shortened to "Sunny," minutes after I was born. There are many jokes my siblings tell about why I was named this… too many kids…ran out names…dad wanted another boy and it was supposed to be spelled "Sonny"…parents where hippies. But I think it was my father knowing he was going to instill this attitude in me. So why not name me this.

I have always tried to surround myself with good positive people. I think that is why I have such an amazing support system around me during this journey. It's been very easy for me to do this because I actually feel ill when I am around a negative soul. I have this great gift, or at times it is a huge fault, that I actually will go out of my way to avoid someone who is always looking into the shadows of life. You know "the glass half empty" type of person. A person that will come up to you, say hello and then go on and on about all the problems everyone has. Or someone who will take a good event or scenario and find some negative in it. For example, I had a situation years ago where I was having a huge surprise party for Mark and I was so excited. We lived in the city in a tiny city home and on a street that had limited parking. You know those city streets where people actually put folding chairs out to save a spots. I eventually learned to put a brick on my chair after losing a dozen or so to a bad gust of wind. Anyways, I actually had one of those downers say to me, "I would not have a party here because where will people park." I did not care if they park in China…all I cared was that

Mark was happy and surprised. The positive people will show and enjoy their ½ mile walk from Stanley Park to get there. The shadows will stay home and the party would be better for that.

How about those who pretend that they are sympathetic of someone less fortunate by telling you all the unfortunates' hopeless problems? Deep down they are gossiping. Those are one's that need to walk in someone else's shoes. Let's not forget the worst of the "boo whooo" bunch, those who just love to be miserable and make others miserable. They are actually not happy until someone is in strife.

I am not saying I am perfect. I have caught myself every once and a while becoming part of the "boo whooo" bunch. But then I turn around and face the sun again. I let the shadows walk behind me and stay in the cold. To be completely understood, these are not the amazing people who are not afraid to speak or just reach out to give me a hug or sincerely ask me how I am doing hoping to hear good news. Nor are they friends who will cry with me when I need to cry. Or the once who cry for me when they know I am hurting. Or those who secretly watch out for my children and every once in a while give them a little hug or a "that a boy." Those are not part of the "boo whooo" bunch. They are my supporting posse.

God, I am so blessed that the list can go on and on of all the positive people I have in my life. I have no time for the negative once. So to be so blunt, I have no time for those who wallow in self-pity or look for the bad in every situation. My whole life I have tried to avoid the "boo whooo" bunch and can tell you I only know a small handful of them. But now my time is so precious and I need more then ever to be with optimistic marvelous people. I think I am doing a good job at that. Karen and I unfortunately were not the best behaved at the concert last night. We actually laughed through the whole thing. We laughed so hard we began to cry. She was embarrassed but I told her, "people probably think we are crying because I have cancer." Just Joking. We were not laughing at the kids performing, after all our babies were up there, we had no idea why we were laughing. We were like little kids who just saw a naked picture in National Geographic's. It was actually shameful that we did this but I know it was great medicine for me and for her.

I watched Jimmy Valvano's last speech to the ESPY in 1993 on You tube the other day with Mark, for anyone who has never heard it; it will change your life. He was in his last stage of liver cancer. He said there are three things you must do every day to have a full life:

1. you should LAUGH
2. you should THINK
3. you should bring your emotions to Tears.

Well last night the day was almost over and I did not laugh yet. So thank you Karen for the help and sorry to the rest of the parents there that thought we were inappropriate. But I will advise you try it sometime, it really felt great.

So on this beautiful spring day walk into the sun and leave the shadows behind you. If you do that you will have a great day.

If you walk towards the Sun the shadows always follow!

March 31, 2009
Tackling Tuesday

First of all, let me lead off by apologizing for the lack of updated posts since Friday. We were actually on a weekend long vacation deep in the Canadian woods and had no access to phones or internet. OK, so those of you who know Sunny realize that there is no way, with or without, cancer she would ever go deep into the Canadian woods. She is all about Carpe Diem as long as it doesn't involve sleeping bags, tents, and bug spray. You might not think so but she does have some diva in her.

The real reason for the lapse in communication is it has been a really long couple of days. If you recall the posts from the week or so after the return from Basel last time, you will remember that it was about a week later that she had excruciating pain and discomfort which unfortunately lasted about 8 or 9 days. When people asked me "How's Sunny doing" my answer was, "it was like being with her during labor for 24 hours a day for a week straight." Well the same type of pain kicked in again over this past weekend and here it is Tuesday morning and we hope and pray that it won't last the rest of the week. The physical nature of the pain this week has also tested her ability to stay positive. I think part of what makes her so special is that she has an uncanny knack for finding the good in things or people. She never let her situation get her down. Just like a boxer after going a strong, hard eight or nine rounds but without a knockout of his opponent may feel tired, discouraged, or worse yet, may question if he has what it takes to finish the bout…just like that boxer needs his corner man to pump him up, needs his cut man to take care of the physical pains, and needs the crowd for encouragement when the bell rings announcing its time to stand up, get back out there and do it all again she needs that now too. She would never let anyone but I hear her but she's been questioning if this is all worth it.

She will get a new type of pain injection on Thursday, which is supposed to be a better option than what she has been taking. I am going to continue to do what I do which is to try to make her see the humor in the world around her and how blessed she really is much like she does for others. However I think that may not be enough; I think she needs you all to be her crowd. Cheer her on and tell her how important she is to this world. Pray for her, call her just to catch up and say hello. Email her a positive note or scripture, let her know that the fight is not over, and re-enforce that it is certainly a fight worth fighting. Don't be afraid to bother her and check on her. She loves people and although she's not at her best, she never likes to be alone.

She is an amazing woman who has touched me in more ways than even I can recall. I could not imagine what my world or I would be like without her believing in me and pushing me to my full potential. Mostly, I could not imagine her giving up right now or ever. I know that from the outpouring of kindness she has touched so many others like she has for me. I also understand that when she talks about how after a year of this suffering she is tired…just drained of fighting. This is hard for her because in her whole life she has never felt defeated like she does right now. She has always been the best at whatever she wants to do and this time the best is not good enough. It is the natural reaction of someone who loves life so much going through the ups and downs of the cancer journey. She isn't going to be down long, you and I all know that, but I think as much as she hates to admit it she can't do this alone. She needs her loved ones to bring back her usual PMA (positive mental attitude) self.

Mark

April 1, 2009
Unanswered Prayers
It's been a rough week but I am finally almost through it. The pain is getting better, not gone, but definitely better. Last night was another sleepless night for Mark and me. I try hard not to keep him up but the

pain and the vomiting just puts me over the edge. When I think back I don't have any idea who that woman is that looks like me. It's like I am having an outer body experience. Despite all that, I feel so thankful this time that I knew what to expect and was prepared. However, even though I was prepared it's easy to get a little discouraged. But once again I feel like I am almost at the top of the mountain and ready to descend to better times.

What I have learned from this experience is that every time I conquer one more treatment I feel so much stronger and so proud that I overcome something else. Don't take this as a pat on my own back…it's just such a high knowing that I got through it again. I have accomplished many things in my life with hard work and perseverance but never has it felt so good as to get through this horrible couple of weeks. I have never asked for this cancer and would give up almost anything to have it taken away, but I know there is a reason for it. Lying in bed sick I get some time to reflect and think. Not always a good thing for someone as intense as me, but it does get my mind working and helps me realize that there is some good in unanswered prayers.

This time I thought about what my life was like before I was struck with this cancer for the second and third time. I remember praying to God not to change anything. I had a perfect family and a perfect life. Sure I wanted more material things – bigger house, nicer car and all the rest money can buy - but I was also content in many ways. I remember when we first bought our home that we are living in now I thought, "we have everything we need. We are so lucky!" I had a hard working husband, three amazing boys and a beautiful home. What else could I have asked for? Little did I know that I was truly not as strong as I could have been? God needed to shake us up a little and teach us to be better people. Each time I get through one treatment or another I look back and thank God for the lessons I learned and the strength I feel in me. Now when I tell the boys to reach deep down inside of them and pull out something you never thought you had to accomplish their goal I truly know how to do it. I hope I am not sounding self praising because I will testify there were a few times this week when I thought I had nothing more to give. I was emotionally and physically exhausted. But with prayer and strength I am almost through it.

Through my thinking I came up with the following testimony:

Unanswered Prayers

I asked for Grace when things get tough and
God gave me cancer.

I asked for knowledge and
God gave me intelligence to find the answers.

I asked for wisdom and
God gave me obstacles to overcome

I asked for strength during treatments and
God gave me pain to make me strong.

I asked for a cure and
God gave me experimental treatments to try
to help others with carcinoid cancer.

I asked for financial security and
God gave me a talent to work.

I asked for courage and
God gave me risky and crazy treatments to overcome.

I asked for love and
God gave me a husband, children, family, and friends
who have been fighting my battle with me.

I asked for patience and
God gave me a rare cancer that I will live with forever.

I asked for peace and
God gave me prayers.

I asked for mercy and
God put me in front of others who are suffering more than I am.

I asked for hope and
God gave me my faith.

I asked for happiness and
God gave me blessings and taught me that happiness is up to me.

I asked to take away my loneliness and
God gave me opportunities to help others.

I asked for help with my family and
God gave me a voice to ask others.

I asked for everything to fight this cancer and
GOD GAVE ME EVERYTHING I NEEDED.

Sometimes God's greatest gifts are unanswered prayers.

April 7, 2009
Tuesday's Gone Again

It's hard to believe that spring is here (the weather outside certainly reaffirms that feeling) and that we are coming up on a year since we learned that cancer had returned with a vengeance in Sunny. Unlike money which you can budget, food which you can ration, clothes and material goods which can be passed down, go on clearance, or just replaced, our time here comes with no knowledge of a best used by date and the only manufacturer that has a true warranty also has complete control of each one of our "lifetime guarantee"…we just don't know if its a twelve month, five year, ten year, etc…let alone tomorrow.

What living with cancer does do is make you reconsider what you are really saying when you tell your wife or your kids "we will do that tomorrow" or "I'm busy, ask me later" or "not now, I am too tired." Sunny has continued to fight this disease with the tenacity of a cornered pit-bull that has only one way out, and in this case the door is blocked by tumors. She has had another rough couple of days pain comes and goes, ranging from aches, to dizziness, to intense sharp jabbing discomfort, to vomiting and has not slept well for about a week. Yet, if you ask her, she will tell you that she is doing better this go around since returning from Basel and to quit making a fuss. She would rather talk about how excited she is to be coming up on the start of a busy photo season or to let me know that I really need to take my time when I help out by folding the laundry (apparently just being a lefty doesn't cut it as an excuse for miss-creasing clothes). But behind her bedroom door she is sick and in so much pain.

Time around the Carney house seems to be measured not by calendars, but by the sports activities our boys happen to be playing. Outdoor soccer practice— mud, gnats, and all for Logan—baseball practices and scrimmages for Austen and Nolan. We had the official close to the basketball season Sunday night with Ace's (nickname Sunny gave him that for some reason stuck) team party and Sunny not only went, she suffered through the heat of the indoor pool area, and watched as the kids open their end of the year gifts which included her individual framed action photos for each boy on the team…unbelievable to me that she still stresses about making sure each 6th grader on the team had the perfect photo that reflected their true personalities. I told her we weren't awarding Pulitzers or Peabody awards for sports photojournalism, but those of you that know her can imagine the fretting that went on as she wrapped each one the night before in the perfect purple and gold paper while in between she would run to the bathroom to vomit (again I was barred from helping because apparently being a man does qualify as an excuse to be dismissed from wrapping detail). It just goes to show that Sunny thinks of every single kid or parent to brighten their day.

Watching the NCAA championship with Austen last night, I realized that some Americans think that we may over-emphasize the importance of sports and athletes in our culture. I have two comments relating to that. One, I can tell you that after returning from Basel in mid-January, having the ability to escape cancer for a few hours every week during the Steelers Super Bowl run meant a lot to the Carney family. Black and gold days at Pivik, planning the back porch tailgates, and the victory parade enabled us to put aside scans, blood counts, pills, bills, and just be a "normal yunzer" family for a little bit. Getting back the second time; we have had first the run to the Elite 8 by my Panthers and now the Penguins playoff chase. (I would mention the Pirates but this is supposed to be the uplifting part of this blog). Again, for a few hours we can just be fans (although I don't scream and shout as much at the refs because I do realize now its just a game and not actually "do or die") and we can share in the experience of just that—being fans. Not a family fighting cancer…not a wonderful woman who can't sit or stand without grimacing, not a husband who gets frustrated at himself for not being able to do more for his wife, not three scared boys that have to figure out what to feel or to know what to ask or say about their mother. For that hour or so that involves a sporting even we are a normal family like the neighbors next door or down the street...not a cancer family.

The second revelation regarding sports is the joy that I know Sunny gets when she is able to go to an indoor soccer game and see Logan score, when she can go to a basketball game and watch Austen as the point guard, lead his teammates to a first place trophy, or go to a baseball game and watch Nolan who works his butt off, get a hit, steal a base, and score a run. But even if they struck out, didn't score, or missed all of their shots, she would still go, still cheer, still feel bad for them...and that's what a mom is supposed to feel. A mom is supposed to jump for joy and aggravate the parent sitting next to her in the process when her little man does something well on the field or court, and a mom is supposed to just want to go out and hug her big guy when he has that bad game and you can just see it in his face. That's what a mom is supposed to do. Just be there. And for Sunny, the ability to be there, rooting, encouraging, and hugging when needed, is something she knows and she does real well. Even though at times I know it takes every thing she has deep inside her to get to that game, when she is there she is there 100%. Because before there was cancer...there was and is one hell of a mom. My kids are blessed because their mom is always in their corner. Something I could never take her place doing. Sunny just always knows how to be that perfect mom and that perfect wife. I just cannot imagine what would happen to us if this treatment does not work. What would these four boys that cannot live without become? Surely we would not know how to love like we do now.

I have asked her at times this past season, "why don't you just skip this one...you look tired...or it's too much pain and too long of a ride." She tells me that she is going to go because she doesn't know if she will be able to next season...but I think deep down she goes because she has put the "can" back in "cancer"...as in I can be a mother...I can fight and beat this...I can be there for my boys...I can cheer for them and I can hug them. But mostly I still can be the best at whatever I am doing....even with cancer. And those of you that know her well certainly understand when I say she has always have been a "can do" person...cancer hasn't taken that from her and I would be surprised if it ever could. Her "can" attitude has radiated throughout this family too.

I know this has been a rather long entry but it was certainly worth my time to write it because to know my wife is to know what true toughness and love is all about. I am now going to hang out with my boys, watch some hockey, hug Sunny, and maybe walk the fat dog. Maybe Sunny will want to walk with me if not I am sure she will try. In any case, please focus on how you choose to invest your time, because life isn't a DVD…there is no rewind…no instant replay…and if you always live like next week or next time is a certainty you may find yourself having regrets at missed opportunities. Opportunities to share your most precious commodity – time - with those that you love and care about. I know the light bulb has come on for me, and my biggest regret is that it took cancer to make me realize that. I only wish I had learned from Sunny earlier.

Continue to keep Sunny in your prayers as you are all in ours and we look forward to seeing you at soccer fields, basketball courts, or the baseball fields….oh ya forgot to add hockey rink too….Nolan just added that sport on to our schedule. Got to love having boys.

Mark

April 9, 2009

I found a book that I had in high school among some things I was cleaning out. It was a book of Helen Steiner Rice poetry and it completely brought me into another place. In the book this poem was marked with a photo of me and my dad on my prom day in my prom dress. Crazy how things just pop up. She was my favorite poet when I was a teenager. How appropriate this is to my life now. Little did I know back then what was to come.

> How often we wish for another chance
> To make a fresh beginning.
> A chance to blot out our mistakes
> And change failure into winning.
> It does not take a new day
> To make a brand new start,
> It only takes a deep desire
> To try with all our heart.

To live a little better
And to always be forgiving
And to add a little sunshine
To the world in which we're living.
So never give up in despair
And think that you are through,
For there's always a tomorrow
And the hope of starting new.

April 14, 2009
Holidays!

Sorry for the delay in posts. My computer crashed and it's a real battle here in the Carney household to fight for the laptop. But tonight I won and I can finally get my mind cleared by blogging. So to answer the number of emails that I've been receiving, "I'm doing well….just having computer problems."

I hope everyone cherished their Easter Holiday. I know that I did. Each and every holiday is so much more meaningful since my re-lapse. I know it's a subject that many hate to hear me talk about but I really try to spend each holiday like it may be my last. I try to wrap all the memories my boys will have in one day. To be perfectly honest, I wish I would have done this so many years ago. It makes all the overboard fuss that I did for years seem like such a waste of time. I always thought that it was my job as a mother to make each holiday "Martha Stewart" perfect. The perfect Easter to me then was having the perfect Easter basket with color-coded candy so each boy knew which one was there by seeing their favorite color dominate the basket. Each one filled so full that it was too heavy for them to lift. I would spend weeks buying the perfect chutzskys so that each boy would have a huge smile on their face when the saw that I listen to what they wished for…for my enjoyment. It was complete unnecessary overindulgence. I realized that what really makes my family happy is that we are getting through each day of our cancer journey together. My oldest son, Austen, and I were just small talking on our way to his baseball practice. Not wanting to end any conversion with him I try really hard to bring up subjects that will keep him talking. So I said to him, "Easter is coming up, and are you excited?" He said in his teenage tone, "I guess, but mom you don't need to go all out this year. Really I don't care so much about all the stuff you stuff that basket in the attic with." So I felt a little sad because I thought that he was saying his too big for the basket I saved since his first Easter. I knew this day was coming, but I still was nowhere near prepared. He continued on by saying, "Mom really we are just happy to be low key and have fun with you." At that time of the comment we were already at the field and he had his hand on the door ready to pop out of the car. I did not make a big issue about how proud I was of him or anything. I just opened the trunk so he could get his equipment for the day. He grabbed all his junk and slammed the trunk of my SUV quite hard, letting me know he is a man now. As I started to put the car in gear he came to the window, with his team near by, and said, "Luv ya Mom, thanks! Thanks for everything you do."

I realized that all my boys want for holidays is to spend time together and making happy memories. I realized that the only gift or present they want right now is for their mom to be able to spend the holiday with them. I finally realized, after three battles with cancer, that the only perfect holiday is being together as a family. There is no basket, no present, or no amount of money that could be more valuable than that. I hope that my boys always keep that in mind when they are celebrating holidays years from now. I hope that they remember that memories are not about what is stuffed in your basket but what is stuffed in your heart.

Of course I did do the whole basket thing but it was so not the focus. We tried to teach the boys this year about what sacrifice our Lord did for us. Mark and I used my cancer as a way of putting Jesus' suffering in perceptive. I think they got it. For years we have read them the whole Easter story starting from the last supper to the resurrection. They have also attended church every Easter of their life and have been drilled over and over again about what Easter is all about. But I am not sure they completely understood the amazement of Jesus' journey until this year. It's another good in cancer. Cancer has brought us closer to our Lord. There is nothing more important than that.

Cancer has also taught us that every sacrifice we make is nothing compared to what our Lord has made for us. The pain and suffering Jesus endured in his last days as an actual human body figure is more than this cancer could ever do to me. It truly puts holidays in perspective.

April 23, 2009
Recent Updates

Sorry for the delay in posting. I know by the emails I am getting my friends are worried. I've been a little under the weather. I have had some dizzy spells and exhaustion. As many of you know by now I hate to post when I am not at my best. I don't want those, especially other carcinoid patients to think that I am taking a turn for the worse. This cancer is going to always be a battle for me. Some days are going to great and I am going to feel like cancer is just a distant memory. Then other days I will feel like have been attacked by a ton of bricks. I understand that this is the way things are and are happy when I have more of the good days than bad ones.

    Anyways, I had a doctor appointment on Monday with my main oncologist and he ran some tests. The blood work showed that my white blood count is low but he still suspects something else is going on because I have been having some agonizing headaches. So we are scheduling an MRI to rule out spreading to the brain. I do however have a tumor in the skull (which we knew about since last May) but it is not in the brain as of my last scan in Switzerland. What we are hoping for however it that this is the lasting effect from the treatment in Switzerland and will eventually go away when the magic drug gets out of my system. I feel very confident that this all just precautionary measures my doctor is taking to rule things out and give me peace of mind (sorry for the pun).

    Meanwhile, Dr. Friedland gave me much encouragement on my fight. He told me that 90% of fighting cancer is attitude. He inspired me to continue my optimism and not give in to the frustration of this prolonged disease. He also said that he is very impressed with all my knowledge on this rare cancer and that I am helping so many others who are suffering from carcinoid. He wished all his patients were as upbeat as me. I sat there quietly and stunned because little did he know that I just got finished lecturing his nurse practitioner that was in the room 20 minutes before for not reading my chart before questioning me about my cancer. I also gave him the "Sunny Smack Down," for not having anyone call me back when I got home from Switzerland to call in my prescriptions. After all I called for three days twice a day and got no return call. Finally on the fourth day without my prescription I called again and told the operator that I will not leave a message but hold for person that could help, after a rude comment from her I got what I needed.

Little did Dr. Friedland know that I told his assistant that I am tired of going over and over again all the ins and outs and reeducating all those who are supposed to be treating me for this rare cancer. I told them what I needed was not more drugs or more people interns reading my files but them to advocates now because I am just worn out. Little did he know that I burst into tears just a few minutes before he knocked on the room the size of a closet door while the nurse and intern just stared at me. I was so angry that my conversation with them was me telling them what test I need and what drugs I should be on which I find from doing hours of research. Little did he know that I was all prepared to give him the very same lecture. Maybe he did know and gave me the prescription of hope. Whatever the case, I wiped my tears, stopped feeling sorry for myself and took more action to help me feel better. So if he was playing mind games they worked and that is exactly what I needed. He is a doctor that knows all it takes to fight this enemy and I am glad he is on my side.

However, I did come home and follow up with my referral in Iowa. I am scheduled for my first appointment with Dr. O'Dorisio, on June 24th. By then I will have all the scans that I need to see if the treatment in Switzerland is doing its thing. He can then better direct me as to which way to go depending on the outcome of those scans. His office wanted to see me sooner but I thought that if I had all the information gathered it would save us some money and the number of trips we need to take. Although I love the two oncologists I have here in Pittsburgh, I am looking forward to talking with the specialist. From what I am told this doctor has dedicated his life to carcinoid cancer and endocrine cancers. I feel so blessed that I can actually get in to see him. I must say I would probably beat down his door if I could not get an appointment.

That is all my updates. Once again I wish I could tell you that I finally woke up from this nightmare and live in castle with many servants, angels for children and half dressed men feeding me grapes. But not yet, however you can shake me when you see me. My next post will be more inspirational and less medical.

Chapter 13: Normal Life with Cancer

"The truly fearless think of themselves as normal"

April 24, 2009
Washington D.C. gets a Carney!
Thank you everyone for all the emails after yesterday's post. I am so blessed to have so many people cheering me on and supporting me. I will keep you all posted on the outcome. I have a good feeling that it is nothing though.

After posting yesterday I realized how good I feel after I write everything down. So you are blessed with a very emotional one to read today.

This morning at 7:00 I dropped Austen off at school with a big tour bus waiting for him. He and his sixth grade class are heading to the nation's capital for a few days. This is the longest field trip he has ever been on and the very first I have not chaperoned. I must say my heart is aching. I feel this huge sense of guilt that I am not experiencing this trip with him. I have this lump in my stomach that I am afraid he will feel abandoned. At least that is what I think he is feeling. Maybe it is me who feels abandoned. I want to hold onto all my children and not face the fact that they are growing up.

As I sit here typing this I am hearing rolling thunder coming from outside and Mark yelling the weather updates from the other room as if a hurricane is on its way. I am trying hard to ignore his annoyance but if he continues to tell me bad news I may just throw him outside in it. My mind is wondering to all the things that could happen when you drive in the rain. At least I am focusing on just the ride now, not like the nightmares I had last night about what could happen to my first born once he got to Washington, DC. It's funny how a mom can fight terminal cancer like it's an itsy bitsy spider climbing your wall, but has a complete anxiety attack with a melt down when her child leaves her for a few days. Last year when the first planning meeting came I was absolutely positive that I was going. In fact I told Mark and Austen that if I don't go then Austen does not go. I was adamant that he will not go so far from home without me. I would have bet the house that I would be better by now. Of course, the meeting was only a few days after my news of my cancer relapse.

I must say again God knows what he is doing. Even though I am not with him now, the last few days, we have gotten closer with all the preparation. Austen and I spent hours together laughing and having a great time preparing for his time away from us. He was so excited about going and had no tension about me not chaperoning. I think he felt a sense of pride that I trusted him, with other parents who know him well of course, to behave and be responsible. He also told me that he cannot wait to get away and have fun. As we packed last night we had the most intense conversation about me and my illness. He really opened up and it felt so good to know what he's been holding in. I don't think he has ever been that honest with me about this whole journey our family has been forced to go on. He is my fist born and feels the need to protect his brothers and me. He told me last night that he's not scared just sad that he may not have me around. At times he feels so much pressure to be there for his brothers but wishes that they could be stronger and not worry….like he does. I didn't say much or ask any questions because I didn't want him to stop talking. I just listen while we packed. I pretended that it was not bothering me but deep down my heart was ripping to pieces. The one thing that really bothered me but I was so glad he got it out was his fear of me leaving his dad. He said, "Dad would be crushed, Mom, and I could not handle him. He would be clueless on what to do for us." I told him that Dad could handle it and loves him more the anything. In his cool tone, he quietly said, "Yah

Right!" It hit me just then, that I need to prepare Mark for when the time comes and I need to do it fast.

When it was his time to get on the bus this morning I just waved bye because I did not want to embarrass him by running up to him and squeezing him tight like I really wanted to do. Plus I did not trust myself to let go when I did hug him. He gave me the "I'm so cool nod" and off he went laughing with one of his best friends. I was so proud of him…so strong and happy. He has come such a far way from the days of hanging on my leg the first day preschool. I remember back then feeling the same lump in my stomach when I left him for two hours. Now he was going for days and did not need me to walk him to the bus. As I walked back to the car stopping a few times to talk to a few of the chaperones, that assured me that they would watch out for him, I hear him yelling "Mom." I looked back, and saw him cooly trotting over to me. I'll I could think was, "God don't let him chicken out." But to my surprise, he actually got off the bus to give me a hug and kiss. He squeezed me so tight that it hurt and said, "I forgot to give you this." A big kiss on the check was his gift to me. He didn't care that everyone was watching and his friends were wondering what he was doing. Nor did it bother him that the buses engine started and it was ready to take off. He just did it. He then said, "Be good Mom and Make Good Choices"…my favorite saying to the boys when they walk out our door. It was one of those breathtaking moments that I write about.

Moments like these are when you can see "The Good in Cancer." Cancer has given Austen a responsibility that only having a mom with cancer can give a kid….a kind of maturity that he is his own person and not just the son of Sunny and Mark. Before my reoccurrence I know for a fact Austen would have never wanted to go on this trip without me. I remember him missing his third grade field trip because I was in the hospital and could not go with him. He was always a little more independent than the rest of my boys but still very needy. I realize now that I made him that way by being a "helicopter mom." Now that Mark has become more hands on he has told me time and time again recently that I enable them to be needy. I think I like my boys to need me. He has been forced to change quickly…for the better I must add. He amazes me everyday. I would love to take this cancer away from my family. However, I would not take back his growth over the past 10 months. I know he will have a wonderful time and have peace that Mom is okay.

Don't wait to make your son a great man - make him a great boy. I wish I could say I did that but I think it was the cancer.

※※

May 1, 2009
MRI

Yesterday was the big day for my MRI of the brain. As stated in a few postings back my oncologist thought that I needed to have one STAT (that word makes me feel so important) on April 21st because of some issues I have been having. So I guess to his nurses STAT meant a week and a half later. I did not fight the issue, like I normally would, when she called me with the time and date of the scheduled appointment. I was not looking forward to having this scan. A brain scan is my least favorite of all the scans I continue to receive. WOW, I am actually rating scans now, like I use to rate movies, restaurants and artist. Note to self…get a life beyond cancer. Besides, deep down I feel that the cancer has not spread to the brain. I personally think my issues are from the treatments in Switzerland. There is not a lot of information on the side effects of this treatment so it's hard to tell. However, if it has spread then I am not in a rush to find out. If you remember me posting before I hate bad news so I really try to avoid it as long as possible.

I decided to do this one on my own. I had many volunteers wanting to take me but sometimes it's nice to test my strength and see what I can do by myself. In addition, I hate having to put others out. Not to mention the sight at Hillman Cancer Center, when you are not use to seeing a huge room full of 100+ very ill cancer patients with their loving ones, can be quite dispiriting. Also, I don't like to stress about having those who go with me feeling sorry for me or any of my fellow cancer victims. I think about the first time, at age 24, when I went to get my very first scan. I thought I had my act together and could handle anything back then. I probably spent two hours the night before picking out my designer outfit. I took my lunch break from my first good paying job out of college and thought I could just run in, get the scan and be back to the office to make the afternoon sales meeting. Well, my ignorance got the best of me. The visions of that waiting room haunted me for months. I think it was then that I started to realize that there is more to life than having a huge career and making tons of money. Although, I am sure the news about the cancer on my ovary a few days later hit it home. I even had Mark stay at work yesterday. I must admit though it was sad being the only one in the whole waiting room with nobody sitting next to me. But when it was all over, I felt exhilerated that I did this on my own. It's like climbing another cancer mountain. I refuse to let this disease take my independence from me. However, now that I know I can do it there is no need to try it again.

I feel very guilty sometimes sitting there with IV's in my arm and looking so well. I know what the others around me are feeling…I've been there and sometimes feel that bad. But for some reason from God I don't look as sick. When the nurse called my name to take me back to insert the IV I stood up in a crowd full of patients and she asked me if the patient is in the restroom. I told her I was the patient and she took a double take. Once we got back to the small medically equipped room she apologized and told me that after reading my records she was expected someone in a wheel chair or at least looking much more ailing. I don't know why I am blessed. I don't know why others lose their hair and some don't. I just know that I have been truly lucky at least on the vanity sense. At that moment I just thanked God for the blessing and then thanked Clinique for the great makeup. Going over my medical history always takes time but for me it's like a broken record. I repeat the same stories over and over again each time I go for a scan, an appointment or a treatment. The nurse asks about each one of my numerous procedures and surgeries over the past so many years as if it could not be true. It's the same each time I go, they give me this implausible tone of voice and say, "you've had knee surgery, shoulder surgery, ovary removed, 2 other tumor surgeries of the other ovary, 3 children, 2 miscarriages, 2 lung surgeries, 1 lung removed, 9 surgical biopsies of 4 different organs, 3 chemo-immobilization's, many chemo and radiation treatments, treatments in Europe" and on and on they go. As if anyone can make this crap up. It is then ended with, "you are 30 what?." I always like to spice things up with "no that's not me, I'm just here for an ingrown toenail?." I then finally get a smile and the sympathetic "I feel sorry for you look" disappears.

After being poked 9 times and looking like my mother's pin cushion she's proudly had for 30+ years, I was told that I am going to need to get a port soon. My good veins are now exhausted and the sooner I get that done the easier it will be. I had to wonder though easier for whom? I finally pointed out my secret good vain and success it was. The MRI lasted about 30 minutes and the tech was amazing. I warned her that I may start to feel trapped and if I yell please get me out STAT (I felt important again). There was no need for that this time but the tech definitely checked on me many times. Last May when I had my first brain scan I think I had to be taken out 3 or 4 times before I could relax. Now it's all getting easier or maybe I am getting stronger. I should have my results back by today but who knows when I will actually get a call. It seems that doctors think that terminal cancer patients have all the time in the world to wait. I guess they don't realize that we are busy living. However, I am pretty sure the scan will show nothing.

Later that Day:
I am sure this is one of those posts that I will not hit the publish button on. I need it to be written and I need to get it off my chest. I have brought up the fact that cancer can tear a family apart if you let it. Every time I think I have a hold on this family and the cancer journey I am smacked in the face again with the reminder that it is not just me who is coping with the morality of this disease. The truth to be told of why I went to the MRI test alone is because Mark was not able to come with me. When I say unable I mean truly unable to get out of bed. He decided last night that on his way to the store for a gallon of milk and some other staples he would take a detour to his local hang out. That detour turned into a 3:30 am stumble through the front door. I received no phone call to let me know that he will not be home later nor did he answer his phone when I tried to call him. I am not shocked about this behavior, truly disappointed. This is just an example of how cancer and the stress of it can absolutely devastate or kill the loved one watching the afflicted suffer. The past two weeks of headaches and cognitive issues have been rough on me but for Mark they are a look into his future with or without me. The fear of the unknown and the possible chance that it could have spread to the brain has beaten him down. So instead of facing the problem head on and finding a solution to fix it, he runs away and tries to erase it. Unfortunately he seems to pick the worst possible times to do that.

 I am by no means making any excuse for his behavior and I am certainly not going to feel guilty for his weakness. However, I do understand the anxiety and hopelessness he must feel. I can't pretend to know what he is thinking because my brain does not work like his. I wonder why the sayings, "Act like a man" or "fight like a man" are used for encouragement. Honestly, I believe they should be "Act like a woman" or "Fight like a woman." I am not telling you that Mark is not coming around. He has changed and he is there for me often. But when things get really tough and I need him the most he becomes a turtle. He sticks his head in his shell and slowly sneaks away. Just once I would like to tag him in and fight this battle for me. I need a break at times. I know I make it seem so easy to handle this journey and my life but honestly it sometimes feels impossible. It is not the disease or what comes with it that makes me feel defeat, it the lack of fight in him at times.

When he came in last night I was awake, yet I pretended to be asleep. I could not go round and round with him this time like I have done so many times before. I don't need the usual assortment of excuses. I just need to get on and for today it was get on all alone.

He left a note on the table for me to wake him for my appointment after I get the kids off to school. I must say that made me even feel sorry for him because he truly has no clue. I quietly got the boys on the bus and then snuck out of the house because I just could not deal with the conflict and really needed peace. When I was finished with the MRI I turned on my phone to see several text message and voice mails from your truly. Guilt has set in with him or is it shame. Whatever the case may be, I was not ready to deal with it so I am waiting to go home until the kids where already home from school. I knew that there would be no talking about last night in front of them.

This evening Mark felt defeated. He has worked so hard the past several months to rebuild our marriage and to prove to me he is strong. One evening destroyed it. We talked about it and what was going through his mind. I did not let him know that I felt pity for him but I do. I am not angry with Mark. I know that deep down inside he is dealing with my cancer the best he knows how to. I am not blaming him for his fall but I cannot let him think I am ok with his weakness and lack of respect. I do wonder what our life would be like if this devil of cancer never came haunting us.

※※

May 3, 2009
Keep Running R4R

Today is the Pittsburgh Marathon. I am so excited I could not sleep. R4R, my running angels, are running for Carcinoid Cancer. I am so proud of the 20+ people that are running today that I feel like I am running myself. Thank you R4R for all your support and passion about Carcinoid Cancer. Awareness is the first start for a cure for Carcinoid Cancer and all of you running with those T-shirts on are doing that. My family and I will be cheering for you along on the sidelines. Look for our HUGE signs. I will feel your pain when you come by us. Stay strong and proud. I wish I could run along with you but know that I am finally able to support you.

WE LOVE YOU,
Sunny, Mark, the boys and ALL CARCINOID CANCER PATIENTS NOW AND TO COME

Look for our Signs:

RUNNING
4a CARCINOID CANCER
REASON

KEEP RUNNING
R4R
FOR
CARCINOID CANCER

THANK YOU
R4R

May 8, 2009
Optmism!

"The optimist sees the rose and not its thorns; the pessimist stares at the thorns, oblivious of the rose."

Later Today:
My Wish for You
"Comfort on difficult days, smiles when sadness intrudes, rainbows to follow the clouds, laughter to kiss your lips, sunsets to warm your heart, hugs when spirits sag, beauty for your eyes to see, friendships to brighten your being, faith so that you can believe, confidence for when you doubt, courage to know yourself, patience to accept the truth, Love to complete your life."

My wishes have come true so I wish it all for you.

Chapter 14:
Family is Why I Fight Like I Fight

"When you look at your life, the greatest happinesses are family happinesses." ~Joyce Brothers

May 10, 2009
Road Trip
The advantage of having cancer is that your impulsive action does not mean you are crazy just dying. The other day Mark approached me and asked, "What can I do to make you happy?" I have never been a girl that likes to be showered with diamonds or material things. I am not saying I don't like to that stuff, because I love it, I like to get it on my own. What I do like is spontaneity. So I told him I wanted to take a family road trip. Eventually I want to end up at my safe haven. My mother's home in Vero Beach, FL, but I want to make crazy stops on the way.

So we took the kids out of school for a week and off we are going. I will post later.

May 13, 2009
The Sunshine State

We made it to the Sunshine state and the road trip was fun and relaxing. Usually we are rushed and Mark gives us a 3 minute bathroom stop every few hours. This time he promised me we would take our time, enjoy ourselves and appreciate the sites that we flew by so many times before. We stopped at every cheesy tourist trap we could find. We pulled over to photograph every amazing site that I use to wish I could photograph before. Mark even pulled over on the side of route 95 so that I can pick the most stunning poppies I had ever seen. We drive by them every May on our way to Florida and I always admire them but this time they seemed so much brighter and denser. I don't know if seeing them through cancer glasses was the reason or if they were actually pretty this time but all I know is that I had to have some. So I softly hint that I would love to have a few of those beautiful orange and yellow flowers and off the road he went. I felt like just laying in the middle of the huge array of them much like Dorothy when she was off to the Land of Oz and she fell asleep in the poppies. That has always been my favorite seen of the whole movie.

I've been waking up the past few mornings around 5:30 A.M. to go out on the beach and photograph the sunrise. It is such a freeing feeling to see the start of a new day in the eyes of God's beauty. Crazy I know, but I feel great after watching that miracle. It just reminds me that anything is possible in Him. Last night at dinner I tried to convince my mom, Mark and the boys what they have been missing while they lay in bed sleeping. I beg them to come with me this morning. They humored me by listeingn but I think they feel like I am going insane. Of course I got the lecture from Mark that I need my sleep and I cannot get better if I don't get my rest. I don't think he get's that I don't have a flu bug, sop I had to say once we were alone and he started the nagging again, "I have an incurable cancer buddy…I can sleep when I am dead." After that comment he gave me that pissed off look that he gets when he knows he cannot win an argument with me. I am not sure if he is truly worried or feels a little bit of guilt that he is missing this wonderful experience with me. Whatever the case, it's his loss and he does not know what he is missing. Yesterday I even spotted some dolphins. I got them on camera and the boys loved looking at the photos. This morning I did actually recruit Nolan to come along (of course I bribed him with breakfast after…he'll do anything for food). I should have tried that with Mark. They are two of a kind.

I know many are thinking what the hell am I doing taking the boys out of school with no notice, packing the car and just going to FL when her blood counts are low and the doctor recommends staying in bed. I also know I don't owe anyone an explanation but I feel I need to give one anyways so that you can understand what goes through the mind of a cancer patient. Have you ever just felt the need to do something and you know if you don't do it now you may never get the chance to do it? It may be something as small as giving into the craving of a food you should not have or as crazy as buying a new home. That is what I was feeling. I just need to go to a place with my family that we have always had happy memories….a place that leaves the cancer behind. Where the boys learned to walk, swim and surf. Where it is just us and no one else and no one knows that I have cancer. There is no pity for me or nobody knows I am sick. Where the sun comes up everyday and warms our faces. After all the treatments, test, scares of spreading and pressure I just needed to be alone with my family. Was it the most responsible thing to do? Absolutely, not. But I have been responsible all my life - not just for me but also for Mark and the boys. I needed to just give into my craving of the one place that has always been my refuge. That is Vero Beach FL.

The kids call this place Zero Beach. They say because there is nothing to do past 7pm. Every places closes expect the beach. I think they have read three full books each in the two days we have been here. They spent some time with my brother and his family. They surfed, boogie board and skim board. They have swam until wee hours. Most importantly they have spent time with just me. Mark has spent his time in the ocean with the boys and I can tell his anxiety has lessened. I know when I get back my full time job as a carcinoid cancer patient and photographer is coming again. But for now I am just a mom living in paradise.

When my father bought his dream home here he said it was for the whole family. At that time I was getting married and working on my career - the last thing I could think about was going to FL. Since I have had the boys we try to come down at least twice a year, when they were small it was sometimes more. It wonders me how much he was preparing us for hard times. He knew that we would all need a place to escape from our worries now and then. Unfortunately he died a few years later, here in Vero, and never got to see how much my boys love this place. I think about him every day I am here because I know that as a 65 year old man he was being a father when he decided to buy this place. He knew that all his children will need a place to run to when life got tough: to regroup and go back fighting. I think that each and everyone of us has done that a few times in the past 15 years. In fact, right after my relapse the first thing my siblings said to me was, "you need to go away to FL...figure things out and then make decisions." I did not do that because I just want to get on with treatment and get better fast. But now a year later reality set in and I needed to regroup. I know now that getting better fast is not going to happen.

I spoke with a new doctor yesterday and unfortunately the news was not as promising as I hoped. I wanted him to tell me that he had the magic pill and I would be cured as soon as I take it. I guess that's the optimist in me. He was my one hope I've been holding on to. Well, it was not the case and I must say I was glad I was in this beautiful place when I got the news. I was glad I had my boys to hug and a beach to hit. Of course, that speeds up my plans a little but it does not give up my fight.

It is storming now - one of those FL storms that if back home the dish and lights would be out. Oh how I would love to just run on the beach in the rain right now. I know Mark is pacing back at the house wondering where I am, so I better complete this later. Oops there my cell ringing now...he is on the hunt for me.

May 17, 2009
Back to Reality

Well the Carney Clan is home and ready to get back to the real life. After a 20 hour car ride to FL and a 17 hour car ride home (don't ask about the three hour difference) we have survived each others love. Many friends think that Mark and I are absolutely nuts for driving to FL with three kids let alone doing it in one day. I must say the first time we did it, when the boys were small, Mark thought we were crazy. The trips before our first driving experiences we would fly and sometimes I would fly with the three boys myself. After hours of stress getting to the airport, two and a half hours of screaming babies on the plane, standing in the rental car line and hoping we get the only mini-van left, and driving from the closest airport to Vero Beach it was more than a 17 hour day...not to mention the expense. So a few years back I talked Mark into doing the driving thing and he was pleasantly surprised how relaxing it actually can be.

Driving was the only way I knew before I met Mark. As a little girl my father loved to take us on vacations. We did not have much money and there were many kids but it never stopped him from giving us the experiences that he thought we deserved. We would all pack up - swimsuit, sandals, two t-shirts and two pairs of shorts (that was all we were allowed to bring) - pile in the car and off to FL we would go. There was no stopping at restaurants on the way, Mom would pack Cool-Aide, fruit and peanut butter sandwiches, we only ate at rest areas out of the trunk of the car. We would stay at a great aunts home and all slept on the floor. We never brought home store bought souvenirs... seashells from the beach and a baby food jar full of sand was our big gift. One night out of the week or two we would be there our Aunt would treat us to a dinner at a "real restaurant" and GOD help us if we did not eat every bit on our plate and use the manners we were so diligently taught by our mother. We never argued...a least not out loud. We would sometimes give each other some sign language or wait until we got alone and give a pinch or tug to the sibling that deserved it, but never let our parents see it. We would spend morning to night at the beach sharing the couple of blow up rafts and sand buckets my father would splurge for once we got there if we were quiet the whole 2 to 3 day ride down. If we did stay in a hotel we never told them how many kids were really in the room. We were never aloud to walk the halls all together because they may guess there was more than a couple of us and out we would go. That was our vacation and it was amazing.

As a college graduate and a middle income woman I never wanted that type of vacation for my kids. Actually I never knew that I really did want that type of vacation for my kids. My father loved the finer things in life and with his career he had it all offered to him but when it came to his children all he wanted was for us to enjoy being together. He had many opportunities to travel with his job but it would be just him and my mother. Those trips were not ones where he could focus on his family so we would stay home with Grandma. As we got older and my father's career progressed our vacations got a little quainter but always a car ride was included. I think that was my parents' time to trap us all together and force us to get along. We still talk about the trips with no air conditioning in the car and the pleather seats that our legs would melt to.

Although the boys are not forced to eat out of the trunk of the car, sleep on the floor or even sit next to each other in the three rows SUV we have, the concept of being together is the same. We enjoy each others company and yes we are forced to even communicate. The boys are now enjoying some of our CDs like U2, Journey, Alman Brothers, Grateful Dead etc., and even singing along. Something they would not dare to do in our neighborhood for fear that someone may recognize them having fun in the car with their parents. The only stress we have is Mark trying to bet my other family members driving time. The bathroom breaks are no more than five minutes and the food is all drive thru (only if there is no line). I of course force him to stop at only respectable places to use the facilities because I am about done with squatting in the woods.

I know that the actual vacation will be great memories for the boys. The beach, the surfing, the boogie boarding, the board game competitions and even the new nickname I earned this trip (I am now know as the Diva of the family because of my outburst at the beach when the boys would not settle down enough to do a full fledged photo shot for me…I really wanted that perfect family portrait) will all be in their mind forever. But the ride to and from will be lasting. Every time I drive to FL since my dad passed I feel this familiarity and comfort. That is what I want for my boys. Of course I have no plans on going anywhere soon but if God's plan is to have this cancer take me, I want my boys to have these memories.

I am so glad that Mark approached me after our huge blow out and asked me what would make me happy. I am also glad that I finally did something on a whim and took off to a place that makes everything seem okay. As my father use to say often, "Everything is going to be awe right." I am relaxed now and ready to start the fight again. I am off to the doctors now. Until next post may you feel blessed.

May 20, 2009
The Winning Sprit: Austen

A friend of mine who created this blog for me often gives me stats on the number of people who read my blog, how they find my blog and where they are located. First I must say I was in complete shock at the number of people who support me by keeping updated on my fight. Not only do I have my fellow friends here in Pittsburgh but I have readers from all over the world. I receive several emails from other carcinoid cancer patients asking me about my children and how they are dealing with my cancer or how Mark and I handle this battle with the boys. I wish I could give them some simple formula to help them understand how we handle things with our boys but to be honest we are just navigating our way through. I have read several books and even spoken with a few experts on children crisis management yet still we never know if what we do for them to help them get through this is correct. What I do know is that I pray every day that God gives us the wisdom to deal with any situation that comes our way.

 Each one of our boys is completely different and has extremely different personalities; because of that we have learned that what we do for one may not work for the other. I felt in my heart the need to share this entry and a few to come, with others. I have mentioned many times in my blog I write many entries that never get posted. Some are just so personal and I don't think they will benefit anyone by reading them. I keep them on the website in case I want to publish them later, but mostly for Mark and the boys to read if ever the day comes. I want them to know my deepest thoughts and what I was really going through at certain times of the journey. I want them to know that I was NOT always strong or as Mark calls me sometimes, "The Tin Woman" and that I do have a heart once in awhile. I want them to realize that I cried at times and was frighten at times. I think that one day when the boys are older and can understand things more they may want to look back and read some things that I wrote just for them. I have written entries with some advice that I know Mark just could not give, like table manners, money saving tips, your first impression on someone is the most important, how to treat the girl you love, follow your dream, etc. I even have a few entries that have answers to questions that they may want to ask me when they are older and I am not around. These entries are written because they are subjects that I obsess over and cannot let them go until I write them down. Things that I want the boys to know but they are just not ready to hear them right now.

Well this is one of those entries. After researching and researching about how to help our children cope with a mother with stage 4 cancer and never coming up with a definite answer, I thought that the next few days of entries will help the mothers who are suffering from cancer too and read my blogs. Talking about some of what my boys are going through (of course the real personal is left out) may help others know that there is no answer to the question, "how to help my child cope with my cancer" unless you have gone through cancer yourself and have children. I have spent hours and hours on the web, at the library and at book stores trying to find one magic answer. I realized that not one of the books or websites I have found was written by an actual person who has cancer and has children dealing with it. All I can say is that Mark and I are just winging it and praying everyday that we are doing the right things. Each one of our boys are completely opposite of the other so it's been a real struggle but I think we are doing an okay job. So I thought that I would dedicate a few entries to how we have dealt with each one of our boys and hope this will help the other mothers who are in the same cancer fight as me. I am not sure if what we are doing is the right "text book" therapist way, but it works for us. Sometimes we have to regroup and figure out a different way to handle them or the situations that come up, but all and all it seems to be good. So as you can see, the next few entries are very personal because it is getting deep into each one of my boys. However, if I could save one mother who is fighting for life like me from hours and hours of useless research then it is worth it.

Of course I have to start with Austen. Everyone who has had children before me warned me about when your loving, affectionate, and caring boy turns 12. Of course the stubborn and somewhat boasting parent I never thought I would see the day my child would change to a person I have no idea who he is. After all, there was nobody more important than me to this little boy of mine. Once in a while the old Austen shines through, like when he gives me a strong hug, tells me I look nice, cheers for his brothers at their sporting events or high fives them when they win a game, but most of the time he is an alien that just got dropped off at our home on September 19, 2008. At that time my sweet red head, curly hair, freckle face boy was taken away. He was exchanged for the unidentified child I have living in the sports decorated bedroom next to mine. He still eats the same enormous amount of food. He still has that cute freckle face and adorable smile. He still likes to play anything that includes a ball, puck or racket. He still watches ESPN all day and reads Sports Illustrated like it is his Bible. But he grunts instead of talking, especially when I ask him a question. This alien forgets that he is part of a family and that the world does not revolve around him. He thinks his brothers are his nemeses. And his parents are absolute idiots and know nothing about living a life of a 12 year old. With all the kidding put aside, Austen is going through so much. I have trouble figuring out if his change in personality is because he is almost a teenager or because he is dealing with my cancer. Whatever the case may be, it's been a roller coaster of fun. I must tell you though he is really a great kid. When I compare notes with other parents of a 12 year old Austen is completely normal.

From what everyone has told me Austen is most like me. Sometimes I feel a little proud of that, but other times I want to put my head under a pillow with just embarrassment that I too have those intense personality traits. On the good side, he was been extremely responsible through this whole journey. He gets amazing grades and works very hard for it. Although at times he gets annoyed at his little brothers, he truly does look out for them always. Of course he reminds me of that every day… he deep down feels the need to be their second father. He sometimes even goes as far as inspecting their clothing before they leave the house for school. He claims that's because he wants them to look cool, but we all truly know it's because he has to walk to the bus with them and does not want to be embarrassed. Austen is the stereo-typical type

A personality oldest child. Whatever Austen does he does it with such conviction and 100% effort. He has a strong self confidence and really believes he can do anything he puts his mind too. Some might say he is even a little cocky at times but once you get to know him you see that it is just an honest to goodness self competition he brings out.

He's got a comedic side to him that used to be cute when he was little but now can be quite annoying. He is very charming and cunning. He uses those traits to talk you into anything; works for me at times, rarely works on Mark. He has a twinkle in his baby blue eyes when he is trying to get away with something that gets me often. He is just a plain old charmer. Of course I know that he does this but he still gets away with it. He is ambitious and goal oriented. Whatever he knows he is not great at, he works twice as hard at to accomplish. He never quits at anything until he does it well. He is his own self motivator. He cannot let his brothers ever get ahead and deep down thinks he can do whatever they can do better. He has this amazing drive and fight that I think he was just born with. My family calls it the "Jennings's trait" (my maiden name) but I am not sure where he gets it from. I love to watch him with his peers. He is a leader but also a motivator. On the baseball field he is the first to run to home plate when teammates hit a home run. On the basketball court he gives the pat on the back to his team mate at the foul line and is always cheering others on. When he becomes passionate about something he obsesses over it until he becomes good at it, which is where he got his nickname ACE from. That is why I think of all the three boys he understands my need to fight through this cancer with all I have. We talk about it all the time. He never wants to hear the negative aspects or any of the test results. He is just interested in what I am doing to feel better. He does not want to know what the doctor says or even how I am feeling. He explains to me that he just can't handle all that "crap"...so he will only listen to the positive things. The other day I was in the kitchen telling Mark my new test result and he walked in to raid the fridge. When he heard what I was talking about he actually covered his ears with his hands and started to hum loudly.

It takes a unique type of person to be like Austen. He has the ability to reach deep down in himself and face any challenge. At times he may seem emotionless or even cold. He can shut someone out faster than anyone I know. If you wrong him or get him angry that is it, he is completely done with you. I have tried to talk to him about forgiveness and that people change but he just won't give in. I have learned through this reaction that is his way of coping and dealing with a hard situation or disappointment. He's got that, "I'm just going to fix it and not think about it" attitude. The evening we sat our boys down to tell them that my cancer was back Austen actually passed out. He was in such complete shock, the memories of the last fight came back and down he went. When he came through, he just wanted to know how to take the cancer away. He did not want hear about how I would be feeling or how bad it was…just how to get it out of me. When we told them the plans we knew at that time, Austen excused himself, went to his room and locked his door. That was it, no more talking to him about it unless it was how to fix it or it was gone. He even told me that he never wants to see me without hair so get a wig fast.

He has come a long way in the months that we have been dealing with it, but he is still very cold and strong. Austen and I have always had a very close and almost friend like relationship. He was my first after being told I could never have children. He has always been my little buddy and helper. Now he is my partner in the fight. He gets me and understands why I do the things I do and I get him the same way. We could talk for hours about anything. He was my protector even at the age of 3 by telling any stranger that talked to me, mostly men, "that he has a big daddy and don't talk to my mommy." He would even cover me up with towels at the beach or swimming pool because he did not want anyone to see me with just a bathing suit on. Last summer he even made me give up the bikini, I hope it was because he was being protective and not embarrassed to be with me. He argued that, "Mom you have Dad and you don't need to wear any bathing suit that other men will look at you in." I respected his feelings on that and tankinis are the closest I get to a two piece now.

Cancer has changed that relationship a little. He has shut done a lot and does not feel the need to talk about things anymore. He says he wants me to focus on getting better and not on his stuff. He is very private and very independent. When I am sick or under the weather he cannot bear to face it. He completely avoids the whole situation by throwing himself into another activity. This winter it was school and basketball. Every time I was not my well self, like clock work Austen would run outside and start shooting hoops. It did not matter if it there was three feet of snow on the ground and the temp was below zero. Austen was fighting with his own demons in the only way he knows how. I must say he did have a good season this year. Now it's baseball and science class. He got a low A in science this last report period so the competitive child is determine to bring that grade up to a high A. Baseball season has started too and I don't think a day has gone by since he found out who his new coach was that he has not been outside with himself practicing. Sometimes he even bribes his brothers with time in his room if they catch with him. It's his way of coping and I am completely understanding of that. Some may say it would hurt their feelings and the text books say this is not a good coping behavior… a teenager should not suppress those feelings and not talk about them, but I am completely comfortable with it.

This is how we deal with Austen. Mark and I only talk to him about my cancer when he wants to bring it up. We have learned that the best time for that is when he is doing some kind of sports activity by himself. For example, if he is outside shooting hoops I may just shoot around with him and then he opens up. However, it is not wise to push any issue or talk to him in detail about the cancer itself especially what the prognosis may be. It's smart to just reassure him that I am doing everything I can to fight this cancer and that it is all I can promise him. We are completely honest with him and don't shelter him from anything. We tell him everything he wants to know. When he asks us the inevitable question "is mommy going to die soon" we answer honestly. I always tell him that I will do everything in my power to stay here but if it is God's will, you will be fine. I will not give him the fantasy that I will live forever. In my opinion that is false hope. The hope I do try to plant in his mind is that I will never give up. I know that he understands that because that is the way he is. Never the less, if you show I child like Austen that you are giving it your all then he is completely satisfied that the cancer is under control. Once you give him a hint of self doubt that I will make it then he falls apart. He feeds off of my efforts and my will to live.

I am so proud of him. His way of handling this journey is his way and it works for him. We have learned that if we show him how much we love him then he will be fine.

❀❀

May 23, 2009
Quiet Soul: My Middle Child, Logan

As promised I am continuing my posts about my children and how Mark and I help them through this cancer journey. To repeat myself again it is so hard for me to write about my children and what they are going through. But I am hoping it helps other moms who are suffering from cancer too.

My middle son, Logan, is probably the hardest of the three to write about. I think it is because Mark being the oldest and me being the youngest of our families we have trouble relating to what he is going through being the middle of three boys. I must say he is absolutely amazing, yet very complex. He is incredibly intelligent and analytical. However, that makes his mind wonder and assume too much. He is a thinker to a fault at times. I am at awe at some of the questions he asks and of course I cannot always answer. Ever since he could talk he has come up with the most complicated and deep conversations. Logan is completely different from Austen. He hates competing with his brothers, especially Austen. We think that is why he plays the only sport, soccer, which his brothers don't play. This year he decided to not play baseball or basketball and focus just on soccer. A few seasons ago Austen decided not to play soccer anymore so I believe that gave Logan the freedom to call it "his sport." He likes to be different and not conform to what society says he should be like. He does not care what anyone thinks about him. If he likes something then no one will change that. He loves buildings, bridges, dams and anything built by man. That is why he inspires to be an architect. He also loves sports and to figure out the stats that go with each player. He reads the sports section and has very intense conversations with Mark about each player.

Logan is extremely compassionate for others. He wears his heart on his sleeve and will go the extra mile to help anyone. Yet he does is quietly and behind the scenes. He has had this quality as far back as a toddler. I always tell him he would be an amazing doctor because he is so kind when others in need. He is the first to check on me when I am having a "sick day" and will get whatever I need. He is a caregiver in so many ways. However, it is a quality that some don't see because Logan is very opinionated. He is always fighting for what is fair and right even when it does not involve him; which sometimes can get him in trouble. He likes to stick up for the underdog and actually befriends anyone who is in need. I can remember one summer when he was about seven. A woman at our community pool with her three very small children came up to Logan, handed him a huge wrapped gift and said thank you. I was in shock and asked her what that was for. She told me that the day before some older children were picking on her son, who we did not know, and taking his pool toys. Logan got so angry at the older kids that he went right up to them, grabbed the toys from them and told them off. He then gave all the toys back to the little boy, who was crying, and walked away. I was not surprised at all. Logan has always been a fighter, no matter what size his opponent is, if he is passionate about what he is fighting for. I sometimes tell him to stay out of things and walk away, especially after a visit to his principal's office. But he cannot let things go if he feels it is not right. I see him with protest sign in Washington DC someday. He is also brutally honest. He will tell you exactly how he feels and never sugar coats his opinion. We are trying to teach him to filter his words but he doesn't understand how that is not lying. He is the one I go to when I need to make sure I look ok before walking out the door.

These qualities make Logan the sensitive child he is today. That is why my cancer has been especially hard on him. He could not hold things in like Austen can. He has to let it all out. The problem is he does not want me to know that he is scared or sad so it frustrates him. He is very emotional but tries so hard not to be because he does not want to bother me. At night is when he does most of his thinking, which causes him to have trouble falling asleep. His mind just wonders and wonders about all kind of things. Night owl is an understatement, never sleeps is more accurate. We joke with him and call him Eeyore because he is always asking "what if?" questions. That is why I let him write a post on this blog called "Wealth over Health" on March 1st. It gave him a chance to clear his mind. I know that it works for me I thought it would help him. Logan is the child that was attached to me at the hip as an infant. I would leave the room that he was in and off he went to go find me. I sometimes wish he would get closer to Mark. I think that would make this time a lot easier on him.

He claims he hates having an older brother but deep down I think he really looks up to Austen. A few days after I was diagnosed I walked by his room and heard Austen talking to him. It was one of those breathtaking moments. Austen was telling him not to worry about Mom, stay tough, and don't let her see you upset because stress is not good for her. I heard them both sniffling and their voices were cracking. Austen then told Logan if you want to get upset come see him and he will help him get through it. He then told Logan that he will take care of him and Nolan if Mom can't. They then must have heard me outside the door and starting arguing over a video game. But for about 2 minutes they were brothers.

Mark and I are trying really hard to show Logan the good in Mom's cancer. We teach him to be thankful for everyday and not take life for granted. When I hear him say something negative I tell him, "today is to be a "Tigger day not an Eeyore day." He is way too old for that analogy and rolls his eyes at me when I say it. However, he began noticing when he is being not so positive and will chime in with, "Sorry mom that's an Eeyore statement not a Tigger statement." I give him the opportunity now to tell me what he is thinking and I reinforce to him no matter how sick I am he can always come to me to talk to. He does not have to worry about going to Austen. I tell him that is a mom's job and by him holding things in I cannot do my job. I gave him a few notebooks and told him to write all his thoughts. It is only for his eyes unless he wants me or dad to read it. He loves doing that because he loves to write. It's been a great release for him; however he has not shared any with me yet. Mark and I try to spend a little more one on one with him, even if it's just playing a video game with him for an hour or so. I have gotten really good at FIFA '09 and he now won't play that with me anymore. He loves to read like me so I thought he and I would do a book club thing together. We would each read the same book at the same time and then once a week talk about it. He is a drummer and takes drum lessons with a great teacher. So I let him teach me what he learned every week. That way he feels some control over me.

He is still a work in progress. Every now and then Mark and I think of something more to help him get through this time. We are no experts on handling a middle child dealing with his mother having stage 4 cancer but we are learning as we go. We take one day at time and try to handle each situation that arises. I have seen a marvelous change in Logan in the past few months. He is happy and is expressing himself in a more positive way. He has not perfected the mind of matter way yet but it is coming. I see great things for Logan in his future and could not ask for a better middle child.

> *"Be careful to leave your sons well instructed rather than rich, for the hopes of the instructed are better than the wealth of the ignorant."* ~Epictetus

I know we have a lot to learn but I think we are doing okay with Logan. I hope I can instruct him to live a happy life long after I am gone.

May 24, 2009
My Baby, Nolan

I am finally alone and ready to post my entry about my sweet baby. Before writing my post about Nolan I had to make sure I stoked up on the tissues because I know that the tears will start flowing. He is just as amazing as his brothers, but like them he is totally different too. I have started this post many times but when I would get deep into it I just had to stop, it was just too emotional for me. I am not sure if it's because Nolan is my baby and I know that because of this cancer I will never have anymore children. Or it may be because Nolan is the one child that feels the most and expresses his feelings so tenderly. It maybe that he is the youngest of the three and would be more affected when the time will come. Or it could be because Nolan is my inspiration when I start to go to the dark side. Whatever the case, he is a true blessing to our family.

What can I say about my sweet child? Nolan was our happy surprise. Austen was a little over a year and Logan was about 4 months old when I found out I was pregnant with Nolan. My father had just passed away, Mark was traveling with job and working long hours, he just bought his dream car (red convertible, not sure of the make but back then I did not know much, but what I did know that it had no room for three car seats) that he worked so hard for. I was going on about two hours a sleep a night. I was in complete shock when the little stick test said positive. After all I was told I was not going to be able to have children and here I am in a little over a year with two babies and one on the way. I actually waited a few months before I told anyone because I was embarrassed. I was petrified that God was trusting me with three little ones all under the age of three. Then Nolan was born and he was another boy. I had a horrified feeling about leaving the hospital and entering a life of diapers and bottles times three. I was scared to death to go home to three boys under 25 months. And as expected, I walked into a house and all three started to cry at once and Nolan did not stop until he was about one. I then blinked and a year went by and I cannot recall any of it.

I am so ashamed of my thoughts back then. I did not trust that God had a plan for me when he gave us Nolan at the time he did. Nolan is our family peacemaker. He evens out the strong personalities we all have trapped between our bricks and mortar. He is the first one up every morning (well after me because we all know I am up before the sun) and never comes out of his room without a smile on his face. He lives each day to the fullest and always sees the bright side of life. He hates conflict and will do what ever it takes to end an argument. I think at times he has more sense than even Mark and I because when we get in our little debates with each other Nolan reminds us how silly we are being.

He is such a kind soul and always puts others needs in front of his own. When I am under the weather Nolan is the first one to slide a hand made card or message under my bedroom door to cheer me up. He hates to see me in discomfort and will sit in bed with me for hours until I start to feel better. He loves to write me letters and reminds me not to give up. When asked by others how he is doing with mom being sick, he always shoots back a confident "she will get better soon," and he really believes that. He has amazing faith in God. My trips to Switzerland were especially hard for him and he really missed both Mark and me. After the first trip I think it occured him that this was not a vacation for mommy and he realized that it was very serious. With that in mind, he spent weeks preparing a surprise for me the second time I left for Basel. Each day he had something for Mark to give me and it had to be given in a special way. For example on St. Patrick's Day I was in the hospital yet I received a beautiful card and a hand written poem about Ireland. My last day at the hotel I was given a CD he recorded with some songs he played for me on his guitar. I had a handmade gift everyday from him and I was to email him an answer to a question that he would ask me in a card or letter that went with the gift. I think that's how he guaranteed that Mark did not forget to give it to me.

Nolan is also very witty. He says the funniest and most whimsical things just at the perfect times. He could have all four of us in stitches for hours. None of it is mean spirited though. We can all count on Nolan to bring us up at bad times. It's one of the things I love about him the most. He is a true joy to be around. This is just what we need in our journey through this horrible disease and he knows that is what we lean on him to do. He is so kind and giving to others. I sometimes ask myself how a ten year old boy knows just what to do to help someone else? It's like he can actually feel the pain others are feeling. This gift of altruism amazes me every time he shows it. I only wish others in this world had half of what Nolan has in his heart for giving.

Although, like his brothers Nolan loves to play sports, his true love is for music. He loves to jam (as he calls it) on his guitar and write songs. I catch him many times throughout the day just humming along to life. His passion for music has actually inspired both his brothers to take up instruments and Nolan will lead the two in a jam session. Music is his escape from my battle. I never have to nag or bribe Nolan to practice. I don't know if that is because of his passion for music or because he is just a pleaser. He loves to please and rarely needs to be asked twice to do something; one trait that makes being his mom easy.

Although it may seem that Nolan is just plugging along with a cheery outlook of life and nothing can get him down, that is not always the case. He is the most optimist child I know but deep down I know he is scared to death. He tries hard not to let me see his worry but as a mother I can see that my cancer has an affect on him. When I see tears in his eyes it nearly breaks me in two. Even as a baby Nolan was always my child that I could count on for a surprise hug at any time. I could just walk into the room were he would be engrossed in playing with his brother and he would be the first one to jump up and just wrap his arms around me. It is still the same but his hugs are just a little more gentle and are held a little longer. They are hugs of compassion instead of just fun. They are comforting hugs that he gives me to let me know he is here for me. There are times when I actually seek Nolan out just to get one of those unique hugs.

I have also seen Nolan's faith in the Lord grow tremendously since the cancer has come back. He truly puts all his fears on God. I love to quietly stand outside his room before bed and just listen to him pray. It is so deep for a ten year old. He is not asking for a new bike or a video game. He is asking for a cure for mommy, or to help his brothers, or to feed those who don't have food, or give homes to those who live in the streets. He prays for others not for his own needs. I think he actually gets what some adults cannot wrap their minds around. He understands that life is not about him but about all of us together. I remember a few years ago when his godmother was very ill. He would pray day and night for her to get better. Eventually she passed away at age 36. Nolan was just in complete peace and understanding. I thought he would be devastated but instead he wiped my tears and said that God needed her. Never once asked why or how come his prays where not answered. He understood and comforted me. Astonishing is all I can say about his deep faith.

After reading this post I am sure you can understand why Nolan was so difficult to write about. I could go on and on but it is just too emotional for me. My heart aches that a child of ten with such a great outlook on life has to see his mom fight for her life. I can only pray, maybe along with him, that he stays as precious as he is today, forever. I now know why God gave us him. I now see clearly and understand.

May 25, 2009
Sum it up!!!
I hope after reading the past three posts you now completely understands why I will not take "no cure" for an answer. Every treatment I have, every doctor I see and every breath I take are because I want to be here for them. I don't want them to feel the pain of losing their mother. I will never give into this cancer. Mostly, I will guarantee them that I will do what ever needs to be done to fight this monster so that they can have a mother. If my battle ends in death, I want them to have pride in me and learn from my perseverance.

Through this battle I will be an example of hope to them. I will show them that giving up is not an option. Strength and toughness comes from within not from words and my fight will teach them that.

Chapter 15:
Keep on Keeping

"Battle is the most magnificent competition in which a human being can indulge. It brings out all that is best. All men are afraid in battle. The coward is the one who lets his fear overcome his sense of duty. Duty is the essence of manhood."
~George S. Patton

May 29, 2009
Catching Up!
Many of you have been asking what is next for me. I am going through so many different steps it is very confusing.

Let me begin with next week. I am schedule for a PET scan next Tuesday. This is the very first scan I have had since my last treatment in Switzerland. This is the one we've been all waiting for to determine if the treatment has helped any. The rest of my moves (it's like a chess game) depends on what the outcome is of these test. The choices are as follows:

Good to worse
1. If the scan shows shrinkage then I will go back to Switzerland ASAP for another treatment.

2. If it's stable—no growth but no shrinkage—then I am scheduled to see a new specialist on June 24th and hopefully I will find out about some other treatments.

3. If there is growth then I will look for other options else where.

I am scheduled to meet with a specialist in Iowa on June 24th. I am praying that he takes me on as a patient. I am not sure what "tricks" he has up his sleeve but I know that he is the best of the best when it comes to Neuroendocrine Cancer. So keep me in your prayers.

June 4, 2009
"The Speech"

A few months ago I was asked by the Plum School District Superintendent and the school board to give the commencement speech to the graduating class of 2009. I must say I was taken back when asked because I did not understand why a mother of three not so perfect little boys…but perfect in my eyes, not so perfect wife, very small business owner with stage 4 cancer could say to a group of excited teenagers with their whole life ahead of them. After much contemplation I said yes because I thought what a great opportunity to thank everyone for all their support this year. The Plum High School students rallied behind me time and time again with my journey and I never got to thank them face to face. Then last week I became ill with an infection and was having trouble breathing and talking. I was close to canceling but after writing my speech I thought it would be very hypocritical of me to preach about taking risk and not giving up then canceling on a small speech. So I said a huge prayer and off I went.

Funny Story:
On our way to the graduation I was in the car explaining to the boys what a "Key Note" speaker talks about and preparing them for what I was going to say so that they did not get upset. I told them that some parts of my speech maybe sad for them but they are not to dwell on the negative and listen to the positive parts. I explained to them that this speech should be inspiring. Nolan, my 10 year old asked, "Mom, does

every graduation have a "Chemo Speaker" and if so how do they find people who have had chemo that everyone knows?." I must say Mark and I laughed for about 15 minutes. His statement summed up my whole speech. If you can't laugh at your struggles then expect to feel sad. Even his older brothers enjoy his innocence.

After the night was over I had several people ask me to post my speech online. So here it is:

Hello. Thank you. Faculty, staff, parents, friends, and most especially the Plum Senior High School graduating class of 2009, I am so honored yet humbled to be here with you all tonight.

Up until this point you have had most of your key decisions made for you. Elementary school, Middle School, then High School…grade to grade…you had few options. From one activity to the next. …someone else, some adult, has made that decision for you. After tonight your future is yours to choose. College, career, military service, or even just slacking is now your call. I was asked to speak tonight by Dr. Nacaretti not because I am a mother, wife, photographer or a business owner, but because I live and fight an incurable disease, carcinoid cancer, which I am told will end my life. In 1994 I was diagnosed with ovarian cancer (year's later finding out that it was actually the start of carcinoid cancer). At that time I was climbing the ladder to success in corporate America and was irritated at the interruption of my life plan. After a small surgery and a few months of treatments, I was in remission and back to succeeding in my career. I became the youngest manager of a fortune 100 company to reach number one in sales in the country. I was quickly promoted to leading an entire division in Pittsburgh. Unfortunately, a year later and a week before my wedding to my husband, the cancer returned. I then had a more invasive surgery, and was told by my doctors that the odds of having children were slim, but if I wanted any chance I had to start right away. Within 26 months I had my three wonderful boys and decided to put my career on hold to raise my amazing gifts. Years went by and I threw my life into my children and slowly progressed in building my own business. Four years ago my youngest son Nolan started kindergarten and I knew it was time to really put energy and time into my business.

Within 8 weeks of that time I was diagnosed again with cancer and this time it was even more serious. A tumor, which the doctors called carcinoid, engulfed my entire right lung and I had my right lung removed. The recovery took almost a year and there were a few very close calls. At that time I was told that there is no cure and that this rare cancer will eventually take my life. Then a little over a year ago, as promised by my doctors, the cancer returned with a vengeance and I was rediganosed with Stage 4 cancer throughout my body – two softball size tumors and many smaller ones are ravaging my liver and the lesions in my skeleton go from my legs through my hips, spine, arm, shoulder, and up through my skull.

However, I was asked to speak tonight not because I have cancer, but because of how I choose to live with it. I know the concept of terminal illness is probably the farthest thing from your mind tonight so I won't dwell on what the disease has done to me, my life, and my family but I will talk about how I choose to fight it…to live each day to the fullest…to being a positive influence on others, and how you can do the same. In some ways, cancer was a wakeup call for me—I had to decide quickly who was going to win—the cancer or me. The tumors and treatments make me tired at times, nauseous at others, and the pain is a constant reminder that this disease is invading my body. But the only way I know to approach this disease is to make sure I am the one in charge of everyday. From my husband to my children and from my brothers and sisters to my closest friends the words I would hear mumbled after I broke the news was WHY HER?

I can only answer —why not me? I, like all of you sitting here tonight, am not unworthy of trials and struggles. God has never guaranteed us a life without tough times. If someone has to take this on, why not someone with a big, supportive family, a strong helping group of friends, and a wonderful community that has rallied on my behalf time and time again. Of course, like most, I would choose a life without cancer but I am grateful for the lessons I have learned while navigating through this journey. I have learned that I can't change the direction of the wind, but I can adjust my sails to always reach my destination.

You cannot let someone tell you the possible is impossible, that the reachable is unreachable, or that your dreams are unattainable. When I was diagnosed this last time I sat in a small doctor's office with the faces of my boys running through my head as I was told, by the same doctor that removed my right lung three years prior, that there is nothing more that can be done. He just shook his head and told me to go home and wait for the cancer to take its toll. At that point I was not accepting that the possible was the impossible. I told that doctor that I would sit in that office for days if need be until he found me someone else that knew more than he did. After all I was in no rush to go home and face my boys with this news. Within in an hour, that doctor came into the room with two oncologist's names that would take my case and see me immediately. Those doctors where willing to take me as a patient but they too had little faith. After hours and days of research I found a treatment that may give me a glimmer of hope but it was not in the United States and was not covered by insurance. But that did not stop me. As many of you know, I have already made two trips to Switzerland with the help of my family, friends and this community. And is hoping to return for more treatments soon.

My question to you tonight is this: what if I went home that day and accepted the very first "no" I got? Eventually I may not beat this disease but I will give it the fight of my life.

And if I can at the age of 38, with tumors throughout my body, with doctors who are ready to give up on me, continue to reach for the impossible, then you all can too. You can achieve whatever it is you set out to do. Don't ever let the "can't syndrome" or the "can't posse" impact your life or your thoughts. A pessimist sees the difficulty in every opportunity; an optimist sees the opportunity in every difficulty. See the opportunities and take advantage of them. Doctors recognized in their community as leaders in their field told me I couldn't have children. I was told to get my long hair cut, by these same experts, because the treatments would take it away and getting it cut first would ease the shock to my kids. I was told over and over that there is nothing that can be done. I have three wonderful, healthy kids.

My real hair. Not a wig. And a little over a year ago, I was told my case was hopeless, I am standing here tonight. Not sure why. Not sure how. Except that I refused to believe what they were telling me was my fate.

So the next time some well-intentioned friend, expert, boss, or advisor tells you you'll never make it, it can't be done, you'll never pull it off, or you will never finish…tell them thanks…and then go make it, go do it, go pull it off, and go finish. You are the only one that can control your path in life with the choices you make. Don't let anyone lead you down the wrong path. Sure there may be speed bumps along the way that may slow you down. In fact I can guarantee you that there will be, but don't allow them to become roadblocks. Never believe that you can't move on. Cancer is something I live with…but it is not who I am. Although at some point it might determine when I go, it does not determine what I will do when I am here. Tonight I get to be here with all of you, apparently, by just doing what I have always done, but doing it with cancer. I am just trying to do the impossible, which I am told inspires others. Being an inspiration just happened. It is not something that I set out to do. I still at times cannot believe what my struggles and my efforts to fight this disease have done for others. I would have never have guessed that I would have articles written about me, that I would be interviewed by radio or news shows, contacted by Senators to speak on Congress, have a blog that is read by thousands across the world or even be asked to address you all tonight. I am no more special then any of you sitting in front of me but my choices are what got me here. My choice to live my life to the fullest despite my challenges. If that choice can inspire just one of you tonight to never doubt yourself, to not let times of trials stop you from reaching for your dreams then I have fought the good fight. The disease has opened up doors I never would have thought possible and has given me an unexpected but urgent reason to make a difference.

Please, I urge each and every one of you to go through each day doing your best at everything you try. Go that extra mile. Everything you do in life is a self-portrait of the person who does it. Autograph your work with excellence. It's OK to reach out to the moon and only be able to grab a star. It's NOT OK to choose not to aim for the moon because everyone else says it's unreachable. There are days when just getting out of bed for me is a chore. The cancer that is throughout my bones often at times gives me horrific pain. But I am determined even at my worst moments to wake up and greet my children every morning. On the days that I feel my worst I may, only get a star but I will always reach for the moon.

As a mother it would be an injustice if I don't encourage you all to always keep a strong relationship with your family. Let me tell you tonight, friends come and go; your family is for life. Tell your parents you love them every chance you get. The love a parent has for a child is the strongest bond any human can feel. Having three children myself I can only imagine the pride your parents are feeling about each one of you today. They are probably holding back the tears for fear of embarrassing you but will go behind closed doors when it's all over and shed a few. Some maybe sitting in their seats today remembering your very first day of school and could probably tell you every detail of that day from the breakfast you ate, to the exact clothes you had on and up until the last word you said before you left to begin the first day of your 13 year adventure. My only hope is that I one day have the opportunity experience what they are feeling right now when it's my children graduating. It is a heartfelt feeling that unfortunately may irritate you today but one day several of you will be able to relate too when you have children. Whatever you parents are going through today you should know that they are your cheerleaders, supporters and will always, love you unconditionally.

I have been given the opportunity to have reality thrust in my face and to recognize what really is important in life as a result. I never sleep in anymore…sunrise is an amazing time of day. I believe there is nothing I cannot do even with my cancer. Don't go through life with a cannot do attitude. You are cheating yourself out of the once in a lifetime chance to know how much you can really achieve. Stay away from negative "can't do," "why me," and "life sucks people." They have no benefits to you and cannot help you reach your goals. I have been to the point where life's alternative has come up and I can say with all my heart life doesn't suck…even during the most difficult of time life is a blessing.

Over the next few weeks as you party…sleep in…party some more….sleep in…remember that at some point the future will be upon you and it won't be "just" tomorrow anymore. It will be time for packing, a call to duty or the start of a new job and this night will slowly become a blur. I hope that you all recognize that you hold your life in the palm of your hands and your choices from this night forward will determine your destination. Enjoy the moment. Plan for tomorrow and never have to regret the past. That is a good life. Be positive…make a difference in your life by getting involved so you can make a difference in someone else's life like many of you have already done this past year in mine. Work your dreams to death and don't get discouraged when life throws you an obstacle. Get up early every morning, give the day your all and lay your head down at night with exhaustion. Whatever it is that you dream to do….do it. Do it giving 100%. As hurdles arise, remember if you can't jump over them you can always run around them. There is always another way. Don't be afraid of the hurdles. Never think tomorrow is going to be anything but a great day. When tomorrow comes and you are part of it, it's a great day.

I am here tonight to let you know that you control how you get up and face each day. I have not done anything special. I certainly am not a hero. Cancer was spelled with can long before I was ever diagnosed. I am a fighter and I refuse to go down without a fight. That's why I was asked to address you tonight. My ultimate message to leave you with tonight is that ordinary people can do extraordinary things if they refuse to allow the expected become reality.

Once again thank you for inviting me tonight. But I mostly want to take this opportunity to thank my family, my friends, the Plum Community, the school district and the students here tonight for all your support throughout my journey. You all make it impossible for me to give into this disease. Be safe tonight and in the weeks ahead. Good night.

When I was done speaking I could not believe I had gotten a standing ovation. I looked out to the students and saw several with tissues wiping away tears. Did I reach some them? I don't know. Will they remember me or what I had to say? I am not sure. But at that moment I redirected their minds from partying and freedom. I hope that just one of them got something and they can see clearer now. "Life is not what is given to you, it's what you give to it."

※※

June 8, 2009
Scan Results!!
Today was my appointment with my liver specialist, Dr. Gamblin. We took the boys because we wanted to take them through Pitt's campus and show them where Mom and Dad spent time studying together before they were even thought of. I thought that it was just another doctor's appointment where they read the scans (I had one Monday) and then out the door I go. Nothing special, no change, let's just wait and see. On Friday I spoke with my overall oncologist and he usually stresses the bone tumors because he knows they give me the most pain and lets Dr. Gamblin handles the liver tumors. So Friday he told me that the PET scan was somewhat inconclusive because not all carcinoid tumors show up on PET Scans but that possible two new tumors showed up in the bones. So I am scheduled for a two day scan, Octreotide Scan, to look at the tumors that we know are there but did not show on the scan and to further look into the two new spots. I was trying to avoid that scan because it is very long and hard on me. But it is what it is.

Anyway, back to the liver specialist news. Dr. Gamblim is a really neat doctor. Extremely smart but really down to earth even in his bow tie. When he came into the small room he had a huge smile on his face so I knew he had to tell me something good. I thought it was about the new carcinoid cancer division he and another doctor friend of mine are starting here in Pittsburgh, which I was really eager to hear about. He always has an entourage of "want to be Dr. Gablim's" with him and Jackie, his trusty and amazing nurse, following behind me. He goes through introduction and then we start talking about my liver. Today he just had to spit it all out. He was so excited to tell me that the two huge tumors I have in my liver have shrunk. Not gone by no means but have SHRUNK!!!! They have only shrunk about ½ a cam. but they shrunk. I tried really hard to keep it together but I could feel my eyes just filling up with tears. I love those happy tears. I knew that Dr. Gamblim, who lives day to day speaking to really sick patients and patients that have lost hope, was so thrilled to offer me the great news. I think he was almost as happy as Mark and I were because the first thing he asks after breaking the good news was, "how are the boys?" He is young and has three very young children so I know it is very concerning to him when a mother is his patient. The boys where waiting outside the small room in the waiting room and I could not wait to run out to hug them.

I was disappointed with Friday's news, especially with two new bone tumors popping up. I wanted to keep this news to myself because I did not want anyone else to feel that their support was useless. I felt like I was letting everyone who has helped me get this "Magic" treatment down. I of course want to be cancer free for me and my family, but it's more than that now. I want to be cancer free for everyone who has supported me. After all the help I went all the way to Switzerland and receive this treatment I need to get better. I owe it too those who have helped me. So yesterday was like a start up the mountain.

"Life is good, even when times are tough." I know that some of you are thinking less then a ½ cem. Shrinkage does not seem like much. To me it means prolonging my life a little longer until a cure is found. It means another trip to Switzerland. It means that all the pain and suffering I went through was worth it. It means some GOOD IN CANCER. Sure it's not gone and I know that I need to still fight for my life but it defiantly helps keep me reaching for the moon.

※※

June 15, 2009
Days Like Today I Hate Cancer!
When I was striuck this time with cancer of the liver, lymph nodes and bones I made up my mind that I was going to fight this disease with everything I got and most importantly with a positive attitude. I did not want to let this cancer define me or determine what I will to or accomplish in my life. I did not want to be a victim of this disease. For the

most part with good organization and planning, I do a good job of not letting this disease interfere with things I enjoy to do or events that I don't want to miss. But there are times no matter how hard I try that cancer gets in the way.

Today is a prime example. Mark had decided to take today and tomorrow off so that he can be with me when I go through this horrific two day Octreotide scan. Little did we know that it was also the day of the Pittsburgh Penguin's Stanley Cup Celebration in Pittsburgh. For those of you who don't live in the US or are not hockey fans the Pittsburgh Penguin's are our home hockey team and YES they won the Stanley Cup on Friday. So the city of Pittsburgh had planned a winning parade, like was had for our Steelers who are the Super Bowl Champs, and my boys (Mark too) where dying to go to. Not to mention it was a picture perfect weather day…blue skies and high 70's. So my heart broke last night when I told the boys that mom had a scan scheduled (which took me 2 weeks to get so I could not cancel) and they could not go to the parade. I wasn't sure who was more disappointed the boys or me because I could not share in their excitement about the parade. So after looking in their big blue eyes, which always gets me, I decided to have Mark take them to the parade and I would go to the scan by myself.

The last time I had this scan was an about a year ago. I have had so many different scans since them so I could not remember the logistics of the whole procedure. What I did remember was that I got something radio active injected in me and have to lay in a confined space for a long time. I also remembered that it is very painful on the spots of the bones and the liver where I have tumors. Mark reminded me that when the scan was over last time I needed a wheelchair because I was in too much pain when I tried to walk. What I did not remember and realized when I got there was that I was injected and then could leave (but don't go near small children) yet had to return in four hours for the actual scan process itself. It was recommended by the tech that I not drive anywhere because the injection could make me feel a little sick. So after finding that out I was really cursing cancer. My family was out on a beautiful day enjoying life and I was alone in a hospital that I have seen way to much of this past year, lighting up like light bright.

For those of you who know me you would not be surprised when I did get in my car and drive home. As I was sitting in the chapel of the hospital finding my "happy place" and I remembered that I did not wash the boys baseball uniforms for their game tonight and would now not be home in time to get them washed. After getting home and putting the uniforms in the washer the boys came home with smiles on their faces. They could not get the words out fast enough about the day and the parade. They had autographs of many of their favorite players and pictures to show me. I was so glad that they got to go but sad that I could not be with them to see them enjoy it. So the uniforms got washed and off I went again back to the hospital for phase two of three for the scan from hell. Mark wanted to come with me but baseball was calling and one of us should be there to cheer them on.

I truly hate when I let this disease take control my mood. Today that is what it did but only for a moment. I was frustrated and felt trapped. Rarely do I like to write a negative post, but I wanted you all to know that I do at times hate what cancer has done to my life. I feel at times that it is a full time job to just stay alive and it is getting really old. But then I come home after lying in a tube in horrible pain to a house full of happy boys, to a dinner made by a friend, to a few cards that I got in the mail and realized that I am truly blessed no matter what the cancer does. Tomorrow is another day of scans but when it is all over my life is still great.

Father's Day

Since my dad has passed Father's Day has always been bitter sweet. I miss my dad with all my heart but I am so happy that my children have an amazing dad to spend this day with them. I think about my dad and how his heart would be broken seeing me so ill. He would not be able to see what I have to endure to fight this cancer. As a parent I can relate to the pain he would feel seeing me grow through this life sentence. My dad was an amazing man….great father but an even more incredible person. He was a man that made a presence everywhere he went. He wasn't loud or obnoxious because he believed when you speak have something to say worth hearing. That is why when he spoke everyone listened. He was the type of person that everyone who knew him admired him and everyone who did not know him wanted to know him. He was strong and tough, yet so generous and kind. As the warden of the Allegheny County Jail he dedicated his career in giving to others and protecting others. I cannot tell you growing up and even today how

Dad
A dad is one that let's you take risks, and then stands behind you to jump in when you need him!

many inmates, parents, teenagers or just ordinary people come up to me and tell me that my dad had helped them through a difficult time. He was the kind of man that never booasted about his good will…he let it humble him. He just made it a way of life and expected us to do the same. He would teach us that no one's life is less important than another's. Yet life's circumstances made some more unfortunate than others and we are less of a person if we don't reach out a hand to help them.

He also instilled in us to do the best at everything we take part in. I learned that anything worth doing is worth doing well. He was strict to a fault at times, but being a parent myself now I understand it a bit. Mark always tells that boys that I grew up in a prison with the warden actually watching every move I made. That was literally true in every aspect. I had a curfew even the night before I got married at 25 years old and I listened with respect. I did not agree with his control issues but I NOW understand them and find myself protecting my children like him. He would to say to all of us, "I will never be your best friend, but always be your dad." That sums it all up. He loved all his children unconditionally no matter what they did. However, he never held back if he did not like your choices. Just what a dad should do.

As a child and especially as a teenager I did not always agree with my father. I can recall several times being so angry with him and his strictness that I would promise myself that to never be a parent like him…only to become a parent like him. I understand his love for his children now and his need to protect us.

Although Mark and my dad are very different I know that the love they have for their children is the same. Mark is more relaxed than my father and likes to be friends with the boys. Mark values every minute he has with his boys, much like my dad use too. Mark is more emotional and expresses his love for the boys with words. With my dad we did not need to hear everyday that he loved us because his action showed us.

Sometimes the poorest man leaves his children the richest inheritance.

Chapter 16: More Hope

"The road that is built in hope is more pleasant to the traveler than the road built in despair."

June 22, 2009
Off to Iowa City!
Tomorrow Mark, my brother Michael and I are off to Iowa to see the guru of Carcinoid Cancer. We are just gathering some information on some new experimental treatments and some clinical trials that may be offered to me. I have been waiting to see this doctor since March so I am really excited to see what he can do to help. The appointment could not have come at a better time because we just got the results back from my two day octreotide scan and the news was mixed. The two large tumors in the liver did shrink a little, so ya for that. Unfortunately there are many new tumors in the bones and some have spread to the ovary. This is why I have been in an enormous amount of pain in the last month. Although, it seems like every time I hear not so great news I have a glimmer of hope that goes with it. Today I am hanging on the hope that this doctor has some options for me.

    I hate posting mixed or bad results on the blog for many reasons. First and most importantly, I don't want my entire carcinoid posse to give up hope. I have not given up, so I don't want them to think that this fight is hopeless. It is true that when one door, or treatment, closes another one opens. I have never accepted the bad news without looking ahead for some good news. Today my good news is this appointment I have in Iowa. I like to think of it as if a hurdle gets in the way of life and it's too high to jump over you can go around it because there is always another way. You just need to be determined to find it and not give up until you find it. Often I hold back posting when I am not at my best for that exact reason. I don't want other carcinoid patients who read my blog to feel down. If each one of us supports each other then this disease will not win.

Another reason why I keep the bad news under lock and key at times is because I don't ever want anyone to feel sorry for me. I don't feel sorry for myself, so the last thing I want is for others to pity me. I do not have time in my life for self-pity. I have this quote inside my Bible beside my bed. Not sure where I heard it, read it or who even claims it but I use it for a book mark. And when I start to feel that "dark side" creeping in I reach for it:

"Each day is a special gift from God, and while life may not always be fair, you must never allow the pains, hurdles, and handicaps of the moment to poison your attitude and plans for yourself and your future. You can never win when you wear the ugly cloak of self-pity, and the sour sound of whining will certainly frighten away any opportunity for success. Never again. There is a better way."

I am so lucky to have my family, my friends and the opportunity to know what is really important in life. It is something that you get when faced with an adversity that is life or death. It is like your eyes get washed with your tears and you see things so much clearer. I know that is deep or difficult to relate to but I also know that some of you who have been through a similar situation are shaking your heads knowing exactly what I am saying. It's like that gift that comes with cancer. Sounds crazy but if you look at this disease as exactly that it makes it a whole hell of a lot easier to navigate through.

Lastly, as I stated over and over again in my blog I hate talking about bad news. I just as well stuff it under a log and never lift it up again. I feel like if the news does not give any benefit by telling it then keep it in. It is the same way I feel about negative people. I avoid them like the plague. No need to spread the germ of negativity.

However, in this case I have up news to go with the new tumors. Some of the liver tumors have decreased in size and that I have an appointment with the "Mac Daddy" of Carcinoid Doctors on Wednesday (some speech influenced by the boys). So as promised I gave you the news of the scans, but now I need a promise form all my supporters: Please do not feel sorry for me…feel inspired by me. Do something this week that will make you a better person. Don't cry for me, cry with me.

Keep me in your prayers Tuesday and Wednesday. I am hoping for a miracle.

June 26, 2009
We Are Back Again!

Well I am back and filled with all kinds of new information. Mark, my brother Michael and I had a good time. It was really nice to spend time with both of them together. Mark was a real trooper because from what I am told Jennings' together can be very difficult to deal with at times. We are very controlling and like to run things our way. We always laugh because we understand each others idiosyncrasies and can relate. It's the ones we married (the outlaws they call themselves) that like to gather around and compare notes about the uniqueness. Anyways Mark just let Mike and I take control as he just went with the flow.

Michael was great too. It was really nice to have someone else come along to actually see what we go through on a day to day basis because of this cancer. I try to hide all the inconveniences of this disease because it is just something we do and there is no need to discuss it. He was very respectful of my choices and did not try to talk me into anything. Since my dad passed Mike has stepped in as the leader of the family. He is wonderful and the big brother anyone would love to have and I am glad he is mine. He has been a huge support through this whole journey. It amazes me how much he is like my dad. Very comforting. My sister-in-law Sue (my brother Happy's wife) and my niece stayed home to watch the boys. She whipped the boys into shape for me and the house was spotless when I got home.

We were so blessed to have a place to stay. My friend Leah hooked me up with friends of her that live in Iowa City and John, the husband, actually is a doctor which specializes in oncology radiation at the same hospital as Dr. O'Dorisio. They were an amazing family and now are great friends. They opened up their home to me anytime I will need to continue my care in Iowa. They were truly the work of God. I cannot thank Leah, Michelle and John for reaching out to me. Thank you again.

The doctor's visit took hours. I had 9 valves of blood taken, few scans and ultra scans, and met with the doctor for almost an hour and a half. He was so knowledgeable about the cancer and has dedicated his life to just this type of cancer. He listened to all our questions and so amazing in helping us understand this cancer. For the very first time I actually felt like I spoke to someone who knew everything there is to know about Carcinoid Cancer. Never ones did he say "I don't know" to any question I asked, and I asked many. He spoke with confidence and hope. He was very straight forward in admitting that this is one of the most difficult cancers to understand but talked with belief. However he did say that there is no cure and it is his job to keep me alive as long as possible.

So here is the game plan for now (subject to change depending on my body and my reactions):

1. The cancer has spread to my gallbladder and ovary (the only one I have left) so I will have surgery to remove both of those soon.

2. I am now going to be given myself injections 3 times a day of sando to help keep the tumors at bay and to help keep the endocrine symptoms in control. I will also go to the hospital every 21 days for an even larger dose.

3. I will go on a drug (undecided which one as of now) that will help with the bone pain and keep the bones as strong as they can be with the cancer invading them. This drug should also help with the pain.

4. I will go on pancreatic enzymes to protect me from the medicine I will be trying in the clinical trial.

5. I will start his clinical trial.

6. I will start a drug called Affinitor. The problem is that this drug is not covered by my insurance and cost $500 a day. YES A DAY!!!! So I am looking into grants to help us out on that. But it is proven to help stop the spread of carcinoid cancer.

7. I will go back to Switzerland in the fall to winter. Gives us more time to come up with the money for that.

8. If all fails then I will have extensive chemo. LAST OPTION because it is very hard on the body with little results.

So that is the game plan. Not once did he tell me to sit and wait. Although many of this treatments are not covered by my insurance I still feel at peace. I will find a way to pay for them but I will not give up. This cancer will not take me down without a fight.

July 6, 2009
It's Not About Me
So tonight I am unable to sleep and I thought I would post. Two weeks ago I got an update about a friend that has been fighting a brain tumor and the news was not promising. I have been thinking about her, her husband and two little girls all night. She, like me, has exhausted all her treatment options and had begun some clinical trials. Unfortunately, the trials have not worked and the tumor has grown. I have not spoken or exchange emails with her lately because she is unable but I have heard from those close to her that she still has her fight in her. We know each other through a mutual friend and I photographed her and her family years back… our cancer reconnected us. She is an amazing inspiration for me. She is determined to do whatever it takes to be here for her daughters. I remember last summer she called me to tell me not to give into this disease she had been diagnosed for about 6 months prior. We talked about alternative medicines, herbs and foods that stop the cancer growth and about doing whatever it takes to be here for our children. At that time she was eating blueberries everyday because she read somewhere that blueberries stop tumors. She is unbelievable.

One summer night I got a knock on my door and it was three of my very good friends from "the field" as we call the neighborhood that I grew up in (Greenfield). They were holding this beautiful huge box for me. Jen was not with them because she was under the weather but she helped with the surprise and gave them the idea. In the box was about 3 dozen individually wrapped gifts for me to open whenever I felt blue. The boys and I loved reaching for one every time something happened and when the last gift came to open it we were sad it was all over. It was so fun to have that gift, but better that my friends whom I sadly don't get to spend much time with since I moved came to my home just hoping I would be home. They are crazy like that. What I could not wrap my mind around was that this woman, mother, wife, attorney and cancer patient thought of me to cheer up. She is very special.

A few months ago Jen emailed me to see how I was doing. She was getting ready to take her girls to Disney World where the cancer was forgotten and the magic will be remembered. I was so excited for her to be able to spend that time with her princesses. We promised each other to get together for coffee when she got back. It's easy for two moms with cancer to talk about things that others cannot understand. Well that coffee meeting never happened and I regret not following through with it. Jen is being taken care of by hospice now and my heart is aching.

Through my whole crazy journey of cancer I have never felt sorry for myself. I don't ask why? I stopped trying to figure out where it's comes from and just accept that I have it. I feel the cancer taking is toll on me more and more, but I just keep chugging along. I try hard not to cry over it, although at times the tears flow. But when I see stories like Jen, I begin to question the fairness in life. This beautiful young mother, a wife and a promising career as an attorney has done everything right in life and now she is suffering. I know God is good but when my time comes I am going to ask him one question, "why do you choose who you choose?" I know I will finally understand the answer. Additionally, I know that I will never wait for a coffee with my friends. So all of you who have noncommittally said let's do lunch or coffee I am making a date with you this week. Look for my call.

Please pray for Jen but more importantly Jen's family who loves her so much.

Friday, July 3, 2009
Sorry for the delay in posting since I've been back from Iowa. It's been a really rough week. The bone pain has increased tremendously and I am doing whatever it takes just to function. I have started several posts in the last few days (I'm determined to finish this one) but just can't get through them. I have not started all the treatments that Dr. O'Dorisio recommended because I am waiting for insurance approval or some kind of grant to help offset the outrageous cost that drug companies charge for your life. I'm not going to get into that frustration. But I am sure once I start those meds the pain will get better.

    Anyway, I just felt the need to post today about how much support I have and how much I appreciate all of it. When a person is in pain, pain that is beyond tolerable, it is so easy to start to go to the "dark side." There were a few times this week when I could of just slipped into the deep abyss of feeling sorry for myself and just give up. But all those who are around me make it completely impossible to do so and Mark is always there to remind me of how blessed I am. The other day after thanking my girlfriend for helping me out with the boys she made a comment about wishing she could do more but she doesn't know how to help me. That is not the first time someone has made that comment to me. I want everyone to know that the little things that are done to help me: phone calls, an email, a card, dinner, planning the dinner list, organizing the sunning, setting up my chair at a baseball game, prayers, invites to lunch, taking my boys out to dinner, loading my car at the grocery store when you see me, etc. mean the world to me. It makes me determined to not give in to this disease. Although at times I feel helpless and embarrassed that I need that help, I have learned that it is worth taking. It is those things that make me appreciate how truly blessed I am. Having cancer has shown me the good in people. Once again my family and I can never pay it back but we can pay it forward, which will make a difference in someone else's life. I have been blessed through this journey and I am going to bless others through their journey.

    At first, last May I had a house full of people around me for weeks then months pitching in and just supporting me. I had two of my dearest friends start a dinner list so my family could eat. I had fundraiser ideas being tossed at me in every direction to help off set the medical bills. I had a group of friends and neighbors planting my flowers and a summer of grass cutting. My mailbox was filled everyday with cards. I had a few packages being sent to me of things to get me through the days when I would be sick. Phone calls filled my answering machine. And I cannot forget the how my family rallied around me. Mark, the boys and me walked around like zombies in complete shock and everyone else just step in. It got us through and still does. But I remember my mind spinning with thoughts repaying or how I did not want anyone to think of me as helpless. I would continue to say over and over again, "I don't want anyone to think I am less of a person because I am sick." I was afraid that all these people that were helping lost respect for me or worse felt sorry for me.

I have come to realize that was not the case in the least bit. But that I needed this support and God has given me amazing people in my life. I have always been able to take care of myself… with or without cancer. I realize now that I never had to do that and that I was surrounded by family and friends who just do for me if I let them be the amazing and caring people they are. The things that many of you do may feel like nothing to you but to me they keep me motivated to keep fighting.

At times our own light goes out and needs to be rekindled by a spark from another person. Last week my light went out. You all have lighted the flame within me this week by your support. It takes weeks like this past one when I am reminded that I have this horrible cancer, to see how truly blessed I am. Monday I will be going for another group of bone scans and X-Ray. Then later that week I will be receiving my first treatment for the actual cancer in the bones. Although the progress for these treatments has not shown the exact results I am hoping and wishing for the cancer has shown me how unbelievably amazing my life is because of all the people around me. Whatever my results may be and whatever the new treatment does to me I know that with all of you I will get through.

Thank you again,
Sunny

July 9, 2009
One Door Closes, Another Door Opens

When God leads you to the edge of the cliff, trust Him fully and let go, only 1 of 2 things will happen, either He'll catch you when you fall, or He'll teach you how to fly! Revelations 3:8

Trusting God and believing he will catch me when I fall is what has gotten me through this cancer journey and many other journeys I have galloped through in my life. There are many times we are hanging off the edge of the cliff and we just stop and not go further because of fear. But we need to trust that He will be there to save us or to teach us how to fight through. I know that is what God has and continues to do for me throughout this whole "cancer thing." I also believe that he is not just teaching me but others around me. So many times others ask me if I am truly at peace with my diagnoses. It has gone as far as having my oncologist giving me names of psychiatrist to talk to because he is afraid I have not accepted what he is telling me. If I was looking in on my life I would think the same thing about me as well, so I don't blame anyone for thinking that. But I will strongly tell you I am truly at peace with this whole cancer.

I am not going to pretend that I never get upset or down. Trust me I have had my times of defeat. But I can say that my hope and faith has gotten me through those times quickly. It seems that I always have some blessings to pick me up. It is those times that he catches me.

The journey itself of stage four cancer is how He teaches me how to fly. There are times when I pray so hard to take this all away. Or I pray to end the treatments. Or to make this treatment be the miracle. Or to give my doctors the knowledge of this rare cancer. Or I may pray to give my family a normal life without sadness and stress. God could easily have me wake up one day and this cancer be over. He can give any miracle. But that is not how he teaches me or my family and friends to fly. By giving into to every request we make to Him, He would not be doing the job of a father. He has given us the tools we need to live with adversity. As a mother I completely understand what He is doing. It takes me to a time when I am in a store with my children and they beg and beg for that one thing they cannot live without. Sure it is easy for me to pick it up and just pay for it and sometimes I do (when I catch them). But other times I make them earn it or pay for it themselves. There are times when my boys want it so bad that they do what ever it takes (that's when I teach them to fly), but other times when they step back they realize they don't really want it anyways.

There have been so many times in my life that one door has closed and right next to me is another that is open. Sometimes I have kept knocking on the closed door afraid to go into the open one. Those are the times when I have missed opportunities because I cannot accept that the door I thought I wanted is now closed. Little did I know then, that on the other side of the open door is what God has planned for me, not what I had planned for myself. I have had many doors closed while navigating through cancer: Doctors telling me there is no hope, financial pressures telling me I cannot afford certain treatments, doctors that are experts in my cancer practicing hundreds of miles away, medications that cost as much as my monthly mortgage payments, doctors that don't return my calls, and family pressures. The difference is I don't have time to keep knocking on those closed doors now. I have learned that when you are faced with a life or death situation God opens another door for you and gives you the courage to go through them quickly. I have gone through them and have had an amazing journey.

So I have to end this by saying I am not crazy, I just have faith. Believing that your life is in God's hands is taking control of any situation.

When God leads you to the edge of the cliff, trust Him fully and let go, only 1 of 2 things will happen, either He'll catch you when you fall, or He'll teach you how to fly! Revelations 3:8

July 14, 2009
What to Do?

Yesterday I went to my liver oncologist, Dr. Gamblin, to follow up on the treatment plan that Dr. Odo has set up for me. As I posted on June 26th, you may want to reread to catch up, part of the plan was to have surgery to remove the gallbladder or the remaining ovary I have, because the cancer has spread to them and I don't need them anyways. Dr. Odo is also trying to find that main source of the cancer and he thinks that maybe it could be the ovaries since that was the first place the cancer popped up. However, Dr. Gamblin, whom I would have perform the surgery, totally disagrees that I should undergoing any type of surgery at this point. He strongly feels that I may not be strong enough or my body well enough with all treatments I have had this past year to undergo any type of surgery that will not save my life. Although, removing these organs is generally a very simple surgery with minimum recovery time it would not be that simple for me. He believes that the benefits to me to undergo another procedure would not out weigh the risks for me. He is looking at the quality of my life and the time it would set me back to go through a surgery that will not save my life. Also he reminded us that I will not recover quickly enough if I had the surgery to return to Switzerland for the next treatment by the fall. He explained to us in his jolly Opey like way that on paper and scans I look a hell of a lot worse than I do in person which he believes fools me, Mark and others. He was very upfront when he summed up that he wants to give me the best life as possible not the longest. He stressed that it is INCUREABLE and I need to think about living a life as well as possible. He went as far as telling me that he will not do the surgery even if I beg and if I was so adamant on having it then I need to look for another surgeon.

Today I have an appointment with my main oncologist, Dr. Fredland, and I will get his opinion on the whole situation. In the end it is mine and Mark's decision. Why can't things just be simple?

July 15, 2009
Option 2

Yesterday I meet with my main oncologist Dr. Freidland to discuss the findings and treatment plan from Dr. O'Dorisio in Iowa. I must say I am completely wiped out and frustrated with the time I am spending on this cancer and the time I am losing with my boys. Austen spent the day with a friend so we brought Logan and Nolan with us. They did not love the fact that they had to come but they don't mind Hillman as much because they have roaming computers with Internet access in the waiting room. To me that just means prepare to wait. The boys stayed in the waiting room while Mark and I saw the doctor and after a 2 hour wait to just get in the examining room, I could care less what they destroyed or how they acted while unattended. Normally I would give the boys the 10 minute lecture of how they should behave and then have them repeat it all back to me to make sure that they understood every single word. But yesterday I was so mad at this cancer and then the 2 hour wait, that I just let the "Carney Crazies" loose. I must say though it did not work because they were little angels. Maybe that's my new discipline plan…say and do nothing. We had planned to take them to a special place after my 2:00 appointment so that they could have a good day. But the 2:00 appointment turned into a 4:30 appointment and we did not get out of there until 5:15 only to rush home to make a 6:00 baseball practice. So I will say another day lost to cancer.

Anyhow, once Dr. Freidland came into the room I was so prepared to just give him a "Sunny Smack Down" for the long wait, as Mark refers to the actions I take when I am really pissed off, but he makes that impossible. He is amazingly kind and so caring about my cancer. He is a general oncologist that sees every type of cancer so it always astonishes me that he is so up to date on the newest treatments for carcinoid. Of course I try to stump him by bringing him a folder full of new meds I've read and researched about, new clinical trials or a group of new questions but once again he was on his game. He spent over 45 minutes with me going over every scan, X-Ray, treatment options and how I am feeling. I always forget how long he spends with me and should realize that is why I wait so long. I am sure he does that with each of his patients. Then he gives me the pep talk about not giving up. So it makes the wait worth it but nothing is worth missing time with the boys.

So to sum this up, he too agrees that the surgery should not be an option at this point. He explains that I need to focus on treatments and having a surgery right now will postpone treatments that I need. He did not rule out the surgery in the near future but as of now he wants to focus on the other treatments. However, he agrees with all other treatment plans that Dr. O'Dorisio suggested. So tomorrow I go back to Hillman and receive my first treatment for my bone tumors. I was told that I will feel lousy for a few days to a week but after that I should get use to it. This treatment most likely will not shrink the tumors in my bones but will help with the pain and possibly slow down the growth. Then a few weeks after that I start the magic drug with the outrageous cost. Then we plan for round 3 in Switzerland.

I am still going to follow up with one more doctor about the surgery options. I have to make sure I am doing everything right. I respect all three of the physicians and their dedication to Carcinoid Cancer and me. But they are not the ones who are going to raise my boys if I make the wrong decision about my care. So next week I will contact Dr. O'do and let him know my doctors' opinions. Then I may contact another specialist, Dr. Warner, in New York and get his opinion. He runs the Carciniod Cancer Foundation where he posts my blog and recommends his patient take a look at my story. I have spoken with him a few times in the past year but maybe it's time for a visit.

Please keep me in your prayers tomorrow. I am a bit nervous about this new treatment for the bones. I don't want to spend a week of my summer sick, but I'll do whatever it takes.

July 19, 2009
The Treatment

On Thursday I had my first treatment to help with the bone tumors. I am told by my doctors that these treatments will not shrink the tumors but will help with the pain that I am having. However, the doctor who administrated the treatment said that he has never given this treatment to a patient with carcinoid cancer so who knows what the results will be. It could be the new miracle. I am glad to be the test rat. When I went to the nuclear treatment center to receive my treatment I felt like I was the prodigal son coming home. The techs are the same techs that give me all my scans. They are amazingly knowledgeable about cancer and the nuclear treatments. Of course they cannot recommend any treatments but I love to pump them for information on what they have seen. So after sitting in tubes for hours and hours and talking with them while they scan me I consider them part of my cancer family. Whenever I stop and think how many fabulous people I have gotten to know through this cancer I am in awe. Once again, "The Good In Cancer." In fact I joke with the few single buff men that I would love to fix up with some of my single girlfriends. They revealed to me this last time that they've known my story the whole time I've been going to this department because they have read all the articles that have been written about me. Some even said they follow my blog. They have mentioned within the last year the scan (octreotide scan) to detect carcinoid cancer has been increasingly ordered and that some patients have even mentioned my blog to them. So my voice is finally spreading. I am always surprised what God can do when you believe.

The doctors have warned me that before the pain gets better it possibly will increase for a few weeks after the treatment. Also, another side affect is a decrease in my white and red blood counts which are already below normal levels. So I prepared myself for a few weeks of being under the weather. I am happy to report as of today I am feeling pretty good. The pain has increased and is really bad at night, but tolerable. I am exhausted which is probably because the blood counts dropping and a little sick to the stomach. But I am functioning and able to be a mom to the boys. What more can I ask for than to be that?

After my counts are monitored and reach a level of normalcy I will start the new clinical trial drug. The one I mentioned cost more than some make in a year. That is one thing I would love to change. I am hoping in mid August. Then we will see what the scans tell us and depending on that we will prepare for trip 3 to Switzerland. So we are looking and hoping for a fall trip. But it is all subject to change.

Chapter 17:
I Think They Get It

"It's what you learn after you know it all that counts"

July 25, 2009
Love Is In the Air
Mark and I celebrated another year of marriage this week. I love to say another year of anything these days. To all of Mark's credit it was almost as amazing as our wedding 14 years ago. He and one of his friends from childhood (whom was a groomsman in our wedding) planned the whole day and evening. This post is just to relive it again.

Because of our children's sports schedule we decided to celebrate a day earlier. I think that is what started it out so special. Mark actually pre-thought about the day and decided that he could not postpone it until we get time, which in the past has meant a bottle of wine a week or two after July 22nd sipped quickly after the boys went to bed. Maybe if I am lucky we would put in the wedding day video and we would actually watch the whole thing through, without fast forwarding, before we fell asleep on the couch. Not this year though. Mark did it all. All I had to do was give him the best night to go out. However, even that was difficult because in between treatments, being ill from the treatments and sporting events there was really no perfect time. So we just forced ourselves to cancel everything and just do it.

The day started with an amazing bouquet of roses. Not just any roses but the exact type of rose that I had in my wedding bouquet. These are wild roses that must be ordered six months in advanced because they have to be cultivated to bloom in July instead of May (so I guess that would cancel out the wild part). I had these roses in my yard as a child growing up and when I was planning my wedding had to have them in my arrangements. They are blush to a very pale pink, almost white, in color with a yellow center and are the most fragrant of the roses. Not to mention the most delicate and I am told are not the most ideal for floral arrangements because of how fragile they are. In fact I remember hunting for a florist when planning my wedding that could actually find these roses. Over the years Mark has tried to replicate these roses with several attempts on past anniversaries or when he has just screwed up. So let's say I think I have been given every pale pink rose ever bloomed. I have never told him that it just could not be done without pre-ordering the rose months in advance until a few months ago when we were in Switzerland. In Switzerland when we had so much time on our hands and the tele only had two English speaking stations we talked about everything and anything. In the Market Plaza there were several street venders that sold the most amazing flowers. Mark being Mark went through every rose and asked, "Is that the one from your wedding bouquet" and I would shake my head no. So I finally let him in on the secret that they need to be ordered months ahead of time or found in May for two weeks only in my mom's backyard. He was amazed that after all these years of receiving bouquets of pale pink roses and hundreds of dollars spent on these arrangements, I never told him he did not get it right nor did I ever expect him too.

 Nevertheless, he did not stop there. A dear friend of ours, John Cinq, and Mark planned a spectacular evening with dinner at Café Zao, Cinq's restaurant, and opening night theater tickets to Barry Manilow's Copacabana The Musical. When we got to the restaurant Cinq had two glasses of champagne with raspberry puree, my favorite, waiting for us and an amazing meal was served. We then had a special dessert of both Mark's and my favorites, chocolate ganche mouse and lavender cheesecake. The desert plate had Happy Anniversary Sunny and Mark written in chocolate. After leaving full and a little buzzed we head across the street to the musical. The evening was amazing.

 We skipped out early on the musical, because we were not sure how long we had until the boys would be calling us to come home, and heading out on the town. We had a blast together. Laughing like BC (before cancer). It was truly like old times when money was not an issue and the theater and dinner was a great date. The most important part of the evening however was the time we spent just talking. Mark finally opened up to me about what it's been like for him during my battle. Although we talk about it at times we never get into the true and actual feelings. The one, and maybe the only thing, that makes Mark and I alike is that we both suppress our negative feelings. I have always felt that it is harder on those who love a cancer patient than it is for the actual patient. I cannot by any means pretend to know what Mark is going through nor do I even want to walk in his shoes for a day, but I can imagine at times it is a helpless feeling. As a patient fighting this cancer I can pretty much take control of almost all of it. Sure I can't change the progression of the disease but if I am in pain I can take a pill, if I have a question I can call the doctor, if I am tired I rest, if I am restless I exercise. I know that eating right and taking vitamins may help, so I do that. I can choose to have treatments or not. And when the time comes for it all to end I can leave this all behind me and know that I did whatever I could to stay alive. With that I can rest in peace.

For Mark it is not that easy. Although I do not always agree with the choices he makes when handling the stress of this difficult voyage, I do try to understand what he is going through. I receive emails from many spouses of patients with carcinoid cancer. Actually when I think about it, I become closer to the families than the actual patients themselves. Some are commenting on my treatments, some ask my advice, some want to know where I get my information from, some just ask how I am doing, some say they read my blogs to their other half and others ask how my husband is dealing with me being sick. Although every email has a different story or topic they all have a certain tone of sorrow and helplessness to it. Much like Mark has at times. For those of you who know my loud fun loving husband it may seem hard to believe that he could ever feel dispirited or powerless. But that is what cancer can do to a man when he watches his wife battle this monster on her own. It is a demon that can take a perfectly stable family and tear it apart. It is a malignant spirit that can take a strong happy go lucky man and bring him to tears at the site of his wife suffering in pain. It is a brutal beast that can destroy a happy spirit and turn it to the dark side. Cancer in my eyes is as evil as the devil. I will not speak for Mark but I will testify I will not let it tear me or my loved ones apart. I will not let them give in to its affliction.

Of course we both did not want the evening to end because it meant we had to go back to navigating our cancer journey. However, we knew that it was just a fantasy night and reality was through the red door of our home. And as we open it and enter a house of sleeping boys we held hands and felt grateful we had one more night together. Thanks Mark for your romantic side. God knows one of us needs it.

July 28, 2009
Austen Gets It

"Strength does not come from winning. Your struggles develop your strengths. When you go through hardships and decide not to surrender, that is strength."

Sunday was Austen's last tournament baseball game for the summer and I must say he was very sad. Unfortunately, this was not a winning season. For a 12 year old boy who lives and dies sports, winning is everything and losing is not an option. As I wrote in my post about Austen on May 22nd, he is extremely intense when it comes to his passions…baseball being his number one. There are several times when he gets into the car to drive home after a game and he will recount every play of the game to try to figure out why they did not win. Or if it's a win he will spend the ride talking about every great hit or play that helped with the win. He would practice every hour of everyday if we did not redirect him to other things. He begs his brothers to practice with him but they have learned that just leads to him smacking the ball out of the yard into the woods and them chasing after it. They will play for a while and then just walk away as he tries to bribe them into staying. On evenings in the summer you can find Austen, his brothers and the neighbor kids all gathered on the street while Austen tries to convince them to play his sport of choice that evening; all of them knowing that Austen will take over the game. At times I actually worry that maybe he is too intense and needs to take a break. In fact some of his punishments for picking on his brothers or possibly not finishing a chore has been a day without sports. Where other parents are taking away privileges like television, video games or leaving the home, we are taking away his sports equipment and sports privileges. Sounds strange but he straightens up real fast.

As much as he loves his sports is as hard as he is on himself. So Sunday when he lost his last game in my old neighborhood of Greenfield, where actually he played against some of his old friends, he was quite distraught to say the least. He shook hands, listened to the coach's great season speech and off he headed to the car, only to be stopped by a few of his old neighborhood friends. He was asked by his preschool best friend to come over to his home and hang out but Austen would not dare spend the day with someone who just beat him. So in the car he went and sat there until the rest of us where ready to go. When I got in the car to go home after the lost I heard some sniffling coming from the back seat. When I started to lecture him about it's not always about winning (knowing I really deep down don't believe that, but that is what a mother should say) and with all our family is going through you need to think of what is important, he stopped me dead in my tracks. And in his mom you don't know anything voice he said, "It not the losing thing anymore mom, it's the escape I got from you being sick and the cancer shit that I will miss." I ignored the swearing and listened as he added that going to baseball even just batting practice made him feel like we were a normal family without cancer. He explained to me that he loved seeing me taking pictures at his game and cheering him on. He told me that is why every home run he hit this season the ball went to me and that was the way he could make me smile. "Mom you don't smile as much as you use too. You are always in pain and I can't help you. But you smile when I am playing and I love playing." He also said that he will miss playing baseball with his friends because they keep him away from all the crap at home. However, he was upset that a few of his teammates were happy that the season was over, "Mom, can you believe some of them where saying that they were happy baseball was done." Yes I believed it.

He continued on to say that he knows that every time he loses it makes him stronger. He even went as far as comparing it to my journey by saying, "like mom when you have to try a new treatment it may not work but you keep trying something else." I started to cry silently like

I do, but the tears just started rolling. Of course the teenage Austen that has appeared in our family a few months ago came back and he made it quite known that I should stop crying before dad gets in the car by saying, "Awe come on Mom, don't be so cheesy." I knew that meant he was done talking about his feelings and I wiped the tears away quickly.

The whole conversation took less than 5 minutes but it made me realize that he finally gets why I am doing all I can do. There are times when I start to feel bad for my boys. They have not asked nor do they deserve to have a mom with a cancer that is incurable. It is not fair that they have to wait for a baseball game to feel that they have a normal life. Although, I try to hide the pain and sickness that I get from the disease progressing it is inevitable that my boys will see some of my suffering. It saddens me at times that they actually look for days that mom is feeling good so that they can have fun with me. But when I look back at moments like this one in the car I truly appreciate what this cancer has taught my family. It proves that your struggles develop your strengths. And when you go through adversities without giving into them you see your strength. That strength that you get going through those hard times will lead you to being a winner one day. I may not win against this cancer, but I will know that my boys have won from my battle. They have learned that regardless of how you feel inside or how close you are to losing, always try to look like a winner with your appearance and attitude. Even if your circumstance looks hopeless, with faith and confidence you can have a victory. It might not be at a game, but it will be at life.

Austen has won so much more than some dust collecting trophies this past season. He has won friendships that will last a lifetime. The Carney family knows first hand how important that is this time in our lives. He has won endurance to not quit when it looks like the end results are not in your favor; much like the endurance that is needed to fight this cancer. He has won the knowledge that winning does not always mean the score at the end of a game, but the lessons you have learned from losing. He has won by learning that winning is not everything, but the will to win is everything. Mostly, he has won the faith to keep trying and believing that a true winner is one that does not quit.

> *"Strength does not come from winning. Your struggles develop your strengths. When you go through hardships and decide not to surrender that is strength."*

August 6, 2009
Sadness

Sorry for the delay in posts. Thanks for the emails my concerned friends, I was a little under the weather but I am feeling good today.

    I had to post today not for me but for all my friends that are going through some hard times. It seems like the past two weeks I have had so many of my good friends just sad. Not for one particular reason all together but they all seem to be going through something. One friend just had surgery and recovery is slow, one has a broken foot that stubbornly will not heal, one has family issues, one has a dear friend that is ill, one has a child that is ill, one misses a loved one that has passed, one's husband lost his job, one lost her job, one just found out the she is ill and has to live with this condition forever, one has financial struggles, one just feels horrible and does not know why, a few have all the above and the list continues. After each and every conversation I have with them they ended by saying some form of I can't believe I am burdening you with all you have going on. Or I am told that when they start to feel sorry for themselves they think of how positive I am and then they try to snap out of it. Some even ask how I get through each day being so sick and having so many worries. But the one comment that really hits me is, "my problems seem so small compared to what you and your family are going through. How I can complain."

    My answer to that statement is no problem is small if it is something that makes you feel sad or worried. I want my friends to know that I am here for them like they are for me and that I never think of them as being a complainer. I never judge or compare their problems with mine. A person that does that is not a true friend. I am honored that they feel they can come to me and let it all out. I only wish I could help them like they have helped me. I wish I could take their pain away. Please don't feel that because I am going through this journey that I don't feel your pain. That is why I like the saying "If you never jump, you'll never know who is there to catch you." I am here to catch my family and friends if you need to be caught. Please know that my heart aches for each and everyone.

    As I don't compare your strife's and struggles with mine, please don't compare the way I handle my situation. I am asked all the time," how do I get through each day without feeling depressed?." My answer to that is my faith. I will not deny that there are moments and sometimes a day that I am not at my best in positive attitude, but those are the times that many of you don't see. I am determined not to go to the "dark side" with this battle. I know that is what will lead me to a losing battle. However, because I do that and it looks so simple does not mean you are expected to do the same. It's okay to cry, tears lead to rainbows. It's also okay to feel sad or down as long as it does not last to long.

I guess to sum up this post I want all of my family and friends to know that I hurt for you like you hurt for me. But what I have learned through this cancer journey is not to let the hurt take over your life. As I am reminded daily, life is a hour glass where the sand moves quickly. Don't let your sadness take any grain of sand away from you. I believe that dying is not the greatest loss of life but the greatest loss is what dies inside you while you are living. Remember you are not burdening me by coming to me with your problems or worries. I will cry with you, but I will not pity you or let you pity yourself. That is what a true friend does.

August 15, 2009

"The steeper the mountain, the harder the climb, the better the view from the finishing line."

I needed to recite this quote many times this week. It's been a rough week for me and my journey. My oncologist decided to double my monthly treatment and shorten the length in between from every 30 days to every 21 days. Before going to my treatment last week, I convinced Mark to stop at Oakmont Bakery (best bakery in Western Pennsylvania for all those not familiar) and to purchase some tasty treats for all the nurses at the treatment center. I believe I was subconsciously thinking that maybe if I bribe them then they will go easy on the treatments, like they have any control of that anyways. But I told myself out loud it was because they are so kind to me and they deserve to know I appreciate them. However, I was not prepared for how horrible I would be feeling. I am on the upswing now and ready to look at the view soon, although my blood work is still not as high the doctors would like it to be.

This quote was sent to me by a wife of a fellow carcinoid patient. Through my blog I have met and corresponded with several carcinoid patient or their loved ones. I have learned that each and every patient is suffering from the same cancer and struggling with the fact that it is incurable and eventually will end their life. Although, we have this cancer in common each story is unique. Some have been misdiagnosed at first, some are at early stages, some are at the end, some are struggling with the emotional hardship, some are struggling with the financial hardship, some have families, others are single, some have amazing doctors, others are frustrated with the little knowledge that is out there about this cancer, whatever the situation is each one is climbing probably the steepest mountain they will ever climb. The question that I know is being asked by each of us is, "Where is the finish line with the great view?"

I, like many others suffering from a terminal illness, need to know what is the definition of a finish line. Is it getting through a treatment? Is it finding a miracle pill to help you with the side effects of this cancer? Is it being able to just have a good day without having the disease take over? Is it finding a cure? Or is it death? I like to believe it's all the above mentioned. There are times when I see the beauty of the view when I am on the recovery from treatment. The feeling is amazing when you realize you made it through those weeks of misery. There are moments when I reach for a pill or a heated pad just to get some relief and then later realize it worked. There are days that I lay my head down at night and thank God for having a day that cancer does not rule it. Those days are more beautiful than any view I have seen or could ever imagine. Of course finding a cure would be one of the most amazing finish lines to my journey. And if it is death, then my faith has led me to believe that the view from that finish line is beyond anything I could conceive.

What I am trying to express is that going through terminal cancer you will experience many finish lines with amazing views if you define them as you like. Sure death is always in the back of your mind. In fact every minute of every day we are fighting to avoid it. So how can the mind not go to that thought when we talk about finish lines? But it is not the only glorious view if you allow yourself to see the other accomplishments while battling to avoid the final finish line.

So I said the "death" word, the word that no one dares to say to someone in my situation. I will address that word in a later post, but for now I will assure you that I will do all I can to stay away from that finish line. However, when that time is here I am not afraid.

> *"The steeper the mountain, the harder the climb, the better the view from the finishing line."*

※※

August 20, 2009
Wade

Below is an email that was sent to me and I need to share it with everyone. I have been corresponding with this family for a few months and am saddened by the news. I rarely like to post depressing or sad news but my heart is leading me to do this for several reasons.

First, I want to stress the need for more research and education to be dedicated to Carcinoid Cancer. Time and time again when I speak to doctors, foundations and even government officials I am told that this is such a rare cancer that money has to be spent on the more "popular" cancers. Like for any reason we need to describe any cancer as popular. Secondly, I would like to correct the misconception that Carcinoid Cancer is slow going and patients can live for many years with this type of cancer. That may be true for some stages of this cancer, just like breast, lung, liver etc., but in many cases that is not true. I get really frustrated when I hear someone, either a doctor, patient, or just a well intentioned person say, "if you have to get cancer this is the one to get." You can live for up to 5 years with Carcinoid Cancer before it takes your life. Tell that to the family of a 58 year old man who dreams of his future with his wife and first grandchild. Or tell that to my boys who in 5 years from my reoccurrence will be 16, 15, and 14. Tell that to Mark when he is a single father or to the doctor who told me to get my affairs in order because it will take a few months before "it" gets too bad. Next, I want to show that there are many stories that are just as heart aching as mine

Lastly, I want to pay honor a man who was loved so dearly by his wife that she dedicated her life to him. A man after sending 2 boys to college had planned to retire soon and spend time just being a husband and a grandfather with complete satisfaction. To a man that raised his children to be caring individuals who is proven by their career choices as a teacher and nurse. This man fought with all he could against his disease so that he would be around for his first grandson who is due in 4 weeks. Some may say he is just an ordinary man because he was not a famous movie star, well known athlete, well liked professor, famous politician or Nobel Prize winner who died from cancer. But to his wife, two sons, daughter-in-law, soon to be grandson, or anyone else whose life he touched he is a hero; a man that lived with courage and strength. A man that did not give in to this horrific cancer and fought with all he had to the very end. After suffering everyday from this cancer I can rightfully say he is a true hero. Good bye to one of my Carcinoid Posse.

Hi Sunny,

It took me awhile to write you, but felt I needed to, because you have been an inspiration to my husband since he was diagnosed last November.

Unfortunately Wade passed away August 6th, he had undergone only 3 embolization treatments since the beginning, and I did take him to UPMC for a 2nd opinion with Dr. Gamblin. Every CT scan he had was worse than the previous, they finally determined the treatments were not working. His initial CT scan 9 months ago was bad, showed "far advanced metastasis lesions to spleen and liver, too numerous to count, so I really feel this was way too advanced when it was first diagnosed, although those doctors always gave him hope. Wade was 58, his obituary is on the Boylan Funeral Home website(Zelienople, PA) if you ever want to read it. He was a wonderful husband and father. I mentioned the type of cancer in the obituary, because I want to bring this very under diagnosed, under detected cancer to everyone's attention. He fought til the end, and never gave up hope. You need to keep up the fight, and getting the word out on this type of cancer is so important. We never got anywhere else for any other opinions, because Wade was too sick. I just wish they would have discovered this so much sooner, so he would've had a better chance of survival.

I will continue to pray for you and cheer you on to good health. Right now I have to stay off all the cancer websites, its too painful because I miss Wade so much. As I said, I hesitated to write you, because I too hate to mention the "d" word, but I thought I should tell you, because he admired your courage, and he followed your blog faithfully.

God Bless,
Trudy

Chapter 18:
Summer Is Over

"Time is free, but it's priceless. You can't own it, but you can use it. You can't keep it, but you can spend it. Once you've lost it you can never get it back."
~Harvey MacKay

August 26, 2009
School Days, School Days, Good Old School Days
Tuesday came. The day I was dreading all summer……the first day of school.

It became a bitter sweet day for me. On one hand I was so sad to see my babies leave on that school bus. I have always loved summer with the boys. From the first day of school I start looking forward to the last day of school, just like the kids. I was determined to make this summer all about our family. I only had mild treatments so that I was not too ill to do all the fun events I had planned. My doctors were not happy about this but for a few months I decided to choose quality of life over quantity. When I was under the weather I just kept telling myself, "It's for them… SUCK IT UP!" I also made it my mission to have my boys become closer to each other. I know that they wanted some separation at times, which I gave them once in awhile, but as a mother I know that soon they will need each other. So I made them have fun together. Yes made them!!!! There were times when play dates were cut short or we missed a few picnics with family and our friends. I am sorry for that, but this summer I had to make about just the five of us. We slowed down on sports and still were running five to six days a week with that. We only did a few camps and we did not renew our neighborhood pool membership. We just hung together.

I also found ways to back off and have Mark do some of the parenting. He was all for that, but it drove me crazy to lose that control at times. However, I noticed by the end of the summer the boys were going to him more often for help, rides, schedules or questions. It has always been that they would walk right by him to find me to ask where something was, for food or drink, ride to a friends or practice, or just to talk. I used to think that Mark was just invisible to them and only could be seen when it's time for fun or of course money. Actually, that would work for me at times too. Of course I'm joking. I don't want the lecture from him that he did not like that comment on the blog…blah, blah, blah.

I am hoping that they had a great summer despite what they are going through. I know that is why it was hard this year to see them off to school. It feels safe to me, and them, when we are together. Some may say I am being greedy, but I wish I could just keep them by me forever.

On the other hand, I feel a sense of relief and accomplishment today. I have relief that they are now a year older and I am still here. I made it through one more summer and I am still here. I have this urgent need to teach them everything they need to know to be a great asset to society. Things that I would once say, "I'll let go until later" are now important. I know that later is now today. I try hard to be subtle about it but they know that I put them on a fast pass to acceptable behavior and believe in yourself. It's not about having them grow up quickly or anything, it's about teaching them all I need to before it's too late. Teaching them how to love each other unconditionally, how to look on the bright side of life, how to treat others with respect, and to respect themselves. I try to instill faith in God, faith in yourself, faith in your family and faith in those around you. I am determined to have them be the best they can be and follow their dreams despite the difficult ride they are currently on. Sometimes they tell me to stop preaching or lecturing so I lay back a little. But usually they are listening and watching. Watching because I believe my example of living is far more potent than any speech I can give them.

I felt accomplished because they seem to understand more what life is all about. Sure they still have lists of what they want. But on the top of the list now instead of PS3 games or sports equipment there are things like: more time with my dad...my mom to get healthy...my neighbor to have her foot feel better...more time with my grandmother or their uncle. These are things that you cannot buy but make a difference in living a full life.

They did fine this morning but I cried for a while. Isn't that what life is all about. I feel so blessed I am able to see them go to the first day of school one more year.

August 27, 2009
Jen!

After finishing my post today I got on to my emails to find one I knew would be coming but I did not want to open. This post is a follow-up to my July 6th post about my friend Jen.

When my friend Jackie sent me an email to call her, I knew what she had to tell me. Jen has passed. A 37-year-old mother of two has been taken by this horrible disease. After talking to Jackie my mind just started racing. What about her girls ages 7 and 5? What about her husband? What about her mother? What about my friend Jackie who was so close to her? WHY HER? Her husband wrote a small entry in her Caring Bridge Blog to let all who loved her know that she went peacefully surrounded by her family. I must have stared at the computer screen for an hour. The words that he wrote were just blurring together, yet they were going through my head over and over again. How hard it must of been for him to write those few sentences? How numb he must feel?

Mark finally came into my office and saw me sitting there just starring at the computer with tears running down my face. He shook me and yelled in his terrified voice thinking it was something happening to me. I could not help but look at him and feel sorry for him. He may have to write that post one day, too. Mark would not let me read what Jen's husband wrote aloud to him, he just closed my emails. He never knew Jen and never knew Jen's husband of course, yet he felt such a connection with him. One that Jen and I will never feel; only a husband who has a wife with cancer can feel.

I reluctantly decided to read the guest book entries. For those of you who are not familiar with Caring Bridge they have a section where you can send a message to the cancer patient and their family. In the guest book there were several post to Bill, Jen's husband, giving sympathy, reminding him how amazing of a woman she was, how kind she was, how unique she was, and how loved she was. All those things he already knows and I am sure he can add a thousand more to the list. Each entry was from someone who has been touched by Jen sometime in her 37 years of life. I started thinking back to a little over a year ago when Jen called me after she heard the news about my cancer. She told me to fight with all I have and to never give up. She gave me advice on vitamins, foods and even meditation techniques to help me through the stress. She was diagnosed about six months before me with an inoperable brain tumor and she was cheering me on. Amazing! We talked about our kids and how our heart was aching for them. We talked about our husbands and how they were handling the news. We also talked about feeling sorrow for ourselves and how it was a waste of our precious time. Both of us knew that our cancer was serious yet we never felt like death was creeping up on us. We just knew that we were in for the fight of our life.

Jen has lost her battle today…or has she? Maybe God had sent her here for only 37 years to make a difference in everyone's life that she has come across. Maybe she was His special Angel and now her work is done. Jen lived life to fullest and embraced everyday. She was a success in love, as a mother, as a daughter, as a sister, a friend, a lawyer and as an angel. Thank you Jen for being you, I only wish I could have known you like others did.

❧❧

August 31, 2009
Today!
It's a good day because I am part of it. I made it to 39.

❧❧

September 6, 2009
Believe!!!
In the hustle and bustle of everyday sometimes cancer is beyond a burden and more of just something that is with me all the time. It's not like I ever forget that I have it because this devil does not let me forget. You never completely learn to live with it, because it changes your situation everyday. You never get use to it, because who gets use to have a terminal illness that effects everything you do? But it's like something that lingers with you and sometimes you can ignore. Not for long but for a short time. Like an annoying fly at your picnic table when you are eating your favorite grilled burger.

    This is what I am noticing lately. I am finding ways to get relief because I have learned to adjust my life so that cancer does not beat me everyday. Since the boys went back to school it's been particularly hard to handle having this disease. I took a break from my extensive treatments this summer so I can spend quality time with my boys and now it's time to get back to work to fight this horrible attacker that is trying to knock me down. So this week my oncologist and I did our fall game plan to fight full force. Even though my blood levels are not where Dr. Friedland would like them to be I am heavily persuading him to okay me to start the Afinator this week. He has agreed to do so if I promise him to be monitored on a weekly basis and agree to stop the meds if my levels do not go up soon. I will be starting the "Golden

Drug" tomorrow and I have faith that this may be the answer. We are not sure of all the side effects because Afinator was just approved in May for renal cancer, not carcinoid, but I will deal with them when they come. I am also scheduled tomorrow for a few heart tests because Carcinoid has a tendency to damage the heart and I have been having some pain in the chest. I blame it on the kids starting school and the stress of getting back into the ring with cancer. I have a good feeling that the tests will come back okay. Our game plan continues but I don't want to bore anyone with the details because who knows what curve balls this cancer will throw me and then the game plan will need to be rewritten.

The purpose of posting today was not just for updates but was to express what I have learned this past week. In the midst of all the crazy planning for the amazing Wiffle Ball event that will be happening this Sunday and with the meetings for the 5k event on Oct. 18th, I have been able to reminisce about my life just one year ago. I thought about how much anxiety and emptiness I felt back then even with all the love I was receiving. I remember the exact moment I realized that I needed to let it all go and just have faith that it is God's plan. At that moment my battle changed from hopelessness to believing…Believing that what ever happens to me I am blessed to no end. This was my cancer turning point and I decided to enjoy my life and to fight to extend it. I made up my mind then that this evil will not take over the time I have left. This is when I photographed the famous "Believe" photo of me and the boys in the sunset. That photo and that moment have changed my life and my journey.

Although at times my faith may teeter a little I have never lost it completely. It is not just having faith that the cancer will one day be miraculously gone. However, I will take that and do believe it could happen. It's the faith that God will always be by my side during these times of strife. It's believing that I can do any type of risky treatment and the outcome will be what it is supposed to be because He has a hand in it. It's having peace that my children will be taken care of if I am not here or if the day is to come. I have faith that my family is there when I need them or my friends will come when I call. It's believing that I can do the impossible if I have faith that God will lead me to do that. The other day Mark said to me in his joking manner, "you think there is nothing you can't do. You are so full of yourself." In all fairness to him I think I told him I could do his job better than him or something like that. I don't always choose the best ways to motivate him. However, if someone said that to me I would not be joking with an answer back. Mark has a way to just shrug my craziness for perfection off with a good sense a humor. I guess that is why we make a good match. At the time of his comment I laughed and shook my head yes but later that night I realized that it's not me that can do anything…it's God. That is what I think. If you believe that, then you should never worry.

At the end of every service at Unity Church in Plum, Pa, Pastor Frank always says, "You go no place by accident. Where ever you are God is sending you." I like to take that further and say, "Whatever you go through God is right beside you. It's never an accident."

September 17, 2009
Thanks—What a Day

Sunny has had one of those cancer weeks and it has taken the best of her at times. Although I kept insisting that I was doing the follow up entry to the Wiffle Ball event on Sunday, somehow it is already Thursday and the week is almost gone. Let me start by saying Sunday was amazing. Sunny, the boys, and I would like to thank everyone who volunteered their time, contributed goods, participated in the tournament or just simply came to Boyce Park to share in the fun. Putting together a fundraiser for 600 to 1000+ people takes a lot of work and although the end result was Sunday the behind the scenes planning and tasks actually began several months ago.

Before I start with the thank yous we want to give thanks to God for blessing us with Sunny simply being here for the <u>2nd Annual Swing Against Cancer Event</u>. A year ago, neither one of us knew what to expect although we both had faith and the belief that she was going to fight the Carcinoid tumors with everything she has. Also we couldn't have been blessed with a more perfect day weather wise and its obvious that when you turn things over to him there are no better hands to put them in.

We began the serious planning around the fourth of July and right from the beginning my sister-in-law Vicki, Sunny's nephew Ray, cousin JulieAnne, Uncle Tom and Aunt Joan, and our good friends Bill and Lisa, have put up with all of the headaches that accompany pulling a day like Sunday off. (Not to mention some bickering, name-calling, and my occasional "its my way or the highway" outbursts) Thanks for helping us stay the course, never wavering in your commitment to help, and always sharing in Sunny's "We will find a way" attitude. You are all extremely dear to us and I thank you in advance for reenlisting for next year's <u>3rd Annual Take A Swing Against Cancer</u> event.

As the big day approached things really got hectic and yes even a bit stressful. Yet we were once again blessed with more help than we ever could have prayed for or expected. Sunny's brother Michael played the recurring role of Mr. Let Me Handle That Loose End No Problem. Mike I know you do what you do because "hey she is my sister" but I know you have a lot going on, and the kids always enjoy seeing Uncle Mike…so raise the cup, here's a tall cold one for you…thanks.

Sunny's brother Happy and my sister-in-law Sue came all the way in from Cleveland to help and we knew that the money and sign-up responsibilities were in the best of hands. Jimmy, Jesse, and Trish, it was great to see you there selling shirts, beer cups, drawing up brackets, and even playing in the games when needed…thanks. Sunny even mentioned that it would not be perfect if you three did not come and decided to do the college thing instead.

Another nephew HOOPS JJ not only did his best to help out around the chaos when needed, but also brought (dare I say forced) the CMU men's basketball team to once again play in the tournament and although one team got bounced early, the other made it all the way to the semi-finals. Talking to several of them I can tell you that besides being good athletes they are also going to be leaders at whatever they ultimately do in life. Sunny really got a kick out of them and I know when "Coach" showed up later in the day, they sort of felt like extended family from Oakland.

Kelly, the Sultan of Chinese Auctions was incredible once again. We literally threw baskets at her, assorted kites, pictures, balls, food, gift cards, and all of the other donations and never doubted for a minute that at least that part of the day was in the right hands. You are not only a great organizer, but the dedication you exhibited with all of the recent changes in your life was not unappreciated. Thanks. (We will start the bringing the baskets for next years event to your house later this month if you are going to be home.) Once again we managed to have the best Chinese Auction in Plum with all the amazing donations, Dooney Purse (Carrie Lou), Penguin tickets (Jackie and Bobby), Sunny's sisters many baskets, The Ward signed photograph (Fred Gleeson), JROTC's basket (Chelsea Getsy) and even custom art work from the famous Sharon

Mitolo. I cannot forget all the donations that John Cinq got. And of course Ray-Ray, as known by in the crazy Jennings' family, for everything. Too many to list.

DJ Louie entertained all day, put up with my long-winded game break announcements, advertised the next activity/event on the slate all day long and played some great tunes. I saw a lot of butts a shaking and hips a swaying on the field as players waited for their next game. (I hope you didn't blow off to0 much of church to get there as early as you did…thanks a bunch)

Our national anthem never sounded better thanks to Plum's own Brittany…who overcame nerves from singing in front of several hundred people whom she goes to school with and right up in front of her…you knocked them dead…broke a leg…yada yada…whatever the right term is you were awesome…and the kids wanted to call the Hoff to see about getting you on NBC next year.

Finally to all of you that came to play and to just be there to support Sunny, Thanks. A lot of work goes behind TAKE A SWING AGAINST CANCER…but without all of you coming, and being so giving, especially as things can be tough out there, we really, really, really want to hug you all if we could. You are all very special and I only hope that we can give back down the road as much as we have been blessed with.

Sunny wanted me to just do a simple thank you at the risk of leaving someone out…and those of you who know me, know I like to keep things short. But that day meant a lot to us, a lot of memories were made, and a lot of prayers were answered. If I did overlook anyone…please accept my apologies…but rest assured your efforts were not unnoticed, unappreciated, and unrewarded. On Tuesday when Sunny got together with some of her family (one of the many days they are together because there are so many and I can only handle a few at a time) we started to plan next year. But according to Sunny she will be better and it will be for other families suffering. By the way, she has donated a percentage of the proceeds to two other families fighting with Carcinoid Cancer……something not unexpected from her. See you next year. I just know that Sunny will be standing on the field again.

September 18, 2009
David

I am posting today with a heavy heart. It's been a rough cancer week with an amazing event dropped in the middle of it. Thank God for the Wiffle Ball tournament and the beauty of the day because without days like those getting through this journey would be unbearable. By doctor's order I've increased my monthly treatment and it has not been without side effects. Times like these are when this cancer smacks me right in the face. It is a test of my strength and desire to win.

On Friday Sept. 11, I received an email letting me know that one of my Carcinoid Posse had passed away. David Lemmink was a father of four, a husband and son. I started corresponding with his family a few months ago when he was preparing to make the trip to Switzerland for his first treatment. Through email and some phone calls I got to know his wife and mother. David did make one trip to Switzerland but unfortunately did not recover enough to make the second trip. He fought with all he had. He did whatever it took to be here for his children and wife Connie. Below is the post his wife wrote on her blog:

> *Today I post with a heavy heart. David is gone and he is finally pain free. We are so happy for him but mourn his loss. Charlie, Angela, Elisabeth, John and I, along with his whole family, feel his loss deeply.*
>
> *The last 17 months have been difficult. David stoically fought his battle with beauty and grace and we are so proud of him. Maybe someday I will be able to post about the months of August and September. Right now, this is all I have. I am sorry not to be able to do more. It is just too painful, but I am sure you will understand.*
>
> *Thank you all for your loving, ongoing support. We are uplifted by the love of those around us. God truly is good to bring so many loving people into our lives that care for us so beautifully.*
>
> *With all my love,*
> *Connie*

Reading this post is why I am rededicated to make a difference for Carcinoid Patients. From what my doctors are telling me, and telling all Carcinoid Cancer patients, my husband will be writing a post like this one day. My children's names will be listed as loved ones left behind. Raising money is extremely helpful for all of us patients but raising awareness is helpful for us and future patients.

After reading my post today some of you will cry for Connie and her family, some will say a pray for them and others will think about them for the rest of the day…she thanks you for that. However, you will finish your work and chores for the day, lay your head down at night and wake up tomorrow to start your day over again. Connie and her children's life will never be the same.

I promise you my next post will be all about butterflies and sunshine, but it would be unjust of me if I don't give my blog readers reality once in a while. And reality is this cancer has no cure and eventually takes every one's life.

September 19, 2009
He Turns 13!
I am here for my oldest to turn 13.

Austen, may you live all the days of your life. I am so proud of you. You have made my life perfect.

You are my sonshine,
Mommy

Chapter 19:
And the Cancer Continues

"Beginning is easy - continuing hard"
Japanese Proverb quotes

Update on the Next Step

It's been awhile since I have updated everyone on my next steps to save my life or as Doc says, "prolong my life," so I thought I would tell you the game plan…subject to change at anytime. I guess the doc has not given in to my begging to just make this monster go away so here is how we are going to keep it under control. After waiting for months for my blood levels to rise I have gotten the okay to start the Afinator. That is the golden radiation/chemo pill that was approved in May for renal cancer. There are some clinical trials going on right now that have shown some positive feedback for Carcinoid Cancer. I was not qualified for the clinical trial so I decided to start my own experiment. Sounds crazy but when death is your other option, what can it hurt? So Monday I will take the first $500 dose. I think I may drink a small glass of champagne with it just to get in the expensive spirit. This drug will be my caviar.

Then on October 1st I will receive my first IV dose of a bone medicine to help strengthen and reverse the damage the cancer is doing to them. I am told the side effects are less but once again there is no precedent for carcinoid patients so we will wait and see. I joked with my doc at the last appointment, but really deep down meant it, that all this first ever I am experiencing better be written down in some journal so that no other carcinoid patient has to wait and see how they react. I'll bite the bullet for the rest but it is my doctor's obligation to spread the word.

Off my soap box so that I can continue. I had planned or hoped that I would have my trip to Switzerland in November but because of my blood counts that is not possible. So I am looking at another January in Basel. I am anxious to get it done, I am told that there is a fine window as to when the best time is for my body. If I go too early it will not work, if I wait too long though it will be too late. So I am just praying God let's me know when and then Dr. Mueller okays it fast. All I can do it stay on top of it and let God do the rest.

In the meantime, I am planning a trip to New York City to see the grandfather of Carcinoid Cancer, Dr. Richard Warren. Hoping that he tells me that I am going down the right road or leads me down the right road if I am lost.

Later in the future if none of these efforts work then we are going to be forced to try massive amounts of chemo. Which has not been too successful but it's all worth the try.

I have not given up hope. Since last May, Afinator has been approved and other meds are being tested. I just need to hold on until that magic cure comes.

September 24, 2009
Dr. Richard Raizman

It seems like in the recent few weeks I have been bombed with news of my fellow Carcinoid posse passing. Today I received the news that the doctor who got me to Switzerland has passed from Carcinoid Cancer. He was passionate about finding a cure and bringing the Y90 treatment to the United States. He was in the process of getting a Carcinoid Cancer Center started here in Pittsburgh which he was funding himself. I have emailed or called him multiple times for just some words of advice. No longer than an hour would it take him to get back to me with his words of wisdom spoken at my level. He has made a difference in mine and many patients care. He was a humble man. I did not realize what he has done not just for the very disease he suffered with but for all cancers until I read about him below. When I met with him for the first time last summer he was so positive and he was suffering just like me. I remember him telling me, "you have to do whatever it takes to stay alive for your boys. The longer you hold on the closer you will get to a cure." "I will never give up," he forcefully told me. He fought to the very end. Please read about him below:

Dr. Richard E. Raizman, of Ligonier, passed away early Tuesday morning, Sept. 22, 2009, after a long and valiant battle with cancer. Dr. Raizman, a gastroenterologist, loved his work and his patients. He loved his family, his daughter, Dr. Emma J. Raizman; his son, Dr. Noah M. Raizman and his wife of 42 years, Dorothy L. Raizman, all of whom were with him at home when he died. Many knew he was never still, always looking for new challenges. He traveled to Bhutan to trek and to India to volunteer his medical knowledge to treat Tibetan refugees in Daram Sala, forming a deep friendship with Dr. Setan Sadutchan, the Dalai Llama's personal physician. On one of his many trips there, he took his children to work with these wonderful people. A graduate of Columbia University and the University of Pittsburgh School of Medicine, he felt strongly that a good life was made better by sharing. He established a scholarship at the medical school, as well as funding a vaccine research laboratory. On his death from neuroendocrine cancer he completes the funding of a neuroendocrine cancer research center that he hoped would help others fight the disease that took his life. He was a member of the Board of Friends of the University of Pittsburgh Medical School, an honor he cherished, as well as being a clinical professor of medicine who taught surgical residents the art of endoscopy. He was an innovator. Along with his friend, Dr. Frank Costa, he developed one of the first out-patient surgical centers in Western Pennsylvania. He was both a polo player and fox hunter. As captain of the Ligonier polo team he created "Polo for the Cure," which over the last 17 years generated more than one million dollars for the Leukemia and Lymphoma Society of Western Pennsylvania. He was named a Master of Foxhounds of the Rolling Rock Hunt, where he had been a member since 1983. He rode to the hunt with his friends, Fritz Teroerde, Dr. John Frazier and Wil Burkland. He is survived by his wife and children as well as his beloved brother, David Seth Raizman, PhD., Head of the Art History Department at Drexel University.

October 2, 2009
Prayers Please

Well I've been postponing this post because I have been hoping to give some inspiring and good news. However with this disease we can never tell when the demon is going to start trying to take over again. For the past 2½ weeks I have been in some tremendous pain in my right leg. Even though I have a few tumors in that leg I really just thought that it would get better. In the past few days it become unbearable, to the point were I could not walk. I had an appointment already scheduled for yesterday to receive my first dose of a new med that is supposed to strengthen the bones, ironic. I actually was not even going to mention the leg pain, because I am always in some pain, but when Dr. Friedland ask me to get up on the table he saw the look of horror in my eyes. To me that high examining table looked like Mt. Everest. Dr. Friendland was in shock that I was not going to tell him after he had to watch Mark lift me on to the table. I guess somewhere deep in my mind I new exactly what was going on and just wanted to stuff it deep down.

It is Dr. Friedland's assumption the cancer has spread pretty quickly in my right leg bones. He wanted to send me immediately to radiation therapy but I panicked. For many reason I am terrified of direct radiation. I need to do some research before I do anything and fifteen minutes is not quite enough time to prepare myself. So he decided to give me an MRI and confirm what we all know is going on. It is Dr. Friedland's style to put the patient at ease before he puts them through hell. In all seriousness, he really does try to make you feel good about every decision of treatment. After waiting an hour for the poor nurse to call every hospital in the UPMC umbrella we were unable to find an available MRI machine ASAP. So we decided to cancel the radiation that was schedule and go home. Today I will be getting my 90 minute MRI and Monday if the results show necessary I will get my first treatment of direct radiation.

I was actually thanking God that there were no MRI's available at the time because I was so overwhelmed, not to mention Mark was on the verge of taking a bridge. I always try to clarify that I truly believe it is harder for the loves ones of a cancer patient than it is for the patient themselves. I still believe that with all my heart, but yesterday I was being selfish. I was so angry that he was frustrated. I felt such a helplessness and complete loss of control. He was upset that our appointment was at 9:30 and we were not seen until 11:30…pissed off that I would not sit in a wheelchair and then when I finally gave into the wheelchair complaining that the handle was to low for him to push it…frustrated with the whole hospital monopoly because we waited an hour and still had no MRI done…annoyed that his phone was ringing continuously with client calls and he cannot pick them up to make some money and then completely angry at me because I insisted on going to Austen's open house last night even after the doctor suggested I just stay in bed and rest. If you know me I refuse to miss my kids' important activities if there is anyway possible I can make it. If I had to crawl I would of been there because Austen made it clear that it was important for him that I don't let Dad go alone. When we got home all hell broke loose when Logan decided to tell us, with his "I don't care attitude," that he forgot a book he needed to study with for a test he had today. I thought at that moment Mark was just going to blow his lid.

This is just a small example of what cancer can do to a family. In just one day it can completely put your home in shambles. The cancer tsunami: in an instant this monster can rip all sense of hope and happiness… If you decide to let it take over. Cancer can take a happy, go lucky, jolly man and turn him into a panicked stranger…if you decide to let it take over. It can take three respectful, amazing, smart, straight A children and turn them into a walking mess…if you decide to let it take over. However, I am not going to let it take over. I am not going to let my family fall apart. My boys will not feel guilt about their mom being sick even when they make a mistake. I refuse to let this monster win.

This week I have been tested. I have had some quiet meltdowns where the tears fell. I had some times anger—at the cancer, at the doctors, at the nurses, at myself, and at my husband. I had a time of frustration that I am unable to do what a mother is supposed to do. All the things I complained about for years before hit with the cancer card…cleaning, laundry, chauffeuring and helping with homework. I even had a time of envy at Mark because he is starting to get the hang of being both a mom and a dad. But, what I refuse to have is a time where I lose hope because that is when this disease has won.

We have hit a road bump which will slow me down a bit, but I promise you it will not become a road block. I will get through this and I will help Mark get through this too. We are resilient and will not let this beast take over our family spirit. However, we know that we cannot do any of this fight without God.

I will fill you in on the results soon.

October 6, 2009
Next Step!

Mark and I have seen enough hospitals, waiting rooms, scan centers and doctors in the past 5 days than I had when I was actually in the hospital. After hearing the news on Thursday (in previous post) I was ordered to receive an MRI of the hip and femur on Friday. I was told that the total time in the MRI tube with a padded weight holding down my hips would be a total of 40 minutes. After about 3 minutes the pain was so bad I felt like I was going to rip my eyes out. But being the stubborn Irish girl I am I said not one word to the tech doing the scan and decide to suck it up. After all, I thought that I only had 37 minutes to go. I have learned in the past year that with bone tumors the pain can get so intense that I actually go to a whole new level of meditation. Not like the Yoga classes I miss so much, but more like an outer body meditation. As I was listening to my favorite station with the headset that the tech was nice enough to give me, I heard the disc jockey (if that is what they are still called) announce a 50 minute music hour. So of course I knew I would be done before the commercial came on. However, I ended up staying in the tube for over two 50 minute music hours. Yes 2½ hours and all I could think about was that Mark is probably freaking out. The pain was so incredible before I got out of that @#$% tube my shirt was completely wet from my tears. The whole meditation thing was thrown about the first half hour. Apparently, the radiologist wanted to make sure he had every single view because he was in awe at the number of tumors for my type of cancer. It is very unusual for carcinoid cancer to spread to the bones. Great, once again I am the freak show that doctors have never seen. Ever since I was a little girl I loved being different and refused to conform to the normal society. Being a teenager in the 80's I had to work really hard to actually stand out. In the era of neon clothes and mohawks different was actually normal. Never did I know that cancer would make that so easy.

When I got home I had an email from Dr. Friedland. He had already checked my scans and informed me that Dr. MGough, an orthopedic oncologist, will be calling me immediately to talk to me. I could tell in the tone of the email that things were not good. However, I think I knew that already when I saw tears in the tech's eyes when she finally freed me from the tube. After talking to Dr. MGough's office, not Dr. MGough, I decided to put all this news aside and wait until my appointment Monday morning, as soon as I can get there. The weekend was great because I knew that Monday was coming quick with a not so positive experience so I savored every minute with Mark and the boys. That's the "Good in Cancer," you sometimes have the advantage of knowing that the days to come are going to be tough so you can appreciate the simple times before hand.

Yesterday came and the news was just what we prepared for. The cancer has spread more in the right leg and moved to the left leg. The scans showed that my bones in the right leg are becoming unstable and brittle. Not as bad as the doctor would of thought with the amount of tumors have grown but still a concern. I guess being forced to drink milk as a child finally paid off a bit. So with that he gave me two alternatives…neither sound like a party. Both options are serious enough to rightfully obtain a second opinion. But as of now this is what I have:

1. The first option will be to have a surgery that will stabilize the bone. The doctor will insert a metal rod in the femur bone. While in there he will try to reduce some of the tumors depending on the mass of the tumor. I will then start immediate radiation. There are several risks for this surgery for me. One main risk being that the fatty acids that fill the bone will be released and fill the lung. Only having one lung would be at a risk of death if this happens. However, if this bone breaks I could risk death as well.

2. The second option is to do radiation first to take care of the pain then do the surgery to stabilize the bone. There are several risk to that as well. The main risk is that the radiation does not work and the bone becomes weaker.

I did schedule the surgery for the end of October even though the doctor wanted sooner. I really just need to think about this all and get a second opinion. Of course I would not do any of this without hours of research.

Nevertheless, I will keep my faith. I am determined to do whatever it takes to be here as long as I can.

October 8, 2009
My Gift

Today a stranger went into my doctor's office and left me a gift. I want that person to know that it meant more to me and my family than he could ever imagine. I don't know your name or even if you want me to know, but I want to tell you that your thoughtfulness has made a difference. Thank you from the bottom of my heart. I always say I wish there was a better way to say it then those two simple words.

> "To give to others and then not feel that you have given is truly the best gift of all."

Chapter 20:
It's All Good

October 10, 2009
Polish the Dull Side

"If you can't see the bright side of life, then polish the dull side"

I heard this quote from my friend Debbie. She is a mother of a three year old little girl that is not just a toddler but a cancer survivor. Although, I knew her story when her family was fighting this battle I did not know her personally. When I had my relapse Debbie reached out to me. We connected immediately. When I heard this quote from her I knew exactly why we connected. She has taken the most unimaginable situation and polished it. She has seen the "Good in Cancer." Her daughter is the light of so many worlds. This three year old little girl has beat all odds and is truly an inspiration to so many. Especially me. She is God's gift.

So many of us go through trials and it is nearly impossible to find the bright side of life. I have been there too. That is when it is time for us to start making the best out of a bad situation. I have realized when you do that you can polish a beautiful gem of a life. And once a dull dirty gem is bright it is priceless. Much like Debbie's daughter Ella. I am asked many times how I don't just give up. The only way I can answer that is, "if I quit then I will miss all the good that is to come."

Let's all polish the dull side of our difficulties this week. I think if we do that we will see that it may just become the bright side again. I know that it has worked for me.

October 21, 2009
My Observations

So today I had a bone scan. Out of all the scans this one is the most pleasant. I can't believe I just used the adjective pleasant to describe a scan. It must be the drugs. But really with all the scans I have gotten in the last few months let alone the last year this one gets a B+. I arrive at 9:30 A.M. where I waited. I am then shuffled to another room where I waited. Then a tech (usually one of "my boys" as I like to call my handsome studs that scan me for all the odd ball scans I need to get) injects me with some type of radiation thing. I wait three hours for it to get to the bones or kill me whatever comes first. Then the scan begins. You are told it takes about 30 minutes but for me it always takes over an hour or so because of the number of metes (never got why they call tumors metes) that I have.

Today I decided to observe some of the things that are going around me in a room full of cancer patients waiting to hear their destiny. Mark, was cracking up at me because I was sitting with my little "notebook" laptop jotting down everything I saw. He leaned into me and whispered, "you always come in here with blinders on. Now what are you doing?" I told him I was living. I am no longer ignoring what is going on in this world of cancer.

This is what I observed:

1. Rude secretary completely clueless that each person she is snapping at have so much more going on in their life than hating there job. God help her.

2. Worried elderly lady holding her husband's hand as he sits in a wheelchair with an IV in his arm and a smile on his face. She is thinking of her future without him, he is looking at the young Drug rep sitting across from him that is wearing a short skirt and sitting with her legs uncrossed. Sorry Mark pointed that one out to me.

3. Mother and Daughter sitting very close to each other while surfing the web for wedding gowns. Mother wearing a beautiful red scarf on her hairless head and daughter hugging her so tight. They are so happy despite the battle.

4. Mark sitting next to me telling dirty jokes to another elderly man. The man is laughing so hard I am scared he is going to fall off his seat. However, the snotty lady in the J. Crew cashmere sweater, I know that because I just got the catalog yesterday, is giving Mark looks that are dirtier than his jokes. "Get a life lady." I just smiled at her and she looked the other way. She must waiting for someone because she's too mean to have cancer.

5. Several names being called out at one time by the mean secretary. The patient jumps up with excitement because it's finally their turn. They quickly lose that excitement when they are asked to stand in line and then follow the nurse into another room to be injected. Like a group of cattle being herded to the next step of their fate. I've been there, done that.

6. Automatic doors opening and closing with patients and their cancer buddies coming and going. Coming with anxiety and leaving with exhaustion.

7. Three televisions in three different corners of the large pen all with different stations and volume turned down. WTF are they doing to these patients….just teasing them. I decided to walk over to one and turn the volume up. Now I see a bunch of happy faces.

8. A husband and wife dressed in designer clothes sitting prim and proper. They are not wanting to look around for fear of what they may see. They are also afraid to get comfortable because they think that they don't belong here. Probably cancer newbies. Reminds me of Mark and I way back when. Not sure which one has the affliction. I would like to see them a few months from now to see how they change.

9. A young girl with a beautiful face but tears in her eyes. She is bald and scared. She is sitting next to me all by herself. I decided to reach over and tell her it will be okay. She puts her hand on my arm and shakes her head. Me in 1995.

10. Oh my favorite nurse just walked in. She has that smile of peace on her face. She shoos Mark to the next seat and sits down next to me to give me a hug. I pull out the big bag of lemon candies that I bring for her other patients. With Hillman's cut backs they discontinued that treat for the chemo patients who have mouth sores. She sneaks the bag in her lab coat like it's a drug deal or something. We laugh.

11. That same nurse moves down next to the young girl who is next to me. She starts to explain the scan to her. I am so relieved that this girl has her today. However, I want her too.

12. A middle age man, okay my age, sits across from me with his brother. He is wearing a black Under Armor running suit. He is fit and looks perfectly healthy. He is drinking that nasty crap they make us drink for some kind of scan that I try to forget. I am lucky that I am small so I only have to drink two bottles…he has three, yuk. He is making faces and gaging. His brother is laughing, but I can see the pain in his eyes. It's that kind of laugh that you get when you are really nervous and don't know what else to do. He asked me if I have ever had to drink it. I shake my head yes. Mark adds, "They should serve it with Jim Beam." God sometimes he is so embarrassing…he got a big laugh today. I told the gentleman to hold his nose and just suck it down. He tries and spits it all over his black jacket. Oh well! Mean secretary is coming over. Oh no!!!!

13. A family of brothers and sisters from Ohio. I know that because they asked the brothers across from me how to get on the PA turnpike and conversation went on. They are sitting close while they take turns pacing back and forth. Each one of them catering to their mothers every need. One brings her a snack, another a drink, another holds her hand,

while the youngest boy hands her a magazine. She hands him back the magazine and tells him it's from May of 2007. He apologizes and tells her he will go to the news stand outside to get her another one. He wants out, but buddy there are no news stands outside. Kinda of cool to listen to the stories. Their mother looks tired and worn out but she is happy to have her kids with her.

My name is being called. It's time for me to get herded with the rest of my cancer posse to the next room…to wait.

To Be Continued for another day.

October 25, 2009
Faith

When you are down to nothing…God is up to something. Faith sees the invisible, believes in the incredible, and receives the impossible. Have faith that God is walking with you and see what amazing things can happen.

November 1, 2009
Heartache

Sometimes I wish I had all the answers to all the heartaches, but all I have is faith. On Tuesday, October 26th a family of a wife, a son and a daughter and dear friends of our family experienced the worst heartache they may every have with the lost of their husband and father. Bob Sovak was a dear friend to our family and to many. His son Justin is one of my son's, Austen, best friends. Bob has always been an amazing influence to Austen. Through my illness Bob has been like a second father to Austen. He took Austen to his first Penguin game and many after that, including the playoffs. He treated Austen like a second son when Austen really needed it. He has taken both Austen and Mark to Steelers' games when they both needed a break. It seems like he would call at the most perfect times through my illness to offer them a night out.

Although the above mentioned sounds like he was a great man, more than that he was a great father. The hurt in his wife's and children's eyes told it all. I wanted to take all their pain away but I realized that is impossible. All I keep thinking is that death leaves a heartache that no one or no action can heal. However the love you have for that person that is gone leaves memories that no one can every steal. Memories that they will cherish until they meet again.

This all brings up the question I have written about so many times…WHY? I am wondering when I will know the answer to why a twelve year old little boy and an eight year old little girl have to feel this pain. Or why a family that has given to so many has to suffer so much. Or why a wife who has been a dear friend to me in my lowest times deserves this loss. When will I get my answers…maybe I should stop asking.

I read this quote in a book that I read to my boys when we lost a dear family member almost two years ago. I wrote it down in my journal even before the cancer returned. I don't know why but it just stuck in my mind and I wanted to remember it. It goes like this:

> *Perhaps they are not stars, but rather openings in heaven where the love of our lost ones pours through and shines down upon us to let us know they are happy.*

I know that Bob is in a better place (I really hate that cliché but it is so true) and I know his wife believes that too. But how is knowing that going to take the pain away from the love ones left behind? I wish I knew just that and then I will stop asking.

Chapter 21:
Don't Let the Sun Go Down

"Some painters transform the sun into a yellow spot, others transform a yellow spot into the sun."~Pablo Picasso

November 12, 2009

Thank you for all the emails and calls. Your concern about my lack of blogging is very touching. I got a kick in the butt today and back at my writing I am.

I have had a difficult week and today Mark decided to give me an intervention to snap me out of the funk I have been spiraling down too. The role reversal of Mark giving me the intervention was quite humbling. The motivational words that were coming out of his mouth were way too familiar. All they way down to actually bullet pointing exact situations to prove his theory that I am slipping into the "dark side" of cancer. He did not pull out the white board and pointer like I have done with him but I think if he knew where I hid it he may have. As he was speaking I can see the wheels in his head turning trying to actually remember my exact words when he is the subject of concern. I realize now that the blank look in his eyes after a few minutes of me having my pump-up meetings with him was him not showing disinterest but him really taking mental notes.

As Mark was talking it clicked to me that my attitude about this disease and the way I choose to battle it affects everyone that I have a relationship with. We have had a few uncharacteristic incidents with one of our children. So this morning Mark and I were summoned to the principal's office where the main topic was this child. I said to one of the many adults in the room, "let's get to the root of the issue" because it just could not be about his mom having cancer. "When did you notice a change?" I asked. She told us almost two weeks ago. So after coming up with some solutions with the group on how to "fix" my already perfect child I decided think back to what went on in our life two weeks ago. On the ride home from our son's school I went over every situation that could have been the root of my son's change in perspective. I started rattling off doctor's appointments, scans, results of scans, death of a friend, my unexpected trip to the emergency room and even rambled about running out of bread and cereal. Finally, Mark looked at me and said, "YOU have changed. Your attitude has changed. Your ambition has changed. Your smile has gone away. Your laugh is not as loud. Your hard work ethic is falling. Your eyes are sad. You are not the Sunny that we all know."

He continued to list things that I would have never let fall by the way side no matter how sick I was. The one that hit me the most was telling me that I am letting go of my passion to beat this cancer. As tears filled my eyes I knew deep down he was right. I've been letting cancer define who I am. When I was told of my relapse I decided to do whatever I could not to let people look at me and see cancer. I would not and still don't accept pity or someone feeling sorry for me. Cancer is part of me but it is not who I am and it does not define what I can do. However, I am afraid that in the past few weeks cancer has beaten me down. I have become tired…too tired to fight. That attitude change has changed the whole dynamics of our family. A change I am not willing to accept until I cannot do anything about it.

I have not given up and will never give up. All the same, I have not been the fighter I usually am and it has affected those around me. I don't think in our 15 years of marriage Mark has ever had to tell me not to give up on anything…until today. He told me that it's always been a given in our family that I am the rock that motivates the rest and when the rock stops being hard the whole mountain falls. With this realization I have learned that my action on how I handle this cancer will teach all those important to me how to fight any obstacle that comes their way. Mark, my boys, my family and my friends will feed from my attitude. If I want them to look at me with hope and not pity then I need to act like I have hope and not fear. My son told me this evening that he knows I am getting sicker and he is scared. I can only think that my action in the past two weeks have made him feel that way. All I can do is go forward and let my strength shine on him. No storm is a match for a "Sunny" attitude. So the fight continues.

November 13, 2009
Two Posts in a Row

So I am told I have to make up for some missing posts. I cannot believe how yesterday's post got so much attention. First, I will confirm I will NEVER give up. I have six little blues eyes watching every way I handle this journey. I made a promise to them and their dad that I will fight as long as God wants me too. However, I guess I needed a reminder of that promise I made. And when I saw two out of the six eyes full of fear and tears I knew that my example was not the best.

One particular email I received today stood out. It was from a cancer survivor that reads my blog. She is waiting for results from a biopsy that her son just had and she is fearful of the outcome. She said that she needs to know the Sunny side of waiting. It brought me back to when waiting for results would overcome my life. I used to pace and pace for days carrying my phone around with me everywhere I went just in case the doctor called. The anxiety of the results would overcome me and my life. I don't do that anymore. I don't let it consume me because I realized that would mean that the cancer is winning. It is affecting me both physically and mentally, which is giving it more power than it deserves.

After reading her amazing email I thought about what I could say to her to let her anxieties not take over her life. All that came to my mind was have faith. Faith that whatever the outcome may be, you are not alone. We must worry about what you can control and let God handle the rest. Do not allow the cancer demons take anymore time away from you then it has to. When you offer it up to Him and Him alone, you get a whole new sense of peace. A peace that I have never felt until I decided to give it to Him and let Him take a hold of the wheel. Let go of trying to control the situation and let God do what he has promised us he will do. Do what ever you are able to do to help the situation then let go of the worry. Sounds easy right! Well it is.

I try very hard to live up to what I say. In fact Mark has at times told me that he wished I would worry just a little bit more about my cancer future. And there have been times when I catch myself trying to play God and control a situation. The famous comment someone says to you when you are finding things difficult is "God never gives you what you cannot handle." Well there are times when I wish God would stop thinking so highly of me. I want to just shout out as loud as I can, "God I am really not that strong….take this back please." However I know that my faith will not let me fail. Faith that I can handle what ever comes my way is what gives me the strength to hold on. Having true faith means you no longer need to have a sense of control over things that our out of your control. You lose worry and gain the greatest sense of strength and calmness.

There are times when I just felt like becoming a turtle and crawling in my shell. I have also had times when I thought it would be a lot easier if I just take a break from the fight for a while. I have become tired and weary so I just want to sleep. But I refuse to lose my faith. Faith gives me the courage to let go and see what God can do. I am not saying that because I have faith God will give me a miracle and cure me. However, I do believe it could happen. But my faith is simpler than that. It knows that while I am climbing this mountain God is right next to me holding my hand. I have seen some amazing things happen because of letting go and letting God take a hold of the situation. And when I feel that faith failing I then pray and God puts someone in my life to bring it back. Yesterday it was Mark. Today it was all the emails, text messages and phone calls I received.

What I am trying to express in this post and to my friend is let it go. Let your faith believe that whatever the result outcome is with Him you can get through it. Then go to the edge of the "faith mountain" and take the leap. I will guarantee you God will be there to catch you.

November 16, 2009
Peacemaker

I have a doctor's appointment today and my laptop has a virus so I am going to do a quick post before I go. I have to write today because I heard an amazing message at church yesterday and I don't want to forget it. Do you know how you wake up on a Sunday morning and find it so easy to just go back to bed instead of going to church? That is how I felt yesterday. The night before I was up with one of my boys most of the night. Yes I know they are tweens but they do have nights where they cannot sleep. Their minds start racing back and forth with the what if question that none of us have the answers to. When your family is fighting cancer there are many sleepless nights of worry and that is when I become a mom and not a cancer patient. However, when a cancer patient does not get enough sleep their whole body shuts down. I was feeling just crappy and did not think I was going to make it to church. Although, as I laid there I just had this feeling that I needed to hear the message. So this is when I reached deep down inside me and pulled out something to get me up and going.

I tried every excuse though not to go. I thought, "If Mark and the boys fight me about church this morning, what they are wearing or slowly get ready…I am just going to give in and go back to bed." But for the first time since Mother's Day, because that day I asked to go to church without any arguments and arrive on time for my gift, they just got up and got dressed. "Darn" I thought, "I guess I cannot use their behavior as an excuse not to go." We actually arrived one minute late which is about 10 minutes early for the Carney Clan. There were no arguments in the extended SUV as to where they where going to sit (which I will never understand anyways because I sat on the arm rest while my other siblings piled in a small car when I was growing up. My boys have a three rows of the finest Italian leather their little butts deserve with headsets to watch a movie. Any seat to me in this automobile looks like luxury. So I figured I was meant to hear Pastor Frank's message since with God's grace my family was the perfect church goers this week.

For the past eight weeks we have been studying the Beatitudes. Yesterday was, "Blessed are the peacemakers" Mathew 5:9. I sat there with one of my three boys on each side of me and decided that this message would be for them. Case in point is that even in church they need to be separated. After all, I know what a peacemaker is because I have three boys, a feisty husband and the youngest of a big family. I've been a peacemaker all my life…so I thought.

After listening more intently I learned what it really means to be a peacemaker. Being a peacemaker is more than just resolving conflict. It's about giving others actual peace when they are going through a battle that you have already experienced. It is the choice of sharing your experiences with others so that it is easier for them. God wants us to be a person who shares hope. As believers we are obligated to be an example to others and be there for others. "Two people are better than one. If one falls down the other can help them up. But it is bad for the person who is alone and falls because no one is there to help." Ecclesiastes 4:9-10

This message helped me understand, somewhat, the answer to the question that we all ask when we go through difficult times…WHY? In my words the answer is: only God knows. I never believed that God gives us evil or hardships because of our actions in the past. But what I learned is that God may let them happen so that we can turn to him and help others turn to him. We need to live through our tragedies so that we can help others get through their tragedies and turn them to faith. Sometimes we don't know that we need God until that's all we have left. Then with our faith we may crawl to him and He then takes over. That is when we see it is never too late to turn to God, but the earlier the better because your pain is less.

We are then to use our brokenness to help others so that they can experience our peace. This is what I want to do with my blog. I want others to learn from what took me so long to learn. It may be with different treatments, new information on this rare cancer I have found or my experiences through this journey. Or I may just inspire one or two of my blog family to not give in to their burdens or give them up to Him. He is waiting for us all to do that. Whatever we all are going through it is tough and I want others to have peace. After all, everyone has their own cancers.

November 24, 2009
The Trip

We are so blessed to have the opportunity to spend Thanksgiving in the Sunshine state of Florida year after year with my family. Unlike most we now enjoy the 20 hour drive just as much as we enjoy our time on the beach. Being trapped in a SUV forces us to focus on spending some quality time with each as well as enjoy the sites on the way. Now that the boys are getting older they do more sleeping than anything else, even more than the "he's looking out my window" arguments. One thing that we do have that I think is so special, but the boys would be so embarrassed that I mention, is our love for the same music. We have a secret love for some of the same artists and bands which we crank up and sing too. I say secret because the boys don't want to admit they actually like the same music as their parents. Of course we each have our favorite type of music but some that are amongst the favorite are U2, Alman Brothers, The Beach Boys, Grateful Dead, Bruce Springsteen and so many more. With the cancer stress and anxiety in our lives music has always been our refuge. Our group is not anything anyone wants to hear nor would my boys ever admit they enjoy actually singing with their family in the car, but to us it is what connects us.

As Mark and the boys belted off U2's finest, "It's a Beautiful Day," I could not help but think what a beautiful day and everyday is if you make the choice to live it to the fullest. The drive to Florida is like second nature to me. I have been on this route at least twice a year ever since I was a little girl. Florida was my father's haven and wanted it to be a haven for his children too. Each road stop, mountain stop or tourist trap has some kind of fun memory. I can still hear my father's voice when we drive through the West Virginia and Virginia mountains that he loved so much. His words, "this is heaven on earth," still ring in my head every time we hit that spot on the trip. In fact, I even repeated it to the boys this time. They gave me the same reaction I gave my dad, "you got to be kidding me. This is all heaven has?" But now I get what he was saying. This whole experience is pure pleasure if you let it be.

As I sat in the front seat and looked out to the most amazing sky I realized that just two years ago I was wishing I was almost to our destination. I did not know then what cancer was going to teach me now. In fact I remember that each of us had our own headset playing our music of choice while we tried to block out Mark's 80's rock. The only communication we would have with each other would be them asking me to pass them some food, them asking Mark the famous, "how much longer?" question, or an occasional "he's touching me." Now we actually talk about things…things that matter, things that don't matter, or the beauty of the sites. We even nicknamed our youngest "Cliff Claven" because he gives us some odd fact every hour or so. He is so funny when he is trying to be serious. He is Mark all over. It sounds like this car ride is a perfect "Hallmark" movie special. Well I will tell you it's not anywhere near perfect. However, to me it's "heaven on earth."

After the song ended Mark turned down the stereo a little before the next track began. He reached over and grabbed my hand. He could see that I was not feeling well and he told me that he would pull over when I needed him to. I told him that I was perfect and that I am enjoying every minute of this day. He assured me that he was not rushing and we can take our time to get to Vero. In my joking manner but I was truly serious I said, "let's take our time forever. When you have what I have there is no need to rush to get where I am going". Unaware that Logan, my middle son, was listening we heard him chime in. With a very low tone, so low we could hardly hear him he whispered, "I wish I could stop time for you Mom." Although that moment was precious it was broken with his older brother comment calling him a dork. Then a shut up followed and a you shut up after that. That is when we knew that life was normal again. Realizing how special simple times are is a gift that cancer has given me. Another "GOOD" in cancer I found just riding in a car.

P.S. Along with spending Thanksgiving with my family, this trip was also planned to fight this incurable cancer. Next week I will be seeing another carcinoid cancer guru in Tampa FL. Please keep me in your prayers.

November 25, 2009
Mark's Birthday
Happy Birthday to my dear hubby, Mark. May we have many more together.

Your Sunshine

December 1, 2009
Sunrise
It is no secret to anyone who knows me, especially Mark and the boys, that I love sunrises. Every morning when I am in Vero Beach, FL I awake well before 6 am to guarantee I am at the beach, camera in hand, plopped on my blanket ready for the magnificent site of a new day starting. I start my recruiting the night before to see who will trug along with me. Since my walking has been a bit shaky lately and my leg pain

has increased Mark has made me promise to not go to the beach alone when it is still dark. However, I did sneak out one day this week and it was well worth the argument when I got back. There is not a moment more peaceful than sitting on a beach when it is still slightly dark waiting for one of the most amazing sites that God has given us. It's as if you are in your own world and He is given you your own personal performance. To say the least it is one of those breath taking moments that I have talked about.

Today's sunrise like everyday's was amazing. After trying hard to wake anyone to come along and getting several roll overs and no answers I almost gave up and went back to bed. Then as I was putting away my favorite hoodie my thirteen year old come yawning down the steps. He rubbed his eyes and said, "Mom can I have a turn to go with you?" Austen has never volunteered nor ever wanted to get up at 5:30 in morning to go sit on the beach with his mother. I was in complete shock but pleasantly surprised when he asked. Of course I took him up on it. I explained to him that it takes about 35 minutes for the sun to completely hit the sky and that I like to watch the whole thing. He said he understood and still wanted to come. So I wasn't going to push it anymore and rushed him out the door. As we were on our way to the beach I could tell that he really was not into it so I did not push conversation. I think he may have just volunteered because he like his dad was afraid I might try to go on my own. So he sucked it up and become my beach bodyguard.

As we sat on the beach in the dark waiting for a glimpse of color Austen asked me why I enjoy this. "It's windy, wet, and dark and there is no one around. I like the beach much better in the afternoon when things are hopping" he chimed in. I really did not know how to answer his question without him thinking I was being nerdy or just emotional Mom. As things go, lately everything I do or say to him is "just not cool." So I tried to explain it in his terms. I explained to him that seeing a sunrise reminds me that no matter how hard the day before was a new day is coming. It's like the night has taken away all your worries and the morning sun will make it all brighter. The sun will always rise again no matter how many problems or battles you have. I basically told him that there is always a new day to look forward to and watching the sun greet the day reminds me of that. There is no better way to see faith and hope than in a sunrise. He shook his head so I think he was getting what I was saying. I ignored his comment when he mumbled under his breath about how bored he was though.

As we sat on the blanket we talked about all kinds of things. Almost like what we use to do a few years ago. We just caught up with each other. I knew that God had a hand in him waking up today. We really needed this reconnection. The sun slowly started pushing its way up over the ocean. Austen then looked at the sky and saw all the amazing colors. All he could say was, "Wow." I started snapping my shots and he asked if he could take a few. I set the camera and handed it off to him. He just started snapping like me…but differently. It was as if he came alive and was seeing something he never thought he would see. He really enjoyed himself. Logan and especially Nolan have been my sunrise buddies several times. Each one enjoying the morning differently. Now Austen can be added to the list.

Right before the sun made its final destination to the sky Austen mumbled behind the camera lens, "Mom, I see why you do this every morning. This is so deep." He handed me the camera and sat down on the blanket to see the last few minutes of the amazing colored sky. I did not say a word because I wanted him to feel the peace that I feel when I am alone and in the zone. After the colors were gone we both got up and started to walk. He could tell I was in some pain so he grabbed my arm. As we walked up the beach to the walkway a morning jogger passed us. I made a comment about how that use to be me a year ago and how I miss being able to do that. He then said, "but you did not notice the sunrise then…like you do now Mom." I felt like kicking myself. I just got finished showing him one of God's miracles and I sounded as if I lost faith. He then added, "Mom you are so tough. Don't worry about that stupid stuff."

Just another moment that shows "The Good In Cancer."

December 6, 2009
Our Trip to Tampa and Dr. Kvols

After a long trip we are back with so much accomplished. As you know if you were keeping up with my blog I spent Thanksgiving in Vero Beach, FL with my family. After the holiday we traveled over to the west coast of Florida to Tampa for an appointment with a carcinoid cancer guru, Dr. Kvols. To our surprise it was also the weekend of the ACC championship. So the boys were thrilled. We stayed at the Hyatt just by chance where they were hosting many of the pre-game events.

I was a little concerned about dragging the boys with us to Tampa for fear that the focus would be on me and they would be bored. Well when we pulled up and the valet asked us if we were here for the ACC championship event I saw the boys bright blue eyes twinkle. Just another time when we were at the right place at the right time.

The real reason for our trip to Tampa was to get more information on my cancer and see about some new clinical trials that I had researched. I had read many articles about Dr. Kvols and was interested in his knowledge about this rare and complicated cancer. With our medical bills pile rising, I was unsure if the benefits of seeing him would outweigh the expense. Then a few months ago I received an email from one of my carcinoid cancer posse, Bob Paver, who highly recommended that I try to get an appointment with Dr. Kvols or Dr. Warner in New York. Bob found my blog when he was doing research for his own carcinoid cancer and felt the urge to reach out to me about his positive experience. This is what I mean when I write about how God puts people in your life just when you need them.

As I was driving over to the west coast through miles and miles of orange groves, I thought about how unselfish it was of Bob to contact me. It is just a true example how we are all in this together. Life with cancer is not just about the individual themselves. It's about all of us reaching out and helping each other. Looking at the bigger picture of this disease can do so much more than just thinking about your own suffering. I don't know if I am explaining myself clearly, perhaps just saying we are all in this together. Spread your wealth of knowledge to others and share your experience to benefit others. That is one of the purposes of my blog but it was actually turned into so much more.

We arrived at Moffit Cancer Center right on time which is actually early for Mark and the boys. After getting the boys set up in the waiting room with their missed school work and portable game systems we checked in. Everyone was so pleasant and positive. The records that I had sent three times were MIA so I started to panic for fear that this whole trip was a waste. After stressing my concern and begging for them to look everywhere because I knew that they were sent the records turned up. To the nurse's surprise, but not mine, there was a box full. Unfortunately because of the mix up Dr. Kvols did not have enough time to read the mounds of records. So instead he spent a considerable amount of time listening to me go over my history with this disease. He listened with such interested and did not rush me a bit. This just amazed me because he is one of the most knowledgeable doctor in the US about carcinoid cancer and he listened like this was the first time he heard this cancer story. He then gave us all his knowledge about the disease and explained things to me that I had always wondered. Just when I thought I had read, researched and learned everything there is to know about this monster growing inside me, there was more to learn.

After I was done he examined me and asked me all about the symptoms I have or had. Then we went into a conference room while he took some time to review all the scans I have had in the past year and half. After some time he came in and went over everything and every option he sees for me. He did not have any clinical trials that I would be eligible for, because of my advancement, but believes that I am doing everything right. He could not give me a formal recommendation until he reads over my box of records. However, he did give an informal:

1. Continue on the Afinator and Stando because he believes that I will see some stability with that drug. In some cases he has even seen shrinkage. But in my case stability is what we will hope for.

2. Next step in the next few months would be to add another drug that has been proven to work along with Afinator. He wants to save that option until we see what the Afinator would do.

3. The last option would be to go back to Switzerland to receive my last two treatments. He suggested that I hold off until we see what the Afinator will do.

He gave me other suggestions but like I said he needs to go over all my records to see if they will actually be my options. The formal report should be finished quickly. What he did confirm was that I am doing everything I can do and not leaving any stone unturned. He told me to not give up and keep on fighting. He stressed that everyday new treatments are being thought of. In fact, I found that with the FDA approval of Afinator just this May. He was so passionate about this cancer and finding ways to keep carcinoid patients alive.

Finally I asked the million dollar question, "How long do you think I can live with this cancer?" I could tell he was a little uncomfortable by this question but has been asked it thousand of times before by others who have come from all over to meet him. I can imagine that he will never get used to giving anyone a time on their life. He cleared his throat and looked me straight in the eyes. He, like every doctor I asked this question to, could not give me any guarantees and told me my cancer is advanced. But what he did say is that if I keep up all that I am doing I could live many more years. The goal is to keep myself alive until a new treatment to cure this disease comes and every minute it gets closer.

At the end of the consult Dr. Kvols gave me a big hug. He then walked out to the waiting room and introduced himself to my boys. He told them to take care of me and to learn from me. I'm not sure what he meant by that but I hope they learn from my will to live everyday for them.

We will make another appointment after the holidays.

December 9, 2009
Christie

Happy Birthday to my dear Christie. It's been two years since you left us but it feels like just yesterday. I think of you always and the battle you so bravely fought. I miss our talks about our physical struggles with this disease. And the boys miss their Aunt Christie especially your Nolan. Your children's hearts will always be yours. I know you are looking down on us from the most glorious place ever and sending us peace. I hate that you are not here for me and I hate that I am so selfish to wish you back. I will fight this cancer with all I have in honor of you. Until we see each other again.

December 15, 2009
12-15-97

Dear Logan,

December 15, 1997 is a date I will remember always and treasure so deep in my heart. On that day God gave me a miracle. God knew exactly what he was doing when he blessed our family with you as our second son. I love you more than you could ever know. I am so glad I can spend your 12th birthday showing you how much you mean to all of us. Thank you for being the best brother and most amazing son.

Here is something I jotted down for you. I wish I could express my wishes more elegantly than this but treasure it and know that it is my gift.

My wish for you Logan

Son, I wish I could fill your life with nothing but Joy
so you can always stay an innocent little boy

Son, I wish I could make all your wishes come true
so that you will never feel sad or blue

Son, I wish I could fulfill every dream you may see
so you can know how happy you have make me

Son, I wish I can gift you all the riches around
so all your frowns are turned upside down

Son, I wish your life could be nothing but fun
and all your nights and days be filled with sun

Son, I wish I can take all of life's pains away
so you can have nothing but glorious days

Son, I wish I could show you how to have strength in times of despair
so you can have faith and never have fear

Son, I wish I could live every single day of your life
so that I can take on all your strife

There is so much I wish for you my dear son
but I cannot give you because your life would then be done.
You need to have all that bad that comes with the good.
Otherwise you will never know were you stood.

You need to learn how to change obstacles into opportunities
that way you will see
how wonderful living your life can be

You need to put your faith in God above
so you can feel His most amazing love

If I could wave a wand and grant all my wishes true
Then you will never see how much I truly love you.

So on your birthday I will gift you all the above
but tomorrow I must continue to fight
so I can teach you to look for the light.

Everyday is a gift I want to say
so that your birthday is not just one day.

Mom

P.S. Happy Birthday my wild loving boy!

December 23, 2009
The Hot Line
I want to share a poem with you that was given to me by a special lady. It was written by her sister when she was a teenager just before cancer took her life on Jan. 7, 1976. Very inspirational:

The Hot Line
By Rosie DePastino

I'm lying and thinking with
Plenty of time
It seems that the world is
Just one up hill to climb.
The question occurs "can we make
It or not?"

If we quit at the middle
It can be a far drop.
We sometimes need courage and
Someone to lean on
It gives us the strength
To manage to see dawn.
They pull us up and out of our
depression
One thing you don't need to be
set back in regression.
It's sometimes hard to
Count our gifts
But thinking about worse others
Should give us a lift.
A gift is nice, a present too
But the best gift is prayers,
Love and a smile
When you're blue.
So in the darkest hour when
You think you're all alone
Remember there's a hot line
To a very special phone.
I won't tell you whose on it
For I guess that you should know
But someone'll *always answer*
And He'll tell you the way to go.
I was climbing up the hill
And I almost had a fall
But I guess you know just
What I did - I slid and slid and crawled.
Until I found my courage
And picked right up the phone
And now I call the Hot Line
When I feel I'm all alone.

I've been waiting until the perfect moment to post this poem. What better time than two days before Christmas. A teenager at the end of her life did not lose faith that anytime she had a special hot line to call

God. She believed that he was there even when she was at her worse possible time. She did not ask him to cure her but to keep up her spirits while she went through this cancer journey.

There is one question I ask when I read this poem. How can a young girl fighting for her life still have faith that God has not forsaken her, when many who have everything don't believe? Something to remember when we open the store brought gifts this season. The greatest gift does not cost a dime and is free to us anytime. GOD!!!!!

Have the MERRIEST CHRISTMAS ever!

Chapter 22:
New Year...A Giving Fight

*"Another fresh new year is here . . .
Another year to live!
To banish worry, doubt, and fear,
To love and laugh and give!*

*This bright new year is given me
To live each day with zest . . .
To daily grow and try to be
My highest and my best!*

*I have the opportunity
Once more to right some wrongs,
To pray for peace, to plant a tree,
And sing more joyful songs!"*
~William Arthur Ward

December 31, 2009
I can't not stop thinking today that my tombstone will not say 1970-2009. I have one more year to add.

January 1, 2010
Reflecting

So the Christmas season is over and a new year, decade, is beginning. Last night before ringing in the new year, I felt such an overwhelming set of emotions come over me. Tears just flooded my eyes and I had no idea why. I started reminiscing about New Years Day 2009 and what my life was like this time last year. Mark and I were packing up our bags and heading to Switzerland on January 2nd. Not knowing what to expect, how we were paying for it, and what the outcome would be. We just knew that we had to try it and felt lead to go this path. As I sit and ponder about it now I cannot help but remember what we were going through then. Although I was acting strong and fearless about my European treatments and my destiny, I now know that deep down inside I was trembling with fear. I was just petrified about what was going to happen to me and my family. I stood strong and confident about my decision to pursue experimental treatments in a foreign land but as I look back it was all an act. I feared for my mortality and my family's welfare. I knew that this treatment was a huge financial burden on my family and was concerned that it was all a farce. Mainly, I never thought I would be around to see 2010. Yes I finally admit I did not think I would be living today. But I knew that I had to do this treatment for my children and other carcinoid patients.

Last night as Mark and I spent a quiet night at home with the boys and some of their friends when it all hit me. Mark looked at me and said, "I cannot believe everything we did this year. We went through more things in 2009 than other families go through in a life time. All because you decided to fight with all you have to be here today." We then talked about how scared he was last year and that he never thought I would be here now. He then continued to tell me that he had to pretend he was not scared because I was so brave and confident. At the end of the conversation, which was interrupted by a group of boys wrestling, I could not lead him on anymore. I admitted to him that I was a frightened little girl and never thought I would see 2010 either. Here I sit blogging away as I listen to my boys laughing together in the next room. I am not the same person I was this time last year. I have changed both physically and mentally. I am sicker, yes, but I have a peace about my destiny now. I have hope.

As many of you have shown me I'm a goal oriented person. Up until my battle I thought that everyone was like that. This year I am setting only one resolution or goal: STAY ALIVE! However I do have a little experiment that I would like everyone who reads this blog to take part in. I will post that tomorrow. Hint though it's about gifts.

I would like to end this post for tonight so that I can go and enjoy whatever it is the boys are cracking up over in the next room. Tomorrow I will give you the details of my experiment. I hope you all participate with me. I believe great joy and peace will come to you if you do. Until then.

Happy New Year!

January 3, 2010
The Giving Challenge

As promised in my previous post, I have an experiment that I would like everyone who reads my blog to participate in. As the Christmas seasons ends and the New Year begins I could not help but think about why this time of year is such a happy time for so many compared to the rest of the year. I believe it's the joy and feeling of worth we get when we give to others. I know for me, I enjoy nothing more than watching those I love open the special gift that I spent so much time to pick out. Especially when I give a gift to someone that is not expecting it. Sometimes I spend weeks or even months thinking about what I will be giving to those on my Christmas list. I have had many of my friends offer to do my shopping for me this year, but that is the one thing about the Christmas season that I so look forward too. It was a little tougher this year, not because of the cancer, but because of a husband who worried every time I went out shopping alone. He said it was because of my health but I think it was really the packages I was caught sneaking in the house a few times. Whatever it was I did not let his anxiety stop my joy.

A few months ago I read a book titled *29 Gifts*. The author, Cami Walker, was suffering severely from MS. She was deep in depression and tremendous pain. A friend and a spiritual counselor she was complaining to told her to stop focusing on herself and start giving to others. To sum it up that is what she did and in 29 straight days of giving she began to feel better. Before this project of generosity she was unable to work, walk or even get out of bed most days. After the month of straight giving her life turned around…even walking daily without a cane. When I finished the book I could not help but think what it would be like if everyone who has some kind of pain...physical or emotional...would try this experiment.

I never thought much about the book after I closed it for the last time...until Christmas night. After all the gifts were opened and we were home from spending the day with family, my youngest said to me, "My favorite part of the day was seeing Dad open the gift I got him." I don't even remember what gift Mark opened was given by Nolan, but I know that it was special to Nolan. He felt the joy of giving. I once again was a proud mom. I have never allowed my boys to do lists for Christmas or cut out pictures of things they are expecting. However, I do get hints right after Thanksgiving. When they start talking about what they want I, like most moms, give them the same, "it's not about getting, it's about giving." I know through them feeling the joy of giving is not something I can force or lecture into them. They just need to experience it. Nolan did that this Christmas. So it got me thinking about the book I read.

I am going to start my days of giving. I would like all those who are going through a struggle or a tough time to give with me. However, I want to change it a tad bit. I don't want to put a time limit on the giving. I would like to see how many days in a row those who are participating can give. The giving can be at all levels but it must be conscious giving. For example it could be holding the door for someone, buying a coffee for another, sending a kind note to a friend, giving a flower to a stranger or much larger. The catch is if you miss a day of conscious giving then you must start over the counting. Cami Walker suggested that you jot down your daily gift or even journal about it. I on the other hand feel better just stealth giving. But whatever works for you. Maybe even share your experience by emailing me.

I would love to hear from anyone who is participating and the changes that have occurred in their life or maybe the difference that you made in someone's life. I have no way of repaying all the gifts and blessing that have been given to me, but this will be one way I can pay it forward. Let's keep the spirit of the holiday all year through.

P.S. After telling Mark about this experiment he thought I was going crazy or had too many pain pills. I have not done either. I just want everyone to experience the joy that I have gotten this Christmas. It cannot do anything but bring good feelings.

January 6, 2010
Giving Ideas

After my post on January 3 I have been bombed with several emails. Some are just sad. I have been prosecuted by some that feel the giving challenge is giving those who are suffering more to worry about. I assure you that was not my intention. I just know from my experience that giving is a great way to think of others instead of yourself. For me it helps me refocus my cancer difficulties into joy. Not to mention it is a great way to pay things forward. This is all the time I am going to waste on this negative subject but I will pray for each person who sent me those emails. My heart aches for anyone who cannot see the joy in giving to others.

On the bright side of my giving challenge I have been bombed with a slew of emails from many who are so excited to take part in this challenge but would like me to elaborate more with ideas. So to make things short and sweet here are some ideas I came up with for my own giving. Feel free to steal them:

1. Drop a thank you note in your mailbox for the postal worker who delivers your mail. They go unnoticed so often. I did this yesterday because I was to sick to get out and my family are wondering why I am being so nice. Today I went to the mailbox only to find six thinking of you cards from others.

2. Hand the coupons you are not using at the store to the cashier and have her pass them on to the next person that needs them

3. Tell your spouse three things that you love about them.

4. Buy a single rose and hand it to the first elderly person you see that day. I did this a few days ago and the lady I gave it to smelled and say, "It smells as sweet as you are." I was beaming all day.

5. Wake up earlier than usual and instead of giving your kids or husband cereal for breakfast make them a feast.

6. Buy a cupcake and give it to your neighbor.

7. Send out an email blast that says something positive and nice.

8. Call someone that you have not spoken to in a while.

9. On your way home from work stop by a nursing home that is on your route and ask if you can visit someone that has not had a visitor in a while. This is a hard one because you have to step out of your comfort zone, but when you leave there you will feel amazing.

10. Send a card to a soldier.

11. If you cannot think of anything than call your mom and tell her you love her. That is the best gift you can give.

January 10, 2010

It's been over a week since I started the giving challenge. It's been an amazing experience. I hate to seem self-serving but I must be honest and admit that I know this is the best medicine for me. It feels so great to know that I am making someone feel good too. I have received several emails from others who seem to be feeling the joy that I am. Please if you have not started the giving challenge jump in and try.

I would love to hear from those who in the past week already feel a change coming. Email me and share your stories.

January 14, 2010
11 Years Old!
Today my baby turns 11.

> Dear Nolan,
> You are the light that brightens up this family. We would be lost without your smile everyday. We can always

count on you to lighten up any situation with your sharp sense of humor. Your kind heart and giving spirit makes you the special person you are today. You have given me more than you will ever know. Where ever you go or whoever you come across you manage to make them smile. Everyone wants to know you and those who do are so blessed. You should be the "Sunny" of the Carney Clan.

I am so proud of you and will love you always.

Happy Birthday!
Mom

January 22, 2010
Poison
Today I will be receiving a new poison. I am praying this will help. Love the irony in that statement.

January 26, 2010
Update
Friday I was scheduled for a new treatment. Unfortunately after six pokes and three nurses they were unable to get a good vein to administrate the cocktail. I like when chemo is referred to as a cocktail because it makes me feel like I am part of a big party. I have had so many treatments given through my vein that scar tissue has built up in them making it difficult to get the needle through. So they wanted to set up an appointment for Monday to receive a port. I begged them to try one more day before putting a port in me.

With that said, on Monday Mark and I went back to Hillman Cancer Center to try again. I am happy to say with nine pokes and four nurses it was a success. I was able to receive the treatment and dodge the port. I have some side-effects (nausea, pain, fatigue and horrible headache), but all and all I am relieved I was able to receive the treatment.

However, on Friday when Mark and I got home from a long day I felt so defeated. I felt horrible that I wasted Mark's time. I started thinking about my obstacles and how they affect everyone in my family financially and emotionally. That evening Austen came into my room and sat down on my bed. He put his arms around me to give me a big hug and told me he was happy I made it to his basketball game earlier that afternoon. He had no idea what my day was like nor did he know that I needed his hug more than ever. Then, he handed me the comics from the Sunday paper and said, "Mom this comic is about you." I was so exhausted and I asked him to read it to me. He holds up the paper to shows me the picture, like I use to do with him when he was unable to read. It was an illustration of a funny looking woman in a superhero costume. He then began reading the following:

Title: SUPER CAREGIVER

SUPERSONIC SIGHT: Knows immediately upon entering a room if anything has been moved. Can find anything anyone is looking for.

SHAPESHIFTING: Can morph from a cook to a nurse to a teacher with ease.

ABILITY TO MUTATE: Can transform an unholy mess into a clean room with amazing speed.

ICY STARE: Can freeze kids in their tracks and send chills down their spines. (not sure I agree with that).

ACCELERATED HEALING: Can cure a boo-boo with a mere kiss.

SUPERHUMAN STRENGTH: Can simultaneously carry an entire family on her shoulders.

He ended with saying again, "Mom that is you." At that moment I learned something from my thirteen year old son. I learned that me feeling sorry for myself is doing more harm to my family than this cancer can ever do. I learned that the person I stared at in the mirror just minutes before with tears running done my face is not the same person they see. They don't see the bags under my eyes, the paleness in my skin or the stress on my face. They sure don't know the anxiety I feel about the medical bills piling up on the dining room table or the stress from every thing falling apart in a house that once was my dream house. All they see is a super mom.

It seems like every time I start to feel like a failure in this journey someone that I love is there to pick me up and make me feel needed. It just reinforces that I cannot let a stumble stop the fight. I can't give into this cancer because it's the easy thing to do. I must do whatever I can do so be my boys' Super Hero.

February 2, 2010
Faithfully Giving

It's been almost a month now since my January 3rd post where I challenged everyone to start consciously giving. I love hearing stories about how amazing it feels to go out of your way to make someone else happy. It seems through the stories that the simplest acts of kindness have brought the most rewards to others. I have been touched the most by those who have told me anonymous act of kindness and how wonderful they felt after it.

Having cancer in the bones and liver I am often in relentless pain. I have learned to refocus my mind most of the time to relieve most of the pain but there are times when it can be so intense that nothing I do can even take the edge off. Once the pain starts to go out off control it can take me days sometimes weeks to get it back in control. However this month several times I began to notice that whenever I turned my thoughts to others instead of dwelling on myself, I experienced an incredible sense of control over my circumstances and pain. I even noticed that recently my entire well-being has improved. I have been laughing more and making others laugh more. I have had several occasions this month when I have laughed until actual tears have streamed down my face.

One of the most difficult aspects of living with cancer in the bones is the immense pain in the morning. It almost always wakes me up before the sun is up. Starting my day I try everything to function somewhat normally before the kids get up so I can get them out the door for school. I usually wake Mark up with my moaning because I am in such agony just trying to get in a hot shower. Sometimes he hears me crying from the pain and he jumps out of bed hoping that something he could do will shut me up. At least once a week he is awakened by the sound of a bottle of pain meds hitting the floor because my hands are so weak I cannot even open the child safety lid; my crazy Irish temper thinks that slamming them on my bedroom's hardwood floor will do the trick. So I decided to try something at night to see if my mornings go smoother. Before turning in each night I write down a name of someone I want to do something nice for. I then start to think of something I could do for that person. It might be as simple as call someone I have not spoken to in awhile, say a long prayer for someone, send someone an email telling them how special they are or even buying someone a gift. Just the other day, Mark said to me, "Sun, I have noticed you have been sleeping in until it's time to get Austen up. How is your pain been in the morning? Are you taking something different?" Sleeping until 6:20 A.M. is huge for me. After racking my brain to see if maybe I have been eating something or added a new magic herb to my already growing pile. Then I realized that just thinking about giving has improved my life and that this challenge is changing me.

Last Monday I had an appointment for the second try with my treatment. I mentioned my new found giving approach of living positive with cancer to one of my favorite nurses. She too is a cancer survivor. She told me that my discovery was supported by not just the Bible but by medical science. She explained to me that doing for others releases endorphins which are the body's natural painkillers. When your mood is good and you are happy the endorphins help your pain. Studies have actually proven that volunteers, devoted givers and those that dedicate their lives to helping others lead happier, healthier and longer lives. She continued to tell me that is why when she went in remission and decided to come back to work she requested this department. She gave me a big hug and whispered in my ear, "every time you are here your attitude changes me. You are a gift to me." Her kind words helped me relax and the needle finally went in one of my veins…an example of the circle of giving.

Since I realized that giving is not just benefiting those receiving, but has really changed my cancer journey I have been feeling better. I have not taken a strong pain medication in at least three weeks. I can go all day with just one morning 600 mg of Ibuprofen. I have come to understand through my silly project I have changed my battle into a life of happiness. I am going to continue this little project because it is not a challenge anymore but a great way of living.

Keep giving,
Sunny

Side Story
This past Friday was a prime example of how this project works. I was horribly sick during the day and once again started to climb the mountain of pain. My mood started to go down and I just felt plain old yucky from the treatments I received earlier in the week. I made up my mind that I was going to skip Austen's basketball game, skip the get together with friends afterwards and just go to bed as soon as my home full of people cleared out. That morning before Austen left for school I told him I would not be going to the game because the new treatment was just kicking my butt. He looked at me with his great big blue eyes and said, "Mom if you don't give to anyone today you may have to give to me and come anyways. Otherwise you will have to start all over on your project." He's been hearing about my project all month and I was surprised it took him this long to use it against me. I spent most of the day feeling sorry for myself and moping around. Yes, I do that sometimes. Then at about 2:45 the phone rang and it was Austen's school on the caller ID. After hardly saying hello I heard my teenage boy on the other end laughing. He said to me, "Mom did you give today?" Not letting me answer, "If not I will see you in about an hour" and click went the call. So of course I got dressed, tried to make myself look like I am not fighting for my life and off I went with Mark and my other boys to the game. After the game we went out with some of my favorite people. I must say the night ended with me laughing so hard that I cried and forgetting totally about how I felt a few hours earlier. I did not get to bed until way past midnight because after coming home Mark and I stayed up and laughed some more. I felt so normal.

Chapter 23:
Need for Inspiration

"Anyone can give up, it's the easiest thing in the world to do. But to hold it together when everyone else would understand if you fell apart, that's true strength."

February 16, 2010
Where to start???
First thank you everyone for all your phone calls and emails. The past two weeks have been a bit of a challenge for me. First the new treatments have been kicking my butt to say the least. I can go into details but I will spare you all. Once I started to feel a little on the up swing I then caught some kind of stomach virus, which spread through out my home with the boys. For the boys it was a 24-hour thing but for me it turned into about 4 to 5 days in bed. The chemo has dropped my ability to rebound from a virus of sorts. Not to mention the several feet of snow that Pittsburgh has been hit with. Yesterday was the first day back to school for the boys in a week.

The past few days I have been feeling better and better. I am still exhausted but I am thinking that is normal for what I am going through.

I will be posting regularly again. I am thinking we need another week of motivation. What do you think?

Start sending your quotes.

February 22, 2010
Ask for Strength

"Don't ask for an easier life. Ask to be a stronger person."

I don't know where I heard this quote or if I just wrote it myself but it came to me last night when I was saying my prayers. How many times have you asked God to make your life easier? I know that for me it's been more then I want to admit. Even those who claim to be well educated Christians ask God to take away some of their obstacles or problems. However, some of God's greatest gifts to us are the troubles that come our way. He is the most powerful of all powers so if it is his will he could give you a life without any adversities. He can change your life for the better in an instants. However that is not what He has promised us.

What he has promised us is that He will never leave our side when we turn to Him. He will carry us through times when we feel we can no longer walk. He will give us the strength we need to get through the impossible and make it possible. All we need to do is trust in him and ask him for strength. There is no need to ask him to make things easier, because if we have the strength given to us by God we can climb the highest mountain and fight the hardest fight.

Throughout my cancer adventure I could count hundreds of times when I did not think I could get through another day. Although those seconds of thoughts have been changed quickly by the strength that I have asked God to give me. Every treatment, every scan, every nasty medicine, every injection I give myself, every pain, every medical bill I cannot pay and every time I hear one of my loved ones cry because of my cancer are times that I wish would just go away. However, I know that my trust in God is what gets me through them. And when those times come, I close my eyes and pray:

God give me the strength to overcome this roadblock. Help me make what seems to be impossible become possible. Let me be an example to others by showing them the gifts that I have received from my cancer. Please Lord give me your strength.

Don't ask for an easier life. Ask to be a stronger person.

February 24, 2010
Walking with God

> *"I would rather walk with God in the dark than go alone in the light."* ~Mary Gardiner Brainar

I pray everyday. I receive peace when I pray. However, these past couple of weeks I seem to be praying a lot harder, more often and with more passion. Why the change? I need more from God right now. When I read this quote, which was emailed to me by my friend Maria, it got me thinking about my walk with God.

I consider myself a Christian; a good Christian. However, I get very frustrated with myself because I seem to be a better Christian in dark times. I know that this quote means more than just turning to God when times are tough but for me, one who tries to always walk with Him, it touched more on how to improve my walk with Him.

In my daily walk with Him I don't ask him to cure me every time I pray. One might think that is strange when you are fighting terminal cancer. I've asked Him once when I first relapsed and I remind Him every once in a while. The rest of the time I trust in Him to do what He needs to do to help me through this journey. On the other hand, when I have a loved one needing prayers or I am suffering from this cancer more than usual I pray harder. That bothers me. I want to walk with God everyday with passion. I want to be a better Christian in both the darkness and the light.

So that is my ambition for today and something I want to work for always.

February 25, 2010
God's Megaphone

> *"God whispers to us in our pleasures, speaks to us in our conscience, but shouts in our pains: It is His megaphone to rouse a deaf world"* ~C.S. Lewis

We have all heard God's voice through a megaphone. The question is have we listened.

February 26, 2010

> *"If you wait to do everything until you're sure it's right, you'll probably never do much of anything."*

How many times in life do we wait until? I have learned through my cancer journey that until may never come.

Chapter 24:
The Fight Will Continue

"Never, never, never give up!"
~ Winston Churchill

March 2, 2010
Yesterday I received my treatment for my bone tumor. The hunt for a vein was easy…first stick. They slowed down the processes into the vein so that the vein would not clot or collapse like has happened times in the past. It was such a relief that everything went so smoothly.

I felt exhausted but pretty good when I got home. Mark did the evening activities with boys while I stayed home and rested. I felt really good considering I had poison running through me. Then this morning I woke up to get the kids off to school and I could not move. It literally felt like my bones where frozen. My body is aching from head to toes. All I can think is the poison eating away at every tumor.

So today will be a day of rest.

March 15, 2010
Time—Our Most Precious Commodity

Yesterday marked the one-year anniversary of Sunny's second treatment in Basel. Not the exact date mind you, but the Monday preceding March Madness 2009 we were in Switzerland, Sunny confined to her room, quarantined like a Chernobyl victim, and I, holed up in the room or the bar at the Hilton Basel. To this day, she is not one who looks back on the two trips at all other to acknowledge that they certainly were worth the efforts, as the Y90 by all accounts has slowed the pace of the cancer. She is not one who looks back on those two trips as anything other than a necessary step to stay alive, not a positive experience, nor one that she cares to talk about, be reminded of, or care to recall. It is not surprising that when I pointed out what Monday was and offered to do a blog, she was more than happy to let me reflect on what the last year has meant, and in order to do so, obviously revisit our time in Basel.

As I write this I wonder if she is going to be comfortable even having this blog published. Basel was a step along the cancer journey and I can understand her uneasiness in recollecting or reflecting back on the two treatments there, and more specifically the anniversary of her most recent one. The same emotions stir inside when she goes back to Presby/Montifiore here in Pittsburgh and is faced with the memories of the chemo-immobilizations preformed there (and by coincidence what could ultimately be our final visit with the liver specialist Dr. Gamblin was yesterday, but more on that to come…) or the same emotions stir when she walks by the kiosk at Hillman. For Dr. Christie who performed the lung surgery years ago and by coincidence is directly across the hall from Dr. Friedland's team and offices…the emotions are strong…we have talked about them…we share them…of course understandably hers are infinitely more intense than mine…these doctors all did their jobs…the lung surgery was deemed a success, the liver treatments as of the scan done just yesterday continue to be what we are all looking at and the Octreotide Scans show that Basel did what it was supposed to do. That is all irrelevant…when you have to look around the waiting room and see the faces of cancer, of advanced cancer staring back…you get angry…then you get angry for being insensitive…you are angry for letting yourself get angry…you wonder why your wife…or in Sunny's case why me? The memories come flooding back and if you let them they can overwhelm.

I have no choice but to realize that even though these memories of Basel may be difficult to revisit, that Sunny is still by my side as I reflect. We have been blessed with a year to date since that scary Swiss treatment and we all know that was never a guarantee. Even AIG wouldn't touch that one. So when I title this "short" little entry "Time-Our Most Precious Commodity," I do so not to repeat a common cliché of the late 20th century, but as a testament to my wife…and to how Sunny chooses to treat each day. She inspires me everyday and as I write this and bring back some of the moments of our time together in Basel last March, I do so not to stir up unpleasant times, but to remember how even then whether she wants to admit it or not she is a unique fighter blessed with an Irish blend of PMA and unfailing tenacity that quite frankly, if the Pittsburgh Pirates could tap into a tenth of, Pittsburgh would be truly be the City of Champions. She doesn't make excuses or look for reasons to procrastinate (although as she will attest to I try to give her outs or force rest) she grabs each day as if it were some kind of steroided beefed up super bull, yanking that big boy's horns until it squeals in defeat. She will not get beat by the clock. She will not get cheated by time. So I can share the memories of our second trip to Basel with fondness because we were together, we were close, and she was to simply put it…Sunny.

Sunny of course brought her camera. I think she knew that even though the treatment was torture that taking pictures would be a distraction. Knowing how much I love to pose for the paparazzi, she had focused on the architecture of the historic city, the people, the river, and had taken a slew of great pictures at one of the better museums during our first trip. (I have to throw out a big props to our good friend Peter, who drove down from Holland on both occasions and without whom, we would have stood out even more than we did as touristy Americans…his insight during the first trip helped us to at least not feel intimidated by the cultural differences during our second visit). But what Sunny had really taken upon herself was to capture pictures of the fronts of buildings…in particular doorways…doors…windows…gates etc…most of them were centuries old and all of them were much more colorful as compared to a typical entrance way here in the states. As she snapped the shot after shot she would say, "I wonder what's on the other side of that door. Or some story like behind that door a little old woman is drinking tea, a mom is rocking her baby, a husband and wife are fighting and on she went." She was determined to put all of these Swiss facades into a book that I kidded would rival Kramer's Coffee Table Book about coffee tables. She was relentless. She actually scaled a five hundred year old wall to peep over bushes to take one and as we marched through cobblestone streets on Saturday before her second treatment she must have taken hundreds of pictures of doors…Jim Morrison wasn't in as many Doors pictures as Sunny shot that afternoon as the sun dropped behind the Alps.

Those of you who read this and see her, please ask her to share with you the "Door Pics" from Basel. She hasn't looked at them since she has been back…but let me tell you they were fantastic. As I chased her through narrow twisting cobblestone streets, my feet hurting (Damn Euro trash hip shoes) and the hunger pains kicked in as our quest for a smoke free, good eats, not too crowded on a Saturday night search continued…she never stopped shooting. She was amazing. I was ready to call it a night. We had just flown from Pittsburgh to DC to Germany to Switzerland, grabbed maybe six hours of sleep, her bones in serious pain, and she wouldn't stop. Time. She kept saying she would have time to rest when she was dead. I would have chuckled, but I was too busy wheezing and geezing chasing her through those Basel Blvds and to be honest I never felt more connected with her…more in tune with what was driving her to press on.

Time. The second trip to Basel was the closest I felt to Sunny since her diagnosis. The fear of the unknown was behind us, the only ones we had to count on were the two of us. It is strange to even write this but it truly was an unbelievable privilege to know that it was just Sunny and I taking this step…of course I don't want in any means to dismiss the pain or emotions of the treatment, I can only comment that the pain for the liver treatments here was worse. At least her appearance post treatment back in da burgh was worse. I just know that we all have one timekeeper in life and he chose to have Sunny and I be in Basel…just the two of us…no other family or friends…(although I felt the prayers)…not our kids, not our intermittent cell phones or pain in the ass wireless Hilton Internet service…it was us…Rickki Lake, Sally Jesse Raphael, Judge Judy, some wacko G5 protesters in London, Nick Nolte and Eddie Murphy, Clint Eastwood, and lots of bar nuts, free lobby apples, stinky ass French cheese and those wonderful Salsa Chips from Papa J's Bistro.

Last St Patrick's day my wife was in a nuclear medicine ward at Hospitaal Basell…Peter and I, not able to see Sunny for 24 hours wandered through that Irish haven of Basel and actually passed the evening drinking green beer and eating "fresh Swiss sushi." Not quite Market Square and Ms. Irish Smiling Eyes. The 17th of March was just another day over there, as was March Madness...and as my week went along I pretended to care about the brackets I had filled in via the Internet Sunday night...I tried to implore my three boys to fill theirs out and email them back home...Sunny rested ten feet from me...did I realize how special TIME was with my three rug rats. I have since mentioned on numerous occasions that we should take the boys the next time...she wants no part of it...I might as well as have invited the boys to visit their mother back in the 80's...big hair...leg warmers...neon bracelets and all.

On Friday, our last day alone together in Basel before the long trek home, I wasn't expecting much more than a quick trolley ride to one of the museums we hadn't yet visited. It was 50 degrees F...I'm sorry, it was like 10 degrees Celsius officially and as I put my shorts on I asked Sunny what she wanted to do...she said lets tackle the zoo. Now mind you, I am all about skipping museums when possible, but it was blustery, she had just been nuked three days prior...her blood count was low enough that if a monkey farted in her general area I was going to have to punch the monkey first and then take her to the Swiss ER.

TIME. I remember to this day what she said next. "I feel bad you have to be inside all of this time, lets do something fun...how about the zoo." It was at this point I realized how nuts my wife really is...in a good-hearted way, but nuts nonetheless. TIME. We grabbed her camera and the Camcorder and left the comforts of the Hilton Basel. We hopped a train that was new, we walked, we walked and then...there we were...Zoolistengher Gardener...the f$#%#$in Zoo. For those of you who personally know Sunny I can only tell you that no matter she may claim now about her time there...she was in heaven...Pictures of swans, hog sex, hippos in their native setting...leopards mooning us...little Swiss kids running from the big American who didn't care for their little school ground song...loose mice in the reptile exhibit...we laughed and laughed, and never once did she complain. She had just got nuked, and we were walking through three and a half miles of odors and animal shit without complaint. I have never been to the Pittsburgh zoo with just my wife. I live 5 miles as the crow flies from it. It's world famous. We take the kids all of the time. My favorite zoo is now in Switzerland.

I hope that none of you have to go through the battle that Sunny has...but if you do, I pray you relish the TIME with each other...don't spend it frivolously, you can never get a refund…so pray…fight the right fight…and remember your life doesn't have a DVR…so be selfish with your time…cancer or not…TIME doesn't play favorites…so just don't take it for granted.

Please keep us in your prayers…huck Sunny for those "door" pictures and I look forward to reaching out to you all the next time Sunny gives me the OK.

Mark

March 19, 2010
What to Say???

After reading Mark's blog from the other day I am speechless. I did not know how wonderful his memories are of Basel, Switzerland. I never like to talk about it with him because I really thought that it was a time he would not want to rehash. He seemed so scared and helpless when I was undergoing these experimental treatments. I remember his anxiety as we boarded the plane from Philly to Germany. I was exhausted, in pain and sick to my stomach yet I was so worried he was going to have a complete break down. At least that is what I thought at the time, only to learn just the other day he was in awe of me. When the subject of our adventure comes up I always see his eyes start to water up so I immediately change the subject. I thought it was because of sadness and fear but now realize those eyes were full of love. Unfortunately, I never let myself see our trips through his eyes so I am so glad he wrote the last post.

He is correct when he says I don't like to remember our trips or the treatments that I underwent while in Basel. I do talk about our experiences but only to other carcinoid patients that call me for information and want to know what it is all about. But I don't like to relive it with anyone else. I don't see myself back then like Mark sees me. I see myself as a sick, insecure, fragile person. I was doing what I needed to do to get through a very hard time. I was really just trying to make the best of a very hard situation. Actually, when I think about it I was truly searching for some happiness and peace. That is why I was dragging Mark all over the Alps while vomiting in several plastic bags. I needed to find any good in the situation we were in. Never did I realize that Mark was just satisfied being with me.

Mark wrote about my photographs. I have not looked at them since we got back and I loaded them in the computer. I am thinking that maybe when I am ready I will sit down with Mark and we will enjoy our memories together. After all, I am alive one year longer then any doctor here in the United States predicted.

March 23, 2010
Daffodil

Sunday was such a glorious day here in Pittsburgh. Of course that means the boys and a large group of their friends will spend most of the day outside. After spending a few hours at a photo shoot I came home to an empty house with the remains of what several messy boys left behind. Drink glasses half full, about a dozen Popsicle wrappers and sticks scatter about the kitchen counter and an empty fridge that was full before I left that morning was proof that they still lived there but only entered the house to refuel theirs and their buddies' bellies. I rushed home because I expected to be greeted by my four favorite boys waiting for me to do something fun with them. I quickly realized that they are now teenagers and they did not even realize I was gone for hours.

As I was cleaning up the mess in the kitchen and feeling very used, I heard my cell phone buzzing that a text just came through. Needing an excuse to not continue I grab my phone to check out what it said. I looked down to see Fav yung son on the name of who the text was sent. That stands for "my favorite youngest son" which is what I jokingly call him at times. I open the text only to see it was a picture of a daffodil from my Nolan and text written above the picture that said, "with the gang and saw this in someone's yard and thought of you. I cannot pick it because I don't want anyone to think I'm weird. I hope you like to just look at it." I must say my heart insistantly melted.

I have to wonder if cancer has made Nolan as thoughtful as he was on Sunday. Has our journey softened my boys? Or would they have become this sensitive and loving even if we had a normal life? I truly believe they have become who they are because of our situation. Believe me when I tell you this surprise does not happen often, but they seem to come at such perfect times. I hate cancer and I hate what it does to others and families. I believe that cancer is somehow a form of the devil.

But I also know that we have become different people for the better because of being struck with this demon.

About an hour after receiving the text, the door flew open and in come a group of about twelve boys ranging from the ages of 11 to 15 to hit our basement to watch the NCAA march madness with Mark. I cringed because I knew this meant mess number two and bad odors entering my freshly cleaned house. I handed each one a bottle of water and warned Mark they were entering the "man cave." At the end of the stampede was Nolan holding that beautiful daffodil he texted me a picture of. Once again I felt my heart melting like candle wax. He handed me the flower and told me to hurry and put it water because he picked it right after he texted me. He claimed that Austen and Logan told him to. I gave him a huge hug and just held him. He then pulled away when he heard someone yelling for him to hurry up because Pitt was on. As he ran downstairs to join the rest of "THE GANG" he turned to me and demanded, "chips mom." Once again I knew that despite my cancer I have a truly perfect life.

March 31, 2010
Control

I have written several posts since the last one but I have not published any of them. My emotions are running crazy. I have been putting off posting because it's been a roller coaster ride of cancer in the past few weeks. Truthfully, I really don't know what to post because I don't understand much anymore. Just when I think I have this cancer life under control I am hit with another wall to climb over.

I had a new set of scans about a week ago and the results were so so. The miracle drug that I have been taking has not shrunk any of the tumors. Some are stable but new ones are popping up faster than I would like them to. After speaking with my liver oncologist after the scans I left his office feeling quite defeated and angry. He, on the other hand, keeps telling me that I am a miracle and I need to remember that I have had a whole year longer than what was expected. I am frustrated because I am doing everything I can do, and looking for more, to fight this fight but keep getting punched down over and over again. I am tired of losing this battle. I am also tired of pretending that everything is going to be allright when deep down I know that the only answer right now for this carcinoid cancer is to slow the process down. I want so badly to just once go into my doctor's office and hear that I am in remission.

I also feel this enormous desire to keep everyone here at home positive and optimistic. I need to keep everything together and tell everyone…including myself…that I will get through this again. I must of said 100 times or more to Mark in the past 2 weeks to stop worrying about something we cannot control only to find myself up all hours of the night worrying for him. I feel this huge pressure to be strong for everyone while I continue my life like I don't have this monster invading every one of my organs. 99% of the time I believe and have faith that I will be here for my children and to see them graduate from high school, college, get married and have children of their own. However, at times there is that 1% that is so hard to overcome.

Today I got a call from my oncologist office and they told me that I need further tests and risky surgery as soon as possible. After I hung up the phone that 1% kicked in and I fell apart. But I had no one to fall apart to because I am the strong one and I have to keep my family thinking that this news is just a little bump in the road. As I started to tell Mark the watered down filtered version of my conversation with the nurse I could tell that it meant him freaking out. As much as I appreciate his need to get upset and angry I really wanted it to be my turn just this once. My turn to scream and cry. My turn to feel sorry for myself and become bitter. Instead as I tried to communicate my frustration, I end up listening to his.

I knew that I had to clear my head so I snuck away for a walk. As I was walking I tried to figure things out and plan my next course of action. I kept asking myself why am I freaking out? Why do I feel like I am losing control of this battle? Why am I so frustrated when I knew this day and many worse days would come? The answer came quick. I don't know if it was God slapping me in the face or me just thinking straight but I realized that I am not supposed to be in control. He is in control. I need to let go of the wheel and let Him drive. I have to put my trust in God and give this up to Him. The answers will come if I open my heart and lose my need to control.

I lost my way for a while. I needed to take control of something I have no control over.

On Tuesday I will see my main oncologist to discuss our new findings. We will lay out a game plan and I will proceed with all my heart again. In the meantime, I am going to enjoy my Easter Holiday with my family and hug my boys every chance I get. I know that I cannot control the outcome of this disease but I control how I handle the outcome.

Thursday, April 1, 2010
Continuation from Yesterday

After reluctantly posting yesterday's blog I felt the weight of the world was lifted off me. At least until Tuesday when I meet with my main oncologist again. I went to my bedroom to get some sleep only to find Mark laying on his side of the bed with a book across his chest and his hands over his eyes. Trying to quickly and quietly slip back out of the room I held my breath and slowly turned towards the door. The thought of rehashing our conversation a few hours ago was just too much for me to bear. I almost made it out of the room when he spotted me and said, "I'm reading your book, I can't believe your notes in the margin. When did you write this stuff?" I did not know what book he was talking about nor did I want to engage in any kind of conversation. I read a ton and always write notes or highlight things I like in my books. I shook my head and tried really hard to escape out the room but he continued to engage in conversation.

"I think you read this book before you got sick. I remember you telling me to read it. In fact I think you brought me a copy." He held up the book and I noticed it was "The Purpose Driven Life," by Rick Warren. He was right, the first time I read the book was the year it came out in 2003 before I had my lung removed. I think I have read it about five more times since then. I did not say much because truthfully I was completely drained and just wanted to be alone. He got the hint and laid the book down open on the bed and left the room.

After putting a few baskets of clothes away, straightening up the room and getting ready for a good night sleep I sat on the bed and lifted the book to find it open to Chapter 4: "Made to Last Forever." I quietly read the chapter without a pencil or highlighter but with an open heart. Like I have mentioned earlier I have read, took notes and highlighted this chapter many times but not until last night did I really get it. I even participated in a group Bible study for this book but I learned more last night than ever before. For those who don't have a copy of this book please get one, read it and keep it next to your bible for reference at times. The chapter, *Made to Last Forever*, was the perfect chapter for me to read last night before laying my head down to sleep. It gave me peace and understanding.

Rick Warren writes:

> *This life is not all there is. Life on earth is the dress rehearsal before the real production……Earth is the staging area, the preschool, the tryout for your life in eternity. It is the practice workout before the actual game; the warm-up lap before the race begins. This life is preparation for the next.*
>
> *At most, you will live a hundred years on earth, but you will spend forever in eternity. Your time on earth is, but a small parenthesis in eternity. You are made to last forever.*
>
> *……This life is preparation for the next. If you have a relationship with God, through Jesus, you don't need to fear death.*

Just as I finished reading that chapter Mark walked back into the room holding his copy of the book. He asked me if I read my notes in the margin. I shook my head yes but I really did not read any of them I just nodded that I did. He turned to me and said, "you were who you are now, then. You understood life even before you had cancer." He continued by saying, "you say cancer changed you and opened your eyes to life. Your eyes were always open." We shut out the lights and I waited until he fell asleep before I turned on my small lamp to read my notes. I could not stand not knowing what I knew back then.

As I read my notes written in cursive, so that even my books looked pretty, I too was surprised. In the margins I wrote things like: "life on earth is just a blink compared to life in eternity," "the way you live your life here determines the way you live in eternity," "live as if today is your last day," "if you live for God and others you should never fear death" and "our life here is to be lived for God. Don't let your life be wasted….do for others." There were several other words I jotted down but those few stood out.

I am guessing it is time for me to listen to what I already know. I need to continue to live with all I have and let Him do His thing.

In Closing

I am continuing my battle and continuing my blog. I hope one day I am writing another book about how I am cured from a cancer that has no cure. However, until then I will live my life with this monster but I will not let this monster be my life. I will always see the "Sunny Side Of Cancer."

To be continued,
Sunny

Acknowledgments

Thank you Lord God. My faith and love for you will never disappear.

To my husband Mark A. Carney, my eternal gratitude to you for encouraging me, supporting me and motivating me through all our challenges. I know it's a very painful time you to watch me go through this journey. I also know that at times I make it very difficult for you to help me. Thank you for your patience and enduring love. Thank you for seeing me at my worst and still thinking I am beautiful. Thank you for your vulnerability. Mostly, thank you for realizing that your family is more important than any other external factors.

To my amazing boys, thank you for just being you. The three of you are truly my most precious achievement. Everything I do in this life is for you. Remember that you are all my sonshines.

To my mother for teaching me to be the mother I am. You have always encouraged me and your faith in me has been my motivation in life. It is because of your unconditional love that I believe I am never alone. Thank you for showing me your quiet strength. Thank you for always being the beautiful face to walk behind me. Mostly thank you for respecting me and building my confidence.

To my departed father. Your example in the way you lived your life has continued on. Thank you for teaching me that family is more important than all the riches in the world.

To my amazing brothers and sisters. The bond that siblings have can never be broken. Thank you for all your support. Thank you for the generosity and kindness you have shown me through out my battle. Thank you for running to me when I call. Mostly thank you for loving me despite my faults. To my extended family. I feel so blessed to be part of the entire Jennings Clan. To my brother-in-laws and sister-in-laws thank you for becoming a part of our family. Thank you for taking on all our quirkiness and skeletons. Mostly, thank you for treating me like one of your sisters. To my aunts and uncles, my deepest gratitude for your continuous support during this journey.

To Dr. David Friedland, thank you for your dedication and compassion. Your encouragement to find other treatments and research clinical trials has meant a lot to me. Thank for listening to me and respecting my need to live no matter what it takes. Thank you for working and organizing my care with all the doctors I have chosen to see. Thank you for not being offended when I wanted to find more. Mostly, thank you for treating me like I was your only patient when I knew your waiting room was filled with others.

To Dr. Gamblin, Dr. O'dorisio, and Dr. Kvols, my eternal gratitude goes out to you for keeping me alive.

To all my dedicated friends who loved me and took care of me through this cancer battle. The cards, fundraisers, dinners, rides, and taking care of my children when I could not will never be forgotten. I am so blessed to have all of you in my life.

To Tracy Reedy for encouraging me to write this book.

To my R4R group, thank you for dedicating your group to help Carcinoid Cancer Patients.

References

Carcinoid Cancer Foundation
333 Mamaroneck Avenue #492
White Plains, NY 10605
1-888-722-3132

Caring for Carcinoid Foundation
198 Tremont St, Box 456
Boston, MA 02116
(617) 948 2514

Carcinoid Cancer Awareness Network
516-781-7814
1-866-850-9555

Sunny Carney
www.sunnycarneycarcinoidcancerfund@blogspot.com

Background

Ever since I was a little girl growing up in prison, I had my life planned out. My father was the warden of the Allegheny County Jail in Pittsburgh, Pennsylvania and for several years I lived in an enormous home connected to the Jail. I interacted with prisoners on a day-to-day basis at the early age of six. They were truly my next-door neighbors for most of my childhood. Although my heart ached for those prisoners, through their lives I knew exactly where I did not want my life to go. I was determined to be the best I could be no matter what curve balls life threw me. At that time, however, I did not know that the curve balls were going to curve so sharply. So I became a dreamer of my future. That dreaming at age seven lead to planning out every step and move I would take to guarantee a life of success. What I did not know is that God had other plans for me!

When I graduated from high school I had my whole life planned out. I completely forgot about the details of my so-called "life plan" until a few years ago, I was going through an old box of high school junk and I found a pink piece of paper with doodling flowers all over it titled "LIFE PLAN FOR THE NEXT 10 to 15 YEARS TO BE A SUCCESS." It is posted later in this book. What I came to realize is that nowhere in that plan did it include: get cancer three times and survive.

In 1994, I was progressing through my list of "Life Plan for the Next 10 to 15 years To Be A Success" and was doing quite well at keeping right on track. I was working for an amazing growing company—number one in their industry—and moving my way quickly up the corporate ladder. At that time I was making more money than several of my peers and actually thought that is what made me important. Additionally, I was planning an amazing wedding to a man that had the same career ambitions as I did. The man I fell in love with had the potential to succeed like me.

Early in our marriage, he was hit with a harsh reality that devastated me as well. For a few months, I was just not feeling right but I could not put my finger on what it was. I was having flushing, trouble breathing, abdominal pain and a small bulge in my stomach that no amount of sit-ups, dieting, or exercise would take away. I went to my general doctor several times and was told that it was just stress and anxiety. It was suggested to me that I find a way to relax and take a break from the stressful career I was in. I began to train for a marathon and thought that maybe my intense training would be a good escape to the everyday stresses of corporate America. However, my condition was getting worse and deep down I knew that there was more to this feeling than the anxiety the doctors were blaming it on. Although they were telling me I was unhappy and stressed, I truly thought that I had a perfect life. Finally, I was taken to the emergency room with severe abdominal pain. I had an immediate surgery to remove a nine-centimeter tumor and my right ovary, which was engulfed by the softball size tumor. At the time I never got a good description of exactly what type of mass it was, but looking back I believe it was Carcinoid Cancer. Before the mass was found I had the clinical symptoms, and after the tumor was removed I was a complete mess. Despite this, I ignored the change in my body and I continued to stay focused on getting back from this interruption.

After a six-week recovery and some other small treatments I continued to work on my "goal list" and I climbed the corporate ladder rather quickly. I never worried about cancer or even thought about what had just happened to me. This brief set back was just that, a brief set back. I did not do any research or even continue to think there would ever be a problem in my life again. I was focused…focused on completing my list. Then a year later and one week before my wedding to my husband (which was already moved back once), another tumor on my other ovary was discovered. After my honeymoon, I went straight to surgery…again. At that time, I was told that my chances of having children were slim to none, but if I wanted any chance at all then I would need to start right away because the longer I waited to conceive the less chance I had. Children were not part of my "life plan" until I hit 35. I was only 25 and my career and life were otherwise quite amazing. I began to conclude that cancer is an annoying interruption of my plan and the sooner I got rid of it, the better. However, I knew that it would not be fair to my husband if he could not be a father. He told me that he loved me and would be fine if we never had children. Although he was trying to be supportive, I knew he did not really grasp what he was saying and I feared that years later he would resent me not even trying to give him a child. Mark grew up in a small family while my large family reproduced like rabbits. As I grew up, I saw my brothers become fathers and knew what an amazing gift it was to be a father. As much as he tried to convince me that he loved me for who I am, I convinced him that he needed to be a father. By the grace of God, within 26 months I had my three wonderful joys of my life and my "life plan" then took a major detour.

When I was about eight months pregnant with my first son, I received a card in the mail from one of my sister-in-laws who I always admired as being the best of the best when it came to mothering. She dedicated her life to her children and even today as her children are becoming adults, I am impressed at her love for them. In the card she wrote a beautiful letter where she expressed that she knew I would be an amazing mother. She did not see me as the driven pretentious career women that I always thought I wanted to be. She told me to give all that I have to this child because life with them is quick and regrets last forever. I don't know if she knows what that simple card did for my children or me or how it changed my life today. I am not sure she would even remember sending it to me. But, because of that letter I put my career on hold, packed my list in an old box to be retrieved later, and decided to raise the incredible gifts God has entrusted to me.

Despite the shortcomings I faced, I loved every minute of being a wife and mother. Sure I may have complained once in a while when my husband worked long hours or when all three babies where sick at one time, but I never regretted giving up the "life plan."

Then five years after my third son was born I started feeling ill again. Like before, I went to the doctor many times with chest pains, a horrible cough, and flu like symptoms. I was put on an antibiotic six times in one year for pneumonia. I was never given a chest x-ray. The same physician told me that I had adult asthma and I needed to change my lifestyle, which meant no more running. I felt the same flushing feeling I did years before but did not connect the two together. I was tired all the time. Finally, after coughing up blood and insisting on a referral to a specialist, I was diagnosed again. It was so different this time when the doctor told me I had Carcinoid Cancer. I am not sure if was because I got a name with the disease and it had cancer at the end of it or if it was it because I had three small boys at home that needed a mother. I felt like someone just shot me in the heart with a bullet that had all three of my boys names engraved on it.

I will never forget the walk across a long bridge from UPMC Hillman's Cancer Center to the garage where my car was parked after the doctor broke the news to me that my cancer had returned and engulfed my entire right lung…another organ. I was alone, because I did not think it was more than just asthma related problems. Making the phone call to Mark to tell him I had lung cancer with a strange name called carcinoid, while walking across the "cancer bridge" was horrific. I write carcinoid with a lower case "c" because at that time I did not give it enough importance to capitalize it. I knew that by the time I got across the bridge to my car my life would never be the same. There was no turning back.

I never understood how some cannot remember what they had for dinner by breakfast the next day, but are able to remember every detail of a tragedy in their life. The phone call to Mark while walking across the "cancer bridge" is one of the moments that is forever in ingrained in my memory. Mark was at his office working hard to help our family fulfill the American Dream that everyone desires. When I rang his line he did not pick up, which was not unusual because he was very driven and talking to me about the kid's mishaps that day was not on his list of importance. Knowing that he was either talking to a client or in a meeting, I decided to hit zero and get the secretary to page him. This is something I never did unless it was a dire emergency, but with three rambunctious boys it happened more often than he would have liked. He picked up sounding annoyed since I interrupted his workday. But like an atom bomb, I dropped the news without a hello. He did not ask one question; he told me he loved me and he would meet me at home right away. I could hear the guilt in his voice for not being with me earlier that day.

When I was diagnosed with cancer in 2004, our boys were seven, six and five. Being that the kids were so young, my husband was by no means ready to be a single dad. Mark was very much invested in his career and HIS life. He loved the kids very much but I was the caregiver. In fact, if I was to leave him alone for more than an hour with the kids he needed a babysitter to come and help out. After I called Mark, the 20 minute ride home from the hospital seemed like hours. My mind was racing. I kept telling myself I needed to keep it together for both Mark and the boys. The cell phone was ringing and ringing but I knew if I picked it up I would have to share the news with whoever was on the other side. The memories of that day seem as vivid as yesterday. I wanted so bad to just pull over and think things through before I entered the door of my home. But I knew if I did that I may have never put my hands on the wheel again. I may have never gone home that night.

The doctor kept saying that this cancer was rare and complicated because it involved the endocrine system. He explained it to Mark and me in clinical textbook terms, which at the time went right over our heads. The only option the doctors had at this time was to remove most of the entire right lung. The recovery took almost a year. The recovery for our family however took years. At that time I was told that there is no cure for carcinoid cancer and that eventually it will take my life.

Then a little over a year ago, as promised by my doctors, the cancer returned with a vengeance and I was re-diagnosed with Stage 4 cancer throughout my body—two softball size tumors and many smaller ones are ravaging my liver and the lesions in my skeleton go from my legs through my hips, spine, arm, shoulder, and up through my skull as well as in my lymph nodes. I am told that this is it. Once it hits the liver it becomes a quick invader. As much as those words are planted in my head, I still cannot wrap my mind around the meaning of them. I cannot accept that this is the end. I have so much more to accomplish. My list is not done and I refuse to turn it into a "Bucket List." I have made up my mind that I will fight this invader with the help of God, with a "Sunny" attitude, and with the determination to make a difference. I hope that through my blog posts and this book I can inspire not only Carcinoid Cancer patients but also anyone who is struggling to overcome any adversity in their life. I don't think I have ever run across anyone whose life is completely without trials and strife. After all, everyone has some kind of cancer in their life.